Martí

José Martí

Martí

MARTYR OF CUBAN INDEPENDENCE

by Félix Lizaso

Translated by Esther Elise Shuler

GREENWOOD PRESS, PUBLISHERS
WESTPORT, CONNECTICUT

Library of Congress Cataloging in Publication Data

Lizaso, Félix, 1891–
 Martí, martyr of Cuban independence.

 Reprint of the ed. published by University of
New Mexico Press, Albuquerque.
  Translation of Martí, místico del deber.
  1. Martí, José, 1853–1895.
[F1783.M38L492 1974]   972.91'05'0924 [B]   73–20502
ISBN 0-8371-7329-9

A Greenwood Archival Edition—reprint editions of classic works
in their respective fields, printed in extremely limited quantities,
and manufactured to the most stringent specifications.

Originally published in 1953 by The University of New Mexico,
Albuquerque

Reprinted in 1974 by Greenwood Press
A division of Congressional Information Service, Inc.
88 Post Road West, Westport, Connecticut 06881

Library of Congress Catalog Card Number 73-20502

ISBN 0-8371-7329-9

Printed in the United States of America

10 9 8 7 6 5 4 3 2

Preface

In order to evaluate the position occupied by José Martí (1853-1895), not only in Cuba's emancipation from Spain but in Latin American culture in general, we must bear in mind that Cuba's political and intellectual history is somewhat different from the rest of Latin America.

Cuba was the only major Spanish possession in the New World that did not achieve independence in the early nineteenth century. The Cubans were forced to fight early and hard for their liberation, but it did not come until the conclusion of the war of 1895-1898.

The Cuban nineteenth century witnessed many uprisings and unsuccessful attempts to gain freedom by the force of arms, as well as several movements for political reforms, with certain degrees of self-government under Spanish rule as a goal. The most important struggle before the War of Liberation of 1895 was the Ten Years' War (1868-1878). This war was preceded by a movement of political reform conducted in an atmosphere of Spanish tolerance, known as *Reformismo* (1862-1867). During that period, the Cuban intellectuals were able to raise their voices in behalf of the interests of the natives of the island, but the movement failed because of Spanish short-sightedness and intransigence. This failure caused the Ten Years' War that ended in the Pact of Zanjón (1878), with Spain victorious and most of the Cuban patriots in exile.

In the quest for a solution to their political problems, the Cubans were divided into three major groups: the Annexionists, with their eyes turned toward the United

States, were hoping that the island could achieve freedom by becoming a State of the Union; the Reformists, later known as Autonomists, were looking for political changes and self-government under Spanish sovereignty; and the Separatists, who desired full independence, wrested, if necessary, from the mother country by violence. The unification of most of the members of these groups, composed of men of different social classes and economic levels, was not an easy task. The man who realized it, and made possible the final united struggle for independence, was José Martí.

Martí's early youth undoubtedly was influenced by the ideas of *Reformismo,* but before he had time to develop any political philosophy of his own, he was greatly affected by the realities of the 1868 war. His exile and studies in Spain made it clear to him that the Spanish Republic of 1873 had a dual conception of liberty, as they refused to grant to the Cubans the political rights they themselves wanted to establish in the peninsula. This convinced Martí that the only way to free Cuba from Spain was by force of arms. Because of his travels in Latin America and long years of residence in the United States, he viewed Cuban problems with a Continental perspective. For him the problems of Cuba were to a certain degree similar to those of the rest of Latin America, and the first task was, of course, to free the island from Spain. Nevertheless, this was not enough. The new republic should not be allowed to fall into the period of anarchy and civil wars that had afflicted the other Latin American countries after independence. For this reason, he planned his important task to begin after the defeat of Spain. Unfortunately, he did not live to see it.

A man of letters, a sensitive poet, a prolific writer and speaker, during his brief life he managed to combine the ideal with the real and became the organizer of the political party that was to liberate his country. Martí was different in this respect from other Latin American leaders, as he combined theory with practice with admirable ability. I do not think that any of the great Latin Americans presents a more formidable challenge to the biographer than José Martí. He confronts the writer with the complexities of intellectual interests covering many fields of the humanities and social sciences, with an extraordinary literary production, and with a dynamic life devoted to revolution and politics.

Mr. Lizaso does not attempt to cover the multiple aspects of Martí's life. He gives a close-up view of Martí's work and thought, reached by faithful study of Martí's writings and his own excellent knowledge of the historical environment. This book is not only a political biography. Lizaso, well versed in Hispanic intellectual history, offers the reader the opportunity to become acquainted with Martí and, at the same time, to enjoy a panoramic view of nearly forty years of the art and thought of Europe and America.

The English translation was prepared by the late Esther E. Shuler, who knew and loved Latin American letters. This publication was made possible by a grant received by the University of New Mexico from the Cuban Commission for Martí's Centennial. We are happy to be able to contribute to the commemoration of this Centennial by including this book in our growing list of Latin American studies.

MIGUEL JORRÍN

School of Inter-American Affairs
University of New Mexico

Contents

Part I:

Formative Years

1. A Morning in 1856

On that limpid September morning the sky was diaphanous, the mild air cool and vibrant. Doña Adelaida de Villalonga left her mansion at number 64 Aguiar Street, seated in her black carriage which rolled down the street toward the Merced Church, where a holy day was being observed with a sermon from eight to nine.

Very stiff and ceremonious on the high coach-box, the driver held the horse's reins firmly in one hand while in the other he displayed his long flexible whip as a sign of authority. The hammering of the horse's hoofs echoed against the stone pavement. The rhythmic clatter lulled the lady's thoughts as memories and desires passed through her mind in vague confusion. In the midst of this placidity the carriage stopped. Another vehicle was in front of it, blocking its way. Both were in front of a house under construction whose scaffolds extended halfway across the street. Simultaneous crossing at this point was impossible. The coachman insisted that the other vehicle, a cart overflowing with merchandise and drawn by strong mules, back up in order to let him pass. The driver did not seem disposed to humor him. He thought it easier for the light carriage to yield the right of way than for his heavy, overloaded cart. He also made a slightly audacious comment: he said that he was doing his work while the lady, on the other hand, was out for a pleasure-drive. The dialogue between the two drivers grew louder. Their arguments revolved around their contrary attitudes.

Doña Adelaida, frowning impatiently, had been waiting for her servant to win the argument. Furious, at last she intervened. But imagine her surprise and indignation when she heard the same refusal to let her pass!

By that time people had begun gathering around to watch the spectacle. Just at that moment an officer of the law passed by. Very ceremoniously he listened to the allegations of the two disputants. Possibly impressed by the lady's rank, he suggested that the cart yield the right of way to the carriage. It was a disconcerting moment for all. The loser did not consider the verdict a fair one. And faced with the latter's refusal to comply with it, the officer excused himself and withdrew.

"This isn't my district," he said, and went off to look for the watchman of that zone.

Near the scene of the incident was the police station of the district of Santa Clara, and inside was the district officer. A few moments later he appeared on the scene.

The disputants once more presented their arguments. No sooner had he heard them than he pronounced the verdict:

"The carriage shall let the cart pass."

Doña Adelaida was extremely indignant. She protested, tried to oppose him. But the officer would not listen to objections. He himself, raising his club, made the horse back up. And he was so violent that he almost broke the carriage.

The crowd broke up, making the most varied comments. Some thought that the officer's decision constituted an insult to a worthy lady. Others believed that he had shown a high sense of justice.

The officer, for his part, did not seem to attach any importance to the incident. His conscience was at rest; he had done his duty.

And thus, swinging his club and taking big strides, the policeman of the Santa Clara district, Don Mariano Martí y Navarro, walked away.

2. The Home

Don Mariano was a tall robust man with a thick black mustache that already revealed a few white hairs and covered part of his mouth. He was a man of few words, a rapid stride, and a brusque authoritarian manner. Born in Valencia, of Valencian parents, forty five years before, he came to Cuba around the year 1850, as a soldier in the Artillery Regiment assigned to Havana with the rank of first sergeant of the First Brigade. In the militia his conduct was exemplary, and he took his position as a soldier very seriously. It had been his pride to belong to the Royal Artillery Corps.

He was not a man of licentious habits, as was frequently the case in the army. On the contrary, his rectitude and reliability brought him recognition from his superiors, who considered him an honor to his corps even though his mediocre intelligence prevented him from being outstanding.

Shortly after his arrival in Cuba he began to frequent the home of a modest but highly respectable family, attracted by the presence of Leonor, a charming, sensible girl of twenty, with bright eyes and wavy hair. Mariano Martí soon resolved to marry. Having obtained permission from his superiors and a certificate declaring the legitimacy, racial purity, life record and character of the betrothed, who needed paternal consent because she was a minor, the marriage arrangements were concluded. In keeping with his class, Mariano Martí registered with the captain of his corps the sum of 500 pesos as a dowry.

The ceremony was performed, not without solemnity, in the parish church of Monserrate, the seventh of February, 1852. The chaplain of his regiment officiated.

5

Less than a year had passed when the same chaplain in the church of Santo Angel Custodio baptized a child born the twenty-eighth of January, 1853, and christened him José Julián.

About two years after the birth of their first child, Don Mariano decided to leave the army in the hope of obtaining a position more in keeping with his present status as father of a rapidly increasing family, for a little girl had just been born to them. As he had saved some money before he married, he decided to take a chance and obtained a discharge as first sergeant of the Artillery Regiment.

His efforts to find a superior position in the Carabineers' Corps were unsuccessful. The lack of vacancies, on the one hand, and the large number of candidates with better qualifications, on the other, prevented Don Mariano from obtaining the position. But he was finally successful when he applied for a position as a policeman. On September 18, 1856, he received his credentials.

What happened, to cause him, four months after his appointment, to resign from his post? In the notice he presented he said that he was unable to continue discharging his duties because he was ill. His intention was to go to Spain with his family. He probably had some of his savings left. Moreover, the five hundred pesos of his wife's dowry were still intact. On May 19, 1857, his resignation was accepted, and a few days later he began the voyage. When he left Cuba, José Julián was four years old.

The family remained in Spain approximately two years. In June, 1859, Don Mariano was back in Havana. He soon took steps to recover his old job as policeman. In his report he gave a good account of his services to His Majesty in the honorable career of arms. He even included the Royal Order in which he was granted a discharge, a great diploma which he was to put to good use on many occasions.

This record of services in the royal army carried much weight. Exactly one month after making application he was appointed as police officer in charge of the district of Santa Clara. But this position was not the kind desired by Don Mariano, who although he claimed to be cured, continued to suffer from frequent attacks of asthma, some so violent that he almost strangled. In February 1860, he applied for a district captaincy which he was not granted, in spite of the favorable recommendation from his superior. On the contrary, a series of events in which he had acted incompetently resulted in his dismissal from the policeman's job which he had obtained so easily.

His son was now seven years old and an excessively serious, thoughtful child who did not play much and was always very close to his mother, often entertaining his little sisters. As it was time for him to learn to read and write, he was enrolled in a small district school. A few months later they were pleased with the facility with which he was learning to read and with his progress in penmanship. Don Mariano was very happy over the accomplishments of his son, always so well-behaved. And Doña Leonor, when she had visitors, always brought the conversation around to the subject of Pepe's progress.

So rapid was his progress that his father began thinking about a way for him to attend a better school, where his son could study English and accounting. Don Mariano had a superstitious awe of that language; the North Americans were the people he most admired. The commercial development of that country seemed extraordinary to him, and he thought that if his son learned English his future would be assured.

Don Mariano did not become discouraged in his attempt to find a new position, and early in January, 1861, he again applied to the Governor General. On October 23, the following year, we find him occupying the coveted post of district captain in La Hanábana, in the jurisdiction of Colón. There we are to find, not only Don Mariano, but also his son, who made an excellent assistant for the paper work of the captaincy. A letter from the boy to his mother, the first indication of his intelligence that has been preserved, is dated from La Hanábana, October 23, 1862. This letter is written in a very firm hand which seems impossible for his nine years. If it were not for its naiveté, we should take it for a letter written by an accomplished amanuensis. It is indeed understandable, when we see that handwriting, that his father should aspire to have him employed as a clerk in some business firm, for it was a position with a future if the boy had a good head and conformed to his employer's interests.

Don Mariano had a few little annoyances in his captaincy in La Hanábana. But he was happy, and he felt like a new man, far from the formal conventions of the police station in Havana. In reality he was not made for administrative details; out there in direct contact with nature he lived in perfect freedom and could breathe better.

His son helped him with what little work the captaincy required. And, like his father, he led a rustic life. It seemed to him that he had little time to take care of the horse Don Mariano had given him; the horse grew fatter and more spirited day by day, and he rode him every afternoon.

This was a new life badly needed by the pale, delicate city-bred child. But the horse was not his only entertainment. Don Lucas de Sotolongo, the well-to-do proprietor of a neighboring farm, had given him a fine cock that also required care if he was to enter the ring soon, as Don Mariano wished.

Unexpectedly, the lieutenant governor of Colón, without giving reasons, requested Don Mariano's dismissal from the captaincy of La Hanábana. And it happened that the decision to dismiss him was reached against the will of the Police Department, which could find no reason for it, and pointed out, on the other hand, that the lieutenant governor proposed to put in his place a person who had occupied the same position previously and had been dismissed on suspicion of participation in the disembarkment of some Negroes. The report very clearly emphasized the fact that the authorities were attempting to dismiss Don Mariano without any justification. Again he was dismissed from the office by which he supported his family.

Back in Havana he obtained a modest position in the Armory, without failing on that account to take new steps toward his reinstatement in the police service.

The family went to live at No 11, Refugios Street. The boy began to be aware of his purposes and his responsibilities. What did he see at the dawning of his life? He would always remember one of his earliest impressions: his father on

Refugios Street. His father, who was discharged from the army shortly after the boy's birth, often said to him:

"I wouldn't be surprised to see you tomorrow defending your country's liberties."

And how well he remembered his father's joy when, at the end of the week, together they traveled from La Hanábana to Havana. The habit persisted. Now Don Mariano gloried in dressing up his children on Sunday and taking them out to visit his friends.

The boy's musings became sombre at times when he recalled the whippings of slaves that he had seen in the country.

3. Mendive's School

The municipal government of Havana had responded to the great need of the humble classes, whose children had only the limited primary instruction of the few existing gratuitous schools, by deciding in 1864 to establish three elementary schools. Thanks to the enthusiasm of the city government and the local board of education, the schools were established.

Rafael María de Mendive, an excellent poet, a great leader of Cuban culture, and a journalist of high merit who had consecrated most of his life to "furthering the advancement and improvement of the society in which he lives" applied to the Civil Governor, on November 22, 1864 for the directorship of the Elementary School for Boys. He had enumerated his qualifications, mentioning the titles of Bachelor of Jurisprudence, fellow of the Royal Economic Society, and Professor of Primary and Secondary Instruction, as well as his editorial activities on the *Revista de la Habana, El Artista, El Correo de la Tarde,* and *El Diario de la Habana,* as well as *La Crónica de Ultramar,* and *La Reforma,* founded and edited in Madrid.

Nineteen of the most distinguished persons in the nation made up the jury that was to evaluate the merits of the candidates, and Mendive was elected.

The election of Mendive was an occasion for rejoicing among Havana society. The Governor, in approving his nomination, emphasized "not only the distinction of his degrees but his literary merits and good record as well."

The newspapers echoed the event in order to express unqualified approval of the wise choice. *El Diario de la Marina* published a note of praise:

"The election of Señor Mendive, widely known and respected as a distinguished gentleman and poet, to this honored though modest post will be applauded because of the professor's indisputable aptitude."

Referring to the Governor's mention, among the reasons considered, of the "fortunate candidate's literary accomplishments," the commentary concluded:

"This tribute to literary merit, which is usually little appreciated in the ordinary affairs of life, is a noble stimulus for those who dedicate themselves to the hard career of art, and it gives proof again of the sincere and enlightened aims of the highest authority of the Island."

There is no doubt that the establishment of this School for Boys and the manner in which its Director was elected were events of resounding importance in the drowsy atmosphere of the colony. An imperative need had been filled, but at the same time the merit of a Cuban of great significance in national letters had been recognized in an unusual manner. The newspapers had mentioned his poetry, his services to Cuban culture. They recalled the influence which he had exercised for many years over the youth that had "most fervently dedicated itself to the study of letters in our country." And who did not recall his famous social gatherings, held in his own home, a meeting place for distinguished men in the fields of letters and sciences, with the sole purpose of reading, studying, and discussing the most interesting questions of the day?

Young Martí was not unaware of this event. He had often expressed his admiration of that great and venerable man who was respected by all and had enjoyed such an unprecedented triumph. He was obsessed by the impression that this event had made on him, and he now had only one great desire: to persuade Don Mariano to enroll him in the School for Boys.

It was not difficult to arouse the enthusiasm of Don Mariano, who continued to want his son to perfect his English, a language on which he based all hopes for the future.

March 19, 1865, the day when the opening of the school was celebrated, was a great event. This act of official solemnity and of rotund affirmation of Cuban nationalism impressed Martí a great deal. But he was most deeply affected by Señor Mendive's very brief discourse, clear and decisive, in which he alluded to the boys before him, eager to learn and "because they belonged to the needy classes especially close to his heart." Mendive's speech even contained a bit of criticism of the school systems of the time, because he emphasized the fact that his instruction would have a "character diametrically opposed to that which unfortunately is observed elsewhere."

So contrary to the practice of the epoch did this discourse appear to the canon Don Domingo García Velayos (who in his character of Vice-President of the local Board of Education presided over the ceremony) that when Mendive finished, he took the floor to suggest that it would be fitting to appoint a priest for the classes in religion and ethics. It is evident that the suggestion was the consequence of Mendive's ideas about teaching in accord with the "spirit of the times," which was "eminently practical" and banished all religious instruction from his program. It was a very difficult moment, saved by the intervention of a good friend of Mendive, Doctor Ramón Zambrana, who declared that he and the director had agreed that he (Zambrana) would be in charge of the classes in religion and ethics. The incident did not pass unnoticed by the numerous audience, nor by the boys who had attended the ceremony. The incident was a revelation for Martí.

Contact with the teacher began to leave an indelible imprint on Martí. And it was no small privilege to have a teacher like Mendive!

A month after the school's inauguration, Mendive became engaged to be married for the second time. Micaela Nin, his bride, was one of the beauties of her time. Mendive's daughters by his previous marriage gladdened the house. Whispering over their embroidery, they sat down in the evenings near the pupils to hear the history class Mendive gave them for the pure pleasure of teaching. How far removed from all rigidity and pedagogical ostentation! Mendive was the great maestro who taught by making himself loved and by putting into his teaching all the artistry of his poetic inspiration.

Mendive's School

How could the gifted pupils help feeling his attraction! The school for them became the center of their existence, the refuge of their illusions. Here they began to dream, to feel, to comprehend.

Mendive's school was once more the center of those literary *tertulias* of 1861, held in his old house on Consulado Street. Now, as then, it was the meeting place of the outstanding Cubans, the men who, in their writings and in their thinking cherished a dream of glory and freedom. Here José de Armas y Céspedes, fleeing from the Spanish police, hid in Mendive's own room; here Tomás Mendoza, Francisco Sellén, Valdés Fauli, Pozos Dulces, Luis Victoriano Betancourt, Ramón Zambrana, Manuel Sellén, Anselmo Suárez y Romero and as many more came to exchange knowledge and inspiration, to read their works and listen to the grave opinions of Mendive. He changed a rhyme in a line of Francisco Sellén's poetry that the censor had suppressed, and he did it in such a way that the latter would not realize that the meaning of the line remained unchanged. Where the censor had stricken "The glory of Bolívar and Washington," he wrote, without arousing suspicions, "The glory of Harmodius and Aristogiton."

This environment exerted upon Martí a powerful attraction which manifested itself in two different fashions: first, he sought every opportunity to be at school; second, he made an ardent attempt to study, to excel, to be the object of Mendive's attention. And he easily became the center of interest both for Mendive and his classmates, who were well aware of this spiritual kinship.

Martí suggested to his teacher that he would like to serve him as an amanuensis, helping him to copy his writings. His large handwriting and good spelling were factors well worth considering, and Mendive gladly accepted his offer because in that way he could get on with the works he had in mind. In the afternoon, before his friends came, he dictated to Martí scenes from his unpublished drama, *La nube negra*, or a chapter from his novel about Havana society, in which he "flagellated with roses, but in such a way that one could see them wince, the petty heroes of gossip and dandyism."

The boy also tried to attend the *tertulias* unobtrusively, in order not to attract too much attention. In this way he could hear, close at hand, the words of many patriots, many truly creative men, and his ideas became more and more definite and precise. One afternoon spent listening to the reading of an article of José Silverio Jorrín or a translation of Moore's *Irish Melodies* by Mendive or the endless comments on art and literature, on Saco's work or on the school directed by La Luz, constituted an apprenticeship infinitely superior to that of many pages of textbooks.

Mendive's beautiful translations brought him as much renown as his own verses. Martí knew, almost by heart, the translations that the maestro had compiled in a little volume which he had managed to acquire, and which bore the title *Melodías Irlandesas, Irish Melodies* of Thomas Moore. As Martí now had a good command of the *American Popular Lessons,* one day he undertook to translate some verses, and for the essay he chose nothing less than *Hamlet.* He could go no further than the grave diggers' scene and thinking it unworthy of a great genius to speak of mice, he contented himself with the translation of the incestuous *A Mystery* of Lord Byron. And so he lived for a few days in a veritable paradise.

This human, direct apprenticeship—how well it revealed to him, little by little, the depths of his own being, how well it served him as an immediate stimulus for his own creative activity, which was gradually taking shape, thanks to such a very fecund contact! And his admiration of the maestro grew increasingly.

When all the friends had gone, he would stay on in the house in order to spend a little more time near the maestro when "in the silent house, by the light of the moon and the rustling of the leaves, he made his verses."

So rapid and notable was Martí's progress in the school that a little more than a year after his entrance, Mendive conceived the idea of paying the cost of the boy's secondary school education. He knew that his family did not have the necessary resources, but he was willing to pay the tuition. Don Mariano gladly gave his consent to Mendive's proposition, and Doña Leonor was happy to hear the news. After all it was really like a prize that the boy had won by his intelligence. He would be a brilliant student and would easily make a career for himself.

At that time Don Mariano was persevering in his efforts to be given some police appointment, and meanwhile he continued to be employed in the Artillery Armory. The registration of his son in the secondary school required his authorization, and he had no objection to accompanying Mendive to the Havana Institute, where on August 27, 1866, the boy's registration was effected. In his petition Mendive stated that he wished to reward his pupil's notable diligence and good conduct by paying for his studies until graduation.

Having passed the examination for admission, given the twenty-seventh of September, he was registered on October 15 for the following first-year subjects: Spanish Grammar, first-year Latin Grammar, Arithmetic, Christian Doctrine, and Sacred History. In this last subject he won an award for attendance and proficiency, and in the Arithmetic examination, the fourth of June 1857, he received the grade of excellent.

With this grade Martí experienced the first flush of triumph and he was so sure of his subject that the day after the examination he went to the Institute in order to ask the day and hour when he could compete for the prize. The fourteenth of that month the contest took place. Martí had only one competitor and the judge awarded Martí the prize. On the seventeenth a list of the prize winners was conspicuously posted in the Institute with Martí named as winner of first place in Arithmetic.

Mendive derived no small satisfaction from this first triumph of his pupil, and he wanted to surprise him with a printed commentary. In *El Siglo,* the great reform paper, an item appeared on June 18:

"Honor to whom honor is due: Young José Martí, former pupil of the Municipal School for Boys, under the direction of Don Rafael María Mendive, won the arithmetic prize in the Institute of Secondary Instruction, of this city, on the fourteenth of this month."

At the same time *El Eco de la Habana* also gave an account of Martí's triumph in an article entitled "Brilliant

Youth," which appeared the nineteenth and ended with special congratulation for his teacher, the learned Rafael María de Mendive.

Martí was examined in the rest of his first-year subjects in September. The third of the month he took the examination in first-year Spanish Grammar and the following day in first-year Latin Grammar. In both he received the grade of excellent. And as in June, he asked to have the day and hour named for him to take part in the competitive exercises. The Latin Grammar competition took place Sept. 13, the subject being "The verb *sum* gives us the theory of the conjugation of all Latin verbs." Martí spoke before the judges long enough to develop the thesis fully, and he was awarded the prize. He was the only contestant. The Spanish Grammar contest took place the following day. José Martí and José del Cueto y Pazos competed. They discussed completely the proposition "Theory and classification of figures of speech. Are they necessary? If they are how does one determine in which cases they are necessary?" Martí was awarded the prize by vote.

His first year of secondary studies having expired, Martí registered again in the Institute. Again Mendive accompanied him to sign as a guarantor and answer for his tuition expenses, on September 30, 1867.

Martí now lived far away from the center of the city at No 53 Peñalver Street. This great distance, which obliged him to walk a long way every day to school, was very hard for the boy. But possibly Don Mariano had lost his modest employment in the Armory and had to seek less expensive living quarters. In February he again solicited a position in the police department, but time went on without his obtaining it, and meanwhile his family increased.

He fell back on his old job as military tailor in order to provide his home with the bare necessities, but he did not care especially for this trade, and he preferred that thankless police job which brought him so much unpleasantness. He knew that it at least assured him a decorous, regular salary with which he could modestly meet the needs of his home.

At the beginning of the year 1868, Don Mariano had not yet found a position. On January 2 he applied again to the

Governor, enumerating all his good services and asking for the office of district captain or watchman in one of the districts of the city. His plea was desperate: "father of seven children, with no means of supporting them." The application, like all his previous ones was favorably recommended, with emphasis on his honesty as a public servant. But at the time it obtained no practical results. Don Mariano would not stop trying: he had friends in the Police Department, people who would make allowances for his rough manners because they knew his rectitude. Besides, one had to wait for a vacancy because jobs like that were highly coveted. And his life alternated between this hope and the gripping anguish of each new day.

For Mendive the year had had a sad beginning. His son by his second marriage, that child who attracted everyone's attention because of his beauty, was the joy but also the grave concern of the household. What was the cause of Micaela's anxiety, her presentiments and invincible fears for their son? No one could understand her frequent somber moods which saddened the other members of the family. Finally Mendive realized that he also had caught that strange despondency.

And Micaela was right; she had glimpsed something, her heart had a presentiment. One day during the carnival Miguel Angel suddenly fell ill. What was his illness? It is not definitely known. But it lasted only a day. He died in February, 1868. What great consternation for Mendive's home, so happy a few days before!

His loyal friends, the professors at the school, his closest pupils, felt this sorrow as their own. With their verses and prose they made a poetic offering to the parents. Those compositions expressed the deep affection and veneration that the great Mendive inspired in them. And Martí also offered his verses, his lines "To Micaela on the death of Miguel Angel," one of his first poetic compositions.

Martí often took charge of the school during Mendive's occasional absence when he spent a few days resting in Guanabacoa at his wife's country home. Martí tried zealously to repay in a modest way Mendive's interest in his education. But Mendive's troubles began to have their effect on his

17

disposition. And Martí was so jealous of his duties that he would not permit anyone, not even Mendive, to remind him of them:

"I do not understand why a generous father should have to remind an adoring son of his duties."

The boy's astonishment on receiving an inopportune note was a lesson for Mendive:

"Therefore your note surprised me, for at any moment, for you I would give my life, which is yours, and yours alone, and a thousand others if I had them."

The school was a part of his life. There he studied and there he also lived his happiest hours. And when Mendive was away he took charge of the cleaning and saw to it that the benches, desks, and blackboards shone. Moreover, he played a little at being Mendive's secretary and helped him in the administration of the new school, a *colegio* which he called San Pablo because La Luz called his El Salvador. He had to establish it in the same building with the Municipal School, because the city government was very slow in paying him and he was in need of some means of support. Martí prepared the receipts, took them to him at Guanabacoa for his signature, and even collected money. Although Mendive was having his own troubles, he continued to succour his most needy friends. Consequently one day he had to pawn his watch in order to lend six *onzas* to a financially embarrassed poet, and it was Martí who undertook the painful errand. Afterwards, the pupils gave him a new watch and Martí presented it to him.

But these tasks did not diminish his enthusiasm for his studies, perhaps because he felt under obligation to perform them as brilliantly as his teacher had predicted. Of the four subjects which he took this year, he was examined in June in Spanish Grammar (second year), Geometry and Descriptive Geography with the grade of excellent in all. He passed the second year of Latin Grammar in September. Unlike the previous year, this time Martí did not compete for any of the prizes, which leads one to suspect some academic difficulty, or lack of time.

But as in previous years, in 1868 he matriculated in the Havana Institute. And for the third time, Mendive accompanied him as guarantor on September 30. At this time Don Mariano's increasing problems forced him to move with his family to Marianao, the boy remaining temporarily in the school. For that reason in his application he gave Mendive's address as his. This was another generous act on the maestro's part. Otherwise he could not have continued his studies. In the school he was now like one of the family, and his attentions proved really useful, especially when Mendive was absent for a few days at the Guanabacoa estate. Sundays Don Mariano came for his son. After making some purchase or doing an urgent errand, they began the trip together to Marianao where the boy's mother was eagerly awaiting them.

Finally Don Mariano's efforts bore fruit; on November 21, 1868, he received the longed-for appointment as watchman. But this time it involved inspection of ships in the port of Batabanó. Five days after his appointment he was at work.

4. Political Initiation

A̶n unexpected event marked a new rhythm in Cuban life: the uprising of Céspedes, leading a group of men pledged to the conquest of freedom.

Although at first the rumors that reached Havana were very few and apparently contradictory, Mendive's school was filled with the constant traffic of visitors; all his friends came to bring or carry away news. A few days after the tenth of October, 1868, a Havana newspaper published the statement that "a handful of deluded, badly armed fellows had uttered the cry of rebellion in Yara." But even this report was retracted afterward, with the statement that what really happened was that a crew of workers in a sugar mill had revolted.

Since the Eastern patriots were obliged to rush into battle before the hour they had agreed upon, in order to prevent a surprise attack (for the Spaniards were already cognizant of their plans), the movement was unexpected even for those in Havana who were connected with the conspiracy. Even they did not know what to believe, and most dissimilar versions were circulated.

The pupils of Mendive's *colegio* shared the general restlessness. Did they not all know by heart, and had they not all recited, in the shade of the banana plants in the patio, Mendive's sonnet to Lersundi?

This personage represented colonial absolutism in Cuba. His attitude was so absurdly incompatible with Cuban dignity, especially in relation to the Spanish revolution of September, that those who knew his conduct felt their anger growing by leaps and bounds, and with it, the conviction that it was impossible to expect any leniency regardless of the changes that might take place in the metropolis. The Cuban reformists, many of them very intimate friends of Mendive, had thought that the provisional government headed by Serrano and Prim would grant Cuba the same rights that it offered Spain. But imagine everyone's surprise at the attitude of Lersundi, who on October 10 celebrated the Queen's birthday in the palace, the same as other years, although she no longer occupied the throne and had been hiding in France since September 30. Would events prove that the new men in the liberal government did not think any differently than Lersundi, the ultra-monarchist, in regard to the government of over-seas possessions?

And this was clearly established in an interview that several prominent Spaniards and a group of Cuban liberals had with Lersundi a few days later on October 24. A revolutionary liberal government was in power in Spain. And Lersundi, it was evident, could not represent the new situation because of his beliefs. Indeed he made patent his loyalty to the so-called "national unity" and facing José Manuel Mestre, who conducted the interview, he concluded:

"Your manifestations are analogous to those which the insurgents of Yara are making with arms. The insurrections of what are now the Spanish American republics began in the same way."

Morales Lemus, in that most critical moment, amid the confusion of all those present, asked to have certain ideas explained. Lersundi made himself even clearer; he hurled forth grave threats of exemplary punishment and made this stern comment to Morales Lemus, at that time editor of *El País:*

"Instead of celebrating public meetings it would be more efficacious if *El País* would denounce the insurgent movement categorically and energetically."

The results of the interview, divulged by the participants, increased the general unrest. In the gatherings at Mendive's home there was much comment on Lersundi's conduct. He had revealed a total lack of consideration for the men who, placing their hopes in the liberal movement of Spain, demanded what it was only human that Cuba should be given: liberal concessions to make her dependency endurable.

Martí

In that sonnet which his pupils recited from memory, Mendive presented the repulsive figure of Lersundi.

Martí knew the course of events point by point. Deeply moved, he hung on Mendive's virbrant words as he extolled the Cuban fervor of Luz, Saco, or Varela or spoke of those who died on the Cuban gallows. And did he not also have a thorough knowledge of the ideas of such patriots as Pozos Dulces, Luis Victoriano Betancourt, and many others who frequently gathered around Mendive?

Now the distant dream was a reality. Now there was a free Cuba. Would there be enough Cubans to extend it and assure its permanence? He felt an impulse that he could hardly dominate and that grew by the moment, as when at night, Mendive, leaning on the piano, and surrounded by the engineer Roberto Escobar, the lawyer Valdés Fauli, the landowner Cristóbal Madan and the student Eugenio Estenza, followed Céspedes' march on the map of Cuba. With what emotion he listened to his burning words, announcing a glorious day of freedom!

At the beginning of January, 1869, there was definite news in Havana that the insurrectionists had defended themselves in several encounters. Enthusiasm for the cause of those who had so heroically hoisted a flag in Yara began to manifest itself. How could they show their sympathy for the fierce fighters? An unexpected happening provided an opportunity for the enthusiasm to manifest itself in turbulent form.

A young man of Havana, Tirso Vázquez, suffered violent death January 6 at the hands of a Spanish officer in a dispute arising from Vázquez' refusal to yield the right of way. As the young man was very well known for his reckless courage, of which he gave proof in the disputes between cadets and students in the Monserrate fiestas, the youth of Havana planned to attend his interment the following day. But to everyone's surprise, at midnight the body was carried to the cemetery by order of the authorities, doubtless to avoid any possible disorder. This measure, far from attaining the desired result, served only to fan the flames. On the following day, all those who were to have attended the burial met in the cemetery.

Political Initiation

An attempt was made to form a demonstration of protest by carrying the body through the streets of Havana, but Don Fernando Vázquez, the victim's father, disapproved. The protest was finally reduced to a parade in front of the garrison with *vivas* to Cuban independence.

This occurrence at least kindled the spirit of the *habaneros*, if not actually heightening their awareness of the times. And this was not the only event that took place in January. Several scenes occurred that some people likened to those famous days in September, 1793, in Paris.

Cuban excitement was countered by the violence of the volunteers, Lersundi's incredibly well organized and fortified militia. He had conceived the idea of founding it as a firm support of his absolutism and the national unity he was trying to defend. As soon as he learned of revolutionary movement in the peninsula, Lersundi asked to be released from his office. We have already seen how he conducted himself in the interim. However, he was kept at his post to maintain order and the *status quo* in Cuba. Finally, General Serrano's government, alarmed by the growing strength of the revolutionary movement initiated at Yara and by Lersundi's failure to restrain it, decided to change tactics and asked to hear the claims of the Cuban reformists. He relieved Lersundi of his charge and named Domingo Dulce captain general.

General Domingo Dulce reached Havana January 4. Immediately he contacted the most influential, respectable people of the reform group, initiating his ancient politics of luring followers with promises of harmonious solutions.

The recall of Lersundi, the guiding light of their organization, greatly displeased the volunteers. They considered him the defender of the rights of national integrity, while they considered Dulce a Cuban sympathizer.

On January 6 Lersundi embarked for Europe. The volunteers gave him an ostentatious farewell demonstration in order to show, in a way that would leave no room for doubt, their great liking for the recalled leader and, of course, their displeasure over the substitution.

Seized with an extraordinary agitation they marched through the streets of Havana demonstrating very clearly their intransigent spirit and their intention of opposing all concessions to the Cubans.

Among General Dulce's first measures was the suppression of the Military Commission and the stay of proceedings of the political cases which the latter was formulating. He also freed the prisoners awaiting the trial of these cases. These measures were followed by the termination of censorship of the press, which action met with very unfavorable comments from the reactionary press.

The state of unrest that had prevailed in Havana continued. Not a day passed without some new provocation or incident. Sometimes a soldier was killed by a bullet which seemed to come from nowhere.

At times the victim was a Cuban. This state of uneasiness was increased by the daily appearance of newspapers and magazines which infuriated the Spaniards, especially the volunteers, who felt persecuted and ridiculed.

At that time Martí's schoolmate and dear friend, Fermín Valdés Domínguez, published a news sheet entitled *El Diablo Cojuelo* (The Little Lame Devil), to which Martí and others contributed. But humor was unquestionably not his forte, and his irresistible urge to write required a more serene, appropriate vehicle of expression. Consequently he, too, with the coöperation of Mendive and Cristóbal Madan, undertook the publication of a newspaper, *La Patria Libre*—a "democratic, cosmopolitan weekly," according to the sub-title. Only one number appeared, dated January 23.

Martí worked steadily on a dramatic poem which he was writing expressly for *La Patria Libre*. In this work he presented, symbolically, the heroism of Cuba, represented by Abdala, the ideal character who sacrificed himself for his country, personified by Nubia. At last Nubia triumphed, thanks to Abdala's efforts.

"Nubia has triumphed! I die happily; death matters little to me, for I have succeeded in saving her. . . . Oh, how sweet it is to die, when one dies fighting boldly to defend one's country!"

All his fervor accumulated during the years he spent in Mendive's school was condensed in this poem. He wrote it when his heart was wrung with mingled anguish and joy—

joy for the country he saw arising, anguish because he was not out there with the heroic armies, helping to forge it.

He saw one of his greatest dreams realized when his poem appeared in print alongside of prose and verse by the maestro. He felt unbounded happiness over that freshly printed sheet which he himself distributed among his schoolmates. Nevertheless he suffered a cruel experience: the censure of his parents, who looked with intense—and understandable—displeasure upon his literary inclinations, and especially his incipient political activities. We must not forget that Don Mariano was a police officer. He had just succeeded in being transferred from Batabanó and had taken charge of the station in the Cruz Verde district of Guanabacoa. After waiting so many years for a position with which he could keep his family from want, it was not fitting for his son to make himself conspicuous as an opponent of the prevailing regime. Moreover, he was risking his own freedom and even his life.

In the protecting shade of General Dulce's tolerance, a company of comic actors in the Villanueva Theatre was presenting programs displeasing to the volunteers. There were those who interpreted the plays as demonstrations in support of Céspedes' cause, and the audience did not conceal its sympathy with the spirit behind the presentations. The women, with flowing hair and tunics of blue and white, the colors of the Yara flag, symbolized a challenge to the authorities. Now it was rumored that the performances were being given to raise funds for the revolution. Without investigating the rumor, a plot was laid for a surprise attack on the defenseless audience. On the night of January 22, groups of volunteers fired upon the Villanueva Theatre, and panic resulted. The instant the first shots rang out, Mendive left his box through a door communicating with the adjoining building, the home of his mother-in-law, joint owner of the theatre. A large portion of the crowd followed him. Martí was at his side.

The news spread through the city. Doña Leonor, knowing that her son frequently attended the Villanueva performances with Mendive and his family, had good reason to think some misfortune might have befallen him. She was well acquainted with his ideas, since he had often spoken to her about *la patria* with spellbinding eloquence. Doña Leonor was not intransigent. At the bottom of her heart she felt great admiration for her son's talent. It was not just because Señor Mendive had told her so; she realized that her son was not like other boys. As time went on and he did not return, she became more and more distressed. After making inquiries she finally learned the truth: her son was hiding in a house surrounded by soldiers next to the Villanueva Theatre.

And Doña Leonor, "on that horrible night of the twenty-second when a multitude of armed men fell upon a multitude of defenseless men," went out to look for her son, with bullets flying past her and men falling dead around her as she crossed the streets.

"A carriage passes, through a rain of bullets. Weeping, they lay a dead woman inside. A hand knocks at the door in the blackness of the night. Not a bullet fails to pierce the door. And the woman who is knocking has given me life; my mother comes for me."

It was his mother. Surrounded by the wounded, with bullets flying across the streets, and shots aimed at another woman just missing her head, she went to seek him out, there where her great love had told her that she would find him.

General Dulce, who had seen his efforts hampered by the volunteers, dominated by the spirit of intransigence which Lersundi had managed so well to instill in them, knew that they were the instigators of this affair. However, he did not have sufficient support to face them. On the following day he issued a proclamation to the *habaneros,* couched in these threatening terms:

"Last night a scandalous incident occurred. It will be punished with all the rigor the law provides.

"Some of the disturbers of the peace are now in the power of the courts.

"Peaceful citizens: have faith in your authorities. Defenders of territorial integrity and national honor: justice will soon be done."

Thus he attempted to calm the prevailing excitement. But terror reigned for three consecutive days while the city was at the mercy of the volunteers. On the twenty-third and twenty-fourth the so-called "Louvre events" occurred. when a force situated at the entrance to San Rafael Street, opposite the Teatro Tacón and the Café Louvre, with the pretext of having been attacked, opened fire upon the buildings and took possession of them. On the twenty-fourth the Palacio de Aldama was sacked, and the volunteers committed the most unheard of outrages, seizing jewels and valuables and destroying everything they could not carry off.

The pro-Spanish press held the Cubans and, more or less covertly, General Dulce responsible for these events. *La Voz de Cuba* declared that a state of general madness must exist, for the events that had taken place could not be otherwise explained. Under the pseudonym Juan Fernández, Gonzalo Castañón, champion of the volunteers and editor of *La Voz de Cuba,* published in the form of a letter a terrible diatribe against General Dulce:

"Unfortunately for the country and for myself, you have not done enough in these days for our mutual satisfaction."

This sentence is sufficient so that one can imagine the rest of the letter, full of accusations and snares, a model of arrogance. If the volunteers' organ addressed the highest governmental authority in this tone, what must have been its procedure against the sons of the nation whom it considered suspect or disaffected?

What was the justification for Mendive's arrest? His mother-in-law's partial ownership of the theatre was not sufficient reason to hold him responsible for the provocation which the volunteers thought they saw in those performances. On the other hand his attitude of manifest sympathy for the separatist cause was well known. His name undoubtedly appeared on the list of enemies of the regime. Was he arrested at once, or on the following day in Guanabacoa, where he had some property and was living at the time? We only know that the next morning, escorted by two guards, he was seen boarding the Havana-bound train at the Guanabacoa depot. The people arriving at the station early in the morning were surprised to recognize as the illustrious poet Don Rafael María de Mendive that distinguished looking man of noble bearing, exquisite manners, prematurely gray hair and a clear gaze from which intelligence and kindness shown forth. Dr. Luis de la Calle, who happened to arrive just then, ran out to press his hand without noticing the soldiers and was met by a rifle blocking his way and the terse, imperious command to step back.

Mendive was taken to the Havana prison where he was kept incommunicado for three days. Afterwards friends came to visit him every day. Martí, inconsolable over his teacher's new sorrow, became Micaela's daily companion and seized every opportunity to be near Mendive. The poet's friends feared for his life because of the spirit of insubordination that prevailed among the troops. Thanks to General Dulce's interest in the petition of José Ignacio Rodríguez, Mendive was transferred to the Castillo del Príncipe.

Months of captivity followed. His friends were refused permission to visit him. His wife was allowed to see him every day, and she tried to stay as long as possible. Martí had a sudden, audacious impulse. Without any sort of recommendation he appeared before the *gobernador político,* Gutiérrez de la Vega, and requested a pass admitting him to Mendive's cell. Gutiérrez de la Vega was moved by the request of this boy who had a man's fortitude. His valor and loyalty won the governor's heart, and Martí obtained the pass. Mendive then had, in Martí, a son to love and serve him.

Martí did not give up his studies, and he continued to attend Mendive's school, which was maintained by his professors in his absence. But the school was finally closed, March 23, and since by the nature of his studies Martí was obliged to attend classes, he requested, on the thirty-first of that same month, the transfer of his registration to San Rafael school. This was accomplished without any difficulty. But it is known that the months of April and May passed without his attending this school. Doubtless Don Mariano's position did not permit him to pay for his studies in such a high-ranking school as this, directed by the educator Francisco María Casado. Meanwhile Martí had been auditing classes in the Institute in order to complete his preparations for the examination. Many of his friends had done the same.

Martí was soon surrounded by a group of companions who admired his exceptional qualities. His patriotic perorations, his literary criticism, his polemics with Pepe Cueto (his rival in the Spanish Grammar Competitions) denoted his outstanding intelligence. This group edited a manuscript newspaper entitled *El Siboney*, which Anastasio Mejías distributed among the students. In this paper Martí published, around the beginning of 1869, his bold, vigorous sonnet *October 10* which distinguished him (if he was not already sufficiently distinguished) as one of the enemies of Spanish domination. The closing lines were sufficient to confirm this impression:

"God be praised that at last Cuba breaks the hangman's noose that oppressed her and raises her head proud and free."

The group considered itself a conspiracy. The meeting place in the intervals between class was the landing on the stone stairway leading to the third floor of the ancient building on Obispo Street, the floor inhabited by Franciscan friars. The nature of these discussions had aroused suspicions; therefore the friars spied on them and afterwards reported them as enemies of the country. Thanks to the mediation of Isaac Carrillo and to the kindness of the rector, Don Antonio Bachiller y Morales, the extreme measures demanded by certain professors and by the secretary, Paulino Alvarez Aguiñica, were not carried out. But the group, now under suspicion, thinned out until only Martí and three more remained.

One morning a paper was found posted on the wall near the meeting place:

"Beware, Cubans! As long as there are friars there will be tyrants."

This time the boys were in danger of having to face a disciplinary council which would mete out harsh punishment. They had to leave the Institute.

Mendive's imprisonment lasted for four months. At the end of this time he was exiled to the town of Pinto, a few leagues from Madrid. Having embarked for Santander he arrived June 1, 1869, on board a mail ship. His letters to his friends, written shortly after reaching Spain, revealed that there, not the slightest respect was shown the sentence pronounced by the military court that tried him. On the contrary, all doors were opened to him, receiving him with cordial generosity. With his great dignity he set an example by "acquiring fame in Madrid without sacrificing his patriotic faith." Those very days when Mendive arrived in Spain a rebellion took place in Havana during which the volunteers burst into the palace of the Captain General, demanding his resignation. Forced to it by the troops, General Dulce embarked for Spain June 5.

When we consider that Martí's character during those last three years had developed in close contact with Mendive, who was more than a father to him, how great must have been his sadness during those months when he saw every refuge of his dreams shattered, and the generous teacher who had tempered his soul now far away, perhaps forever.

Now more than ever he was crushed by the terrible reality which had pursued him and from which he had tried to escape, as from a prison; the mediocre reality of his home, where he could find no spiritual warmth or understanding. He sensed within his heart a growing inspiration that called him, but without he heard only the incessant, brusque call to another reality which tried to destroy his inner life.

A great apathy, an "almost English sadness" took possession of him. For a few months he was almost an automaton. He understood the great abyss between his thoughts and the interests of his home. And he awaited resignedly the arrival of something unexpected that might free him from this situation to which he believed himself condemned.

The interruption of Martí's studies influenced Don Mariano to look for work for him. Not only so that he might help with the household expenses but also to free him from bad company, and more serious mishaps. The job he obtained for him in Don Cristóbal Madan's warehouse was indeed work that left him no spare time. He worked from six in the morning to eight at night and earned four and a half *onzas,* which he turned over to his father.

His only pleasant moments were those he experienced when Micaela received a letter from Mendive. The idea of joining his teacher obsessed him.

In a letter to Mendive he poured forth all his sorrow and made this confession:

"I confess to you with all my rude frankness, which you know so well, that only the hope of seeing you again has kept me from killing myself. Your letter yesterday saved me."

Martí's letter also informed Mendive of the latest events, and these were extremely important, having resulted in the arrest of his best friends. Only Martí remained free, suffering the most frightful loneliness and bound to a mean occupation. And well did God know that his greatest desire was to suffer punishment, as they had. Perhaps the punishment would be deportation. That would permit him at last to realize his dream: rejoin his teacher.

"The Domínguez brothers and Sellén," he wrote, "are still in jail. They released Fortier, the Frenchman, immediately upon the council's protest. These people, who are as cowardly as they are sanguinary, think that a Frenchman is innocent and a *criollo* guilty, when if it is a case of guilt at all, both are guilty."

5. Chains and Blood

In the year 1869, which had a tragic beginning, the course of Martí's life was determined.

On October 4, the birthday of His Most Serene Highness, the Regent of Spain, was celebrated. A great military parade was held in Havana. The troops were lined up from the Fuente de la India to the Castillo del Príncipe.

The city was filled with excitement as the parade began. The first battalion of Infantry Volunteers began marching down Industria Street. All the windows were crowded with people watching the parade. The division of army sanitation with its little burro carrying a medicine chest attracted everyone's attention. As the troops passed number 122, the Valdés Domínguez home, a terrible thing happened: the volunteers heard the laughter of some young people leaning out of the windows and frowned at them menacingly. The solemnity of the occasion prevented them from venting their indignation at that moment. They continued marching solemnly, but it was certain that they would return, as they had promised, to punish some unspecified crime, undoubtedly the irrepressible laughter which the little animal drew from the three young men named Eusebio Valdés Domínguez, Manuel Sellén, and Anastasio Fortier.

The youths attached no importance to the event. Perhaps they even thought that the volunteers' indignation was occasioned not so much by their laughter as by certain news. It was generally known by that time that the United States had sent a notice to the Madrid government "threatening to recognize the Cuban insurrectionists as belligerents."

Chains and Blood

A few moments after the incident, Sellén and Fortier withdrew, leaving Eusebio alone in his house. His brother Fermín soon arrived. He had just left Martí, who was also on his way home. Fermín found his parents extremely distressed, especially his mother, who had a premonition that the soldiers would return and the apparently insignificant occurrence would have lamentable results. While Fermín was being informed about what had taken place, the enemy rifle butts were heard pounding on the door.

Rudely the soldiers broke into the house. Fermín tried to keep them from arresting his brother without a warrant. His aged father stepped between Eusebio and the soldier who was attempting to arrest him, and the soldier raised his rifle to strike him with the butt. Fermín intercepted the blow by dealing the "defender of national unity" a well-timed blow with a chair.

The outcome of the day's events was that finally the volunteers apprehended the two brothers. At about eight in the evening they began the march through the streets of Havana. That night they slept in the municipal army quarters, each in a different cell. A few hours later they were joined by the two friends involved in the incident. They had also been arrested in their homes.

That same night when the four youths were behind bars, the Valdés Domínguez home was thoroughly searched. The volunteers seized a number of newspapers branded as *mambises* (or favoring the Cuban insurrectionists), broadsides published during those fleeting days of freedom of the press, with their waggish headlines and crackling ironies. They also found a good supply of the papers in which Fermín Valdés Domínguez and Martí had uttered their first childish words of rebellion: *El Diablo Cojuelo* and *La Patria Libre*. But among all their discoveries there was one that made them stop for a moment to look at each other with satisfaction as if they had found what they sought so eagerly—proof that the house was a den of conspirators. It was a letter addressed to Carlos de Castro y de Castro, a schoolmate who, forgetting Mendive's lessons, had enlisted as an officer in the Spanish army. The letter read:

33

Martí

"Have you ever dreamed of the glory of the apostates? Do you know how apostacy was punished in ancient times?" . . .

These opening sentences made a strong impression on the volunteers conducting the search. No doubt a grave offense against national unity was involved.

Two signatures appeared at the end of the letter, another cause for suspicion. Was it necessary for two persons to sign a letter like this? Were its contents that important?

When the search was finished late at night, they carried off many compromising papers, at least enough to send to jail for a year these boys who had the audacity to insult the worthy, battle-proven First Infantry Batallion.

In his letters to Mendive, Martí related all these happenings. To his grief over his teacher's absence was added this new worry over his friends' imprisonment. Had he not spent his happiest hours—his few free hours in the evening—since Mendive's imprisonment and deportation, at the Valdés Domínguez home? There he studied at the same desk with his friend, there he kept his poems and notes for prospective literary works, there he wrote Mendive, far from the disapproving atmosphere of his own home. During Fermín's imprisonment he visited his friend's parents everyday to inquire about him. On one of those days he wrote his teacher that letter which revealed so much pent-up sorrow, informing him: "The Domínguez brothers and Sellén are still in prison." No sooner had he mailed the letter than Martí was arrested in his home, on October 21.

Why was this arrest made seventeen days after that of his friends? That compromising letter to Carlos de Castro y de Castro was accomplishing its purpose. Martí's signature along with Fermín's was sufficient cause for suspicion. Martí was held for disloyalty after a minute investigation. In that investigation facts concerning Martí's recent activities were collected. His authorship of the sonnet *October 10*, published in *El Siboney,* was revealed, as well as his participation in the Institute conspiracy and the fact that it was he who obtained permission to publish *La Patria Libre.* His activities on the night of the Villanueva incident were also brought to light.

Chains and Blood

While preparations for the trial were under way, Martí had a visit from the prosecutor and was surprised at the interest which the latter showed in his case. "It is very strange that the one who is to try my case should ask me why I am a prisoner," he mused. But he was obsessed by his own ideas, which led him to ominous conclusions:

"The Domínguez brothers and Sellén will finally be released, and I shall remain a prisoner."

And he added:

"The outcome of my imprisonment hardly frightens me at all; but I shall not long endure being a prisoner. And this is all I ask: that they do no harm to one who in turn did no harm. At least they cannot accuse me of anything that I cannot undo."

His days of confinement matured his ideas and strengthened his character. If he was sorry to be behind bars, he was also grateful to his prison for the lessons he was receiving for life. He would not fail to profit by those lessons.

"I am sixteen years old," he wrote, and already many old men have told me that I seem old. And to a certain extent they are right, for if I have in its full strength, the recklessness and effervescence of youth, I have, on the other hand, a heart as small as it is wounded.

"It is true that you suffer intensely," he told his mother, "but it is also true that I suffer more. God grant that I may some day tell you of my sorrows in the midst of happiness."

The gravity with which Martí hurled himself into the maelstrom of life, faced his responsibilities, and prepared to discharge them, is surprising. These words to his mother are an indication of his character.

In jail his wants were few. He needed only an occasional two or three *reales* for coffee. His father had given him some money, but he had given part of it away as alms and loaned the rest.

His greatest pleasure during his imprisonment was derived from the interest with which the inmates surrounded him in order to hear about his teacher Mendive. Then Martí had moments of great eloquence, and they all understood that that slim, slightly pale boy with a strange glow in his sad eyes

Martí

was not like anyone they had ever seen before. For indeed it was as if the wisdom and experience of an old man spoke through the mouth of a boy.

Why was he unable to write a single line of poetry while he was in prison? "To a certain extent I am glad of it, because you know what the poetry I write or shall write is like," he told his mother.

But although he did not write verses, he wanted books to read, especially poetry, and one large book called *El Museo Universal*. In the immense solitude of those days, he found comfort in being still close to Fermín, who, like him and the other prisoners, was still awaiting the outcome of their case.

During the trial Martí acknowledged the letter taken from the Valdés Domínguez home and assumed the responsibility of writing it and signing both his name and his friend's. Fermín made the same affirmation, which roused the judge's suspicion in view of the similarity between the two signatures. On March 4, 1870, the date indicated for the court martial, the court was faced with the same problem, since each one insisted that he wrote the letter and signed for both. The court, perplexed, decided to cross-examine them together. Martí took advantage of the opportunity not only to assume all the blame very emphatically, but also to attack the Spanish regime and proclaim Cuba's right to independence. So unexpected was his burst of oratory that it shocked Fermín into silence and drew all the attention to Martí. It was his first political discourse and surely one of his most sublime, for he staked his life on it.

In thus resolutely challenging the ruling power, he committed the greatest crime of which a son of Cuba could be guilty. With inspired determination and brave eloquence he chose the course which he was to follow for the rest of his life: uncompromising dignity. It was as if the idea of suicide which had sometimes crossed his mind had now pointed out to him the hard road which he must follow. Or as if he had taken a secret vow to crusade for an ideal now firmly enshrined in his heart. The courage with which he uttered phrases that fell like sacrilege on the judge's ears, because they upheld his country's right to independence, could only spring from a firm conviction. He knew how to distinguish between a child's impulse and a carefully weighted resolution, as he had said a few days previous in a letter to Mendive.

Despite the harshness of the military men who judged Martí, it must be admitted that for a moment they were touched by that seventeen-year old lad's courage, eloquence, and sense of dignity. Dignity, when it appears in an atmosphere of submission, has the power of momentarily crushing even tyranny itself.

The penalty unanimously accorded Martí by the court martial that same day was six years' imprisonment whereas Fermín was sentenced to only six months of arrest. His friends Eusebio and Fortier were deported from the island for "as long as present conditions exist."

The enormous difference in the sentences shows that Martí was convicted of a much more serious crime. He was tried for two offenses: insulting the company of sappers of the First Battalion of Infantry Volunteers and suspicion of disloyalty. The suspicion fell conclusively upon Martí. Even if this were not true, Martí had just dispelled before the jury any doubts that might have been entertained.

The sentence also specified that Martí was to serve his term in the *presidio* or penitentiary. Fermín was to be confined in the fortress of La Cabaña.

April 4, 1870, a few minutes before leaving the jail to enter the penitentiary, he wrote in the notebook which he always carried with him a few lines declaring his belief in the joy of sacrificing oneself for one's country:

"Within you I locked my hours of joy and bitter pain. Permit me, at least, to leave my soul with my farewell upon your pages. I am going to a great house where they tell me that to live is to die. My country leads me there. For my country, to die is to know greater joy."

Martí arrived at his dark cell and went in behind the bars. The following personal details were entered on his registration blank: medium weight, white race, brown eyes, brown hair, beardless.

Then the blows of the hammer rang out lugubriously as chains were fastened to his feet. He put on the uniform of the institution; from then on he was number 113 in the first brigade.

Then, feeling no fear, only pity, he awaited the arrival of the men who were to be his companions the next day at forced labor in the quarry.

Finally those companions arrived. Their heads were bent, their faces thin, their hands covered with sores. They did not walk, they dragged themselves along, their sunken eyes glowing with mute despair. Among them Martí discovered one who was more bent, emaciated, and exhausted than all the others, a venerable man whose hair had turned completely white. His soiled clothes were stained with blood. An uncontainable impulse made Martí run toward the old man. On seeing the youth Don Nicolás de Castillo pressed Martí's hands in his own while the tears ran down his wrinkled face.

"Poor thing! Poor lad!" he said.

When the old man raised his shirt and asked Martí to look, he saw a sore that covered his back, oozing blood and pus. That was the condition in which the old man had just come from work—work in the stone quarries of San Lázaro!

Martí could hardly believe what his eyes told him. The horror reflected in his eyes was his only comment. Such cruelty and undeserved suffering pained him deeply.

"Why did they do this to you?" he said at last.

"My son, you would probably not believe me. Ask any one of the others and he will tell you."

That very night Martí's companions in misery told him of the sufferings of old Castillo. The chains that shackled their bodies became a firm bond uniting their souls. Martí trembled, not with terror, but with indignation at that account of the suffering of Castillo, whose only offense consisted in desiring his country's independence. Martí felt great admiration for the martyred man. And he was more firmly convinced than ever before that he must live in order to denounce such shame and crime to the world and consecrate himself to the redemption of his brothers.

On the following day he began the daily trip to the quarry. The penitentiary was more than a league away from the quarries. At half past four the morning call aroused him. He had hardly slept all night, stretched out on the wretched canvas which served him as a bed. When he arose he felt like one of those ailing spectres which had occupied his thoughts since the previous night. Mechanically his hands moved the reservoir pumps, beginning the morning tasks, and then he took his place in line and marched to work.

The men marched silently in the cold of the early morning, dragging their chains, which made a noise resembling an infernal saraband as they walked. It was still completely dark when they reached the quarry. A few minutes later, pick in hand, Martí began to split rocks under the gaze of the watchmen who occasionally brought their rods down on the men's bent backs. Their backs also smarted under the whip, which drew blood. More than in his own flesh, Martí felt it cut into the flesh of the many poor wretches around him.

The quarry occupied an extensive area over a hundred yards deep. The bottom was covered with piles of broken rock. The spaces between the piles were so narrow that a man with a load could hardly pass through. At the sides were extremely narrow niches where the huge masses of stone frequently fell thundering down. There they threw the men who had fallen to the ground in a faint and lain in the hot sun for hours. Carrying the broad loading boxes on their backs, the men climbed up the steep hills to the lime kilns, often coming back blind. The heat was so stifling that their sweating bodies received the refreshing rain avidly. They did not cease work unless it rained very hard, in which case they rested briefly beneath the excavations. And ceaselessly the noise of the chains, the thud of the club against flesh, the blasphemies of the cudgelers and the terrible silence of the beaten ones continued from dawn until far into the night when fifty pale, emaciated, scourged men returned over the same road in a plaintive, spectral procession.

The quarry was situated next to the road to La Chorrera, a road of vice and opprobrium. In the afternoon the uniformed hordes from Cangas and Covadonga came arm in arm with drunken women adorned with red and yellow ribbons. They amused themselves by aiming their rifles at the old men and children who, blinded by impotent ire, ascended their *via crucis* from the depths of the quarry with chains around their feet and stones hurled at their heads. Bitter thoughts passed through Martí's mind as the wicked jibes, punctuated with shrieks and laughter, reached the depths of that inferno. The gravity of the Cuban problem was revealed to him with increasing clarity. It was not a matter of political liberties. It was a matter of dishonor, of corruption and vice which made it impossible to live an honorable life. It was not being able to eat a loaf of bread that was not broken with shame.

What a bitter day it was when his father managed to see him and he tried to conceal from him the sores on his body! Don Mariano could not restrain his grief when he approached him and found him so resigned and superior to the suffering which had been inflicted upon him. His son spoke to him about the others, but Don Mariano guessed all that he was holding back. One detail which José told him broke his heart: the chain constantly dug into his flesh and bruised it. What a tragic scene took place when the good father brought the soft cushion which Doña Leonor had made and bathed in her tears! Don Mariano insisted on placing it himself over his son's wounded flesh. He was horrified at the sight of those sores covered with dust and blood and continuously irritated by walking, under the guard's unappealable orders.

Martí could imagine his mother's tears as well, in that heart breaking moment when Don Mariano's deep love of him was revealed. As he returned, on wounded feet, to the task that would not be finished until night, he thought of the sad scene that would take place in his house when Don Mariano went back with that new pain in his soul and between sobs revealed the truth to his mother.

On August 28 when he sent her a recent photograph in which he was dressed as an inmate of the penitentiary with the chain extending from his waist to his foot, he wrote her some verses of consolation and resignation which also concealed a hope—the great hope he now cherished:

"Look at me, mother, and do not weep because of your love! If as a slave of my age and my doctrines I filled your martyred heart with thorns, remember that flowers are born among thorns!"

Don Mariano had hoped his son would be given a light sentence. He saw that the penalty had been made extremely severe. How could they give Fermín only six months' punishment and his son six years, when the offense was the same?—

Chains and Blood

if there was an offense. For some time he had been displeased with the course that events were taking. A professional soldier who had always honored the army he represented and was proud to have belonged to it, he despised the cruel, stupid volunteers. Now that he saw injustice preying upon his young son, Don Mariano felt greater admiration and affection for the boy, for his sincerity, his valor, his keen sense of justice.

Don Mariano had made use of his connections with certain army leaders to see if he could do something to help his son. His position as policeman gave him an opportunity to approach certain authorities, but the best promise of help had come from Don José María Sardá. Don Mariano made his acquaintance during the intervals spent waiting for the ship, and he even had the opportunity of doing him certain small favors. Sardá's influence with the authorities through his firm friendship with the Captain General was well known. Furthermore he was the concessionary of the quarries where Martí worked. Sardá made a real effort to answer Don Mariano's plea. He verified the account of the boy's suffering. The lamentable state in which he found him, with his eyes burned by the lime and the sun, touched him so deeply that he immediately had him transferred to the penitentiary cigar factory. There with his arms fastened to the worktable in the shop, the days passed no less terribly than those he had spent in the quarries. From this table to which he had been sent by a benevolent order he contemplated his companions' torture. He would have liked to sacrifice at their sides, sharing their pain. But it would have been a futile sacrifice; he needed to recover his freedom if he was to consecrate his life, as was his most vehement desire, to the fight for his country's liberty.

Sardá took a very personal interest in Martí's problem. At the same time and most likely at Sardá's suggestion, Doña Leonor submitted a petition to the Captain General asking for her son's pardon.

"Behold the little sisters and the sad mother of the unfortunate José Martí, a youth of barely seventeen years sentenced to six years of imprisonment for three words written when he was hardly fifteen, in a letter he wrote to a schoolmate when he was attending the *colegio*."

Martí

Doña Leonor presented this petition in August, and a month later "taking into consideration Don José Martí's youth," the Captain General changed his sentence of six years in the penitentiary to exile to the Isle of Pines. He was ordered transferred to the Havana jail. At that time, however, Martí was in the fortress of La Cabaña, where he had undoubtedly been sent because of his health.

September 30, as a result of the change of sentence, he entered the Havana jail, remaining there until October 13, when he was transferred to the Isle of Pines. Although the decree of pardon was communicated to the lieutenant governor of the island, Martí was delivered directly to his protector, who had agreed to take care of him. Indeed, Sardá took the boy to his country home, *El Abra*. Here he was given a room in the spacious old house. He won the love of Don José María's wife and his small children. Absorbed in his own thoughts, he spent most of the time in his room writing or reading. Sometimes he strolled around in the vicinity of the house, or sat in the shade of the trees for hours. During his walks he carried with him, fastened to his waist, the chains that had accompanied him during those unforgettable months. He refused to part with them, as if he did not want the thought of the horrors he had witnessed to be erased from his mind. Such was his state of mind and his firm resolution that at night he even put them under his bed in order not to be separated from them more than was necessary.

His aptitude for teaching became more clearly defined as he dedicated several hours every day to the instruction of Sardá's daughters, just as he had done before with his little sisters. He thought of his sisters when the little girls surrounded him, eager to hear his explanations. The memory of Mendive also came to his mind. If only he could join his teacher!

When the classes were over he went into the village in the family coach, to pick up or to send mail. When he received letters from his mother and sisters or from the companions with whom he had studied and shared ideals, he experienced a few moments of happiness.

Martí had won the love of the Sardá family. Don José María, who, like a good Catalan, was inclined to understand the boy's ideas, had promised to help him obtain complete pardon in order to realize his ambition to go to Spain. Martí reminded him of this ambition several times until one day on returning from Havana, Sardá showed him a document addressed to the lieutenant governor of the Isle of Pines. It was a notice that permission had been granted to Don José Martí y Pérez to return to Havana with the object of going to Spain and "with the understanding that the above mentioned will stand the expense of the passage."

December 18 Martí left the Isle of Pines bound for Havana. His generous protector accompanied him. Don Mariano met them in Batabanó.

By dint of great sacrifices he managed to acquire the necessary sum to pay for his transportation, and to have a little reserve until he found a means of supporting himself in Spain. Sardá's generosity probably contributed in great measure to make the trip possible, for of course he wanted to give him the great pleasure of joining his teacher.

The thirty-first of December he was issued a passport, and January 15, 1871 he embarked for Spain on board the mail ship *Guipúzcoa*, bound for Cádiz.

Two hours before embarking, he wrote to Mendive, who was then in the United States, "I have suffered much, but I am confident that I have known how to suffer. And if I have had the strength for all this, and if I feel strong enough to really be a man, I owe it to you only; and all the good, loving part of my character is yours, and only yours."

The next day when Martí went on deck to gaze at the blue sky and feel against his face the cool sea breeze, he had a disagreeable encounter that revived all his bloody memories of the quarry. On the same boat was the Head of the Penitentiary, Commandant Mariano Gil de Palacio, the man directly responsible for the inhuman punishments inflicted upon old Castillo, Lino Figueredo, the little twelve-year old Negro boy and so many others whose tortures had made Martí's soul rebel. At that point he made a firm resolution from which no one could dissuade him. There was the man who had been worse than a wild beast toward his companions and toward him. His opportunity for revenge was at hand. At the moment when the officer was near a group of passengers whom Martí was entertaining with his talk, he volunteered: "Do you want me to tell you some of the things I saw in prison?" They all grouped around him, and he told the story of a prisoner who managed to send the Captain General an account of the conduct of the Head of the Penitentiary. The Captain General turned over the letter to the Head of the Penitentiary, and the latter took his vengeance:

"Are you the author of this letter?"

"Yes sir," answered the man.

"Well, now you are going to eat this whole sheet of paper, or I'll shoot you."

And he forced the prisoner to swallow, not only the written half of the folded sheet, but the blank half as well. Then he ordered twenty-five lashes for the culprit, who received the first, and as a consequence had to be taken to the infirmary. When he was returned to the penitentiary for the second one, he died.

When the passengers expressed their indignation after Martí had finished, he added these words:

"Well, gentlemen, that man of whose deeds you have just learned, that man for whom you feel such great and well-deserved contempt is the gentleman seated over there."

Part II:

Years of Exile

6. Exiles in Madrid

While intransigence in Cuba had been growing more acute ever since the September revolutionary movements, in Spain too the idea of Cuban independence was struggling to gain ground. Prim, a friend of Céspedes and the leader of the government that replaced Isabel the Second, sought a means of offering Cuba autonomy similar to that enjoyed by Canada, or incorporation into Spain as a federal province.

Aware that the real obstacle was in Cuba, not Spain, he pondered over the only plan he considered feasible: the disarmament of the volunteers with the pretext of reorganization. From Vichy, on September 9, 1869, he wrote to Caballero de Rodas concerning this plan. Caballero de Rodas belonged to the same insurgent military group as Serrano, Topete, and Prim. He answered the suggestion in terms as violent as they were final, definitely aligning himself with the volunteers. In his reply he informed Prim that when a government does not support individuals or even collectivities, the latter have no other recourse than to take justice into their own hands, with the pen, the garrote, or the rifle.

And carrying his indignation to extreme limits, he wrote:

"Fortunately, we Spaniards here have not degenerated, as apparently is the case over there; and as long as there is a single one to hold on high the flag of Castile, Cuba will be Spanish, in defiance of that government and of the whole world."

What hopes could the Cubans possibly entertain after hearing these words with which the supreme authority of the Island received the first hint of a just solution?

47

Martí

From that moment on, a new classification of Spaniards was established: the good and the bad, the pure and the degenerate. The good Spaniards were those in favor of continuation in Cuba of the régime of oppression and negation of all freedom, all right, a régime propitious to fraud and slave trade and profitable to the exploiters, many of whom were Cubans. The bad Spaniards were those who proclaimed the necessity of abolishing the infamous slave trade and wished to see the colonies given treatment analogous to that received by the other provinces of Spain.

From this atmosphere charged with rancor, hatred, and injustice, Martí departed. And the very day that he was issued a passport for Spain, December 30, 1870, Prim died as the result of a savage attempt on his life in which the slave traders of Cuba undoubtedly participated, determined to suppress the threat that his liberal ideas signified for them.

Martí had just arrived in Madrid. Now he saw more clearly Cuba's problem. A newspaper branded as a *"filibustero"** because it was a champion of liberty and attempted to clarify everything pertaining to colonial affairs, gave an account of a telegram published by *The New York World*. The telegram stated that on the same night when the official notice of General Prim's death was received, the Count of Valmaseda attended the Teatro de Albisu; that during the performance he was very pleased, and that in his private room in the theatre there was a profusion of dainties, refreshments, and champagne.

Aside from these incidents, Martí found in Spain an atmosphere of liberty and consideration. Those who were called bad Spaniards in Cuba because they tried to listen to the complaints of the oppressed, were able here to understand the *good* Cubans, those who fought for freedom in their own country.

Martí conceived the idea of making himself heard in this environment so different from that of his distant island. During his stay on the Isle of Pines, he had decided to write a poem based on the suffering he had seen and endured in the stone-quarry. He considered himself the symbol of the vindi-

* *Filibustero:* A pirate, but also a person who worked for or favored the cause of emancipation of the Spanish colonies. (Ed.)

cating spirit of his brothers who stayed behind, crushed by that agony of chains and blood. He represented all those who were waiting for a little justice and liberty. He had made them a promise; the time had come to begin to keep it.

In Madrid he established himself in a small sunny room. Immediately he began to contact Cubans who had liberal ideas concerning their country. Many of them were exiles like himself; others were living there in freedom because they could not endure the polluted air of the Colony. Most of them were men of letters and political figures, well known for their participation in public affairs. Martí was received with open arms by these compatriots who perceived that he was already, in spite of his youth, a man inspired by the idea of liberty. Martí was impressed by such distinguished men as José Calixto Bernal and José Ramón Betancourt.

Most of the time during his first months in Madrid he visited José Ramón Betancourt's hospitable, cultured home, a pleasant refuge for those who worked unceasingly for their country's independence.

Gathered around the fireplace, the visitors read *La Cuestión Cubana*, published in Seville by Nicolás Sterling's son, or admiringly turned the pages of *Las Dos Banderas*, which their host had just published in Seville. They spoke of men like Francisco Díaz Quintero, the editor of *El Jurado Federal*, which defended Cuba's right to clemency and freedom. They spoke of Gaspar Betancourt Cisneros, whose works, carefully compiled in notebooks, Martí read reverently. The meetings were attended by Calixto Bernal, the valiant author of *La Vindicación*.

In that atmosphere of love of Cuba Martí submitted some of the pages he had written about the penitentiary. The most impressive part was doubtless the heartrending story of old Castillo, whom he had loved ever since his first day in prison. This account was so moving that from then on Martí was respected; a few days later it was published in *La Soberanía Nacional* of Cádiz. It was a fragment of a work that he was preparing for publication. Shortly afterward he assembled his friends in Betancourt's house to read them the entire manuscript, on which he had worked night and day.

49

Martí

He attained memorable success the night he read *El Presidio Político en Cuba* (The Military Prison in Cuba), as he called his essay into which he had put so much ardor, so much ire restrained by love.

Martí began slowly in a muffled voice. Gradually he progressed from spiritual and philosophical considerations to a gloomy evocation of the Dantesque scene, and across his pages filed the figures of the martyrs, old men and children converted into living sores, blood and pain. What he saw, what he felt, what he remembered like a persistent, unhealed burn in his breast; that which he could never erase from his thoughts and would pursue him like a perennial nightmare, —it was all there, evoked in strong pictures, between entreaties to heaven and execrations of men, between outbursts of infinite indignation and of infinite compassion.

Vacillations of a faith shaken by so much evil among men; a desire to burst out weeping and to utter blasphemies; a child's faltering and a vindicator's lightning blows. How great was their anguish as they heard the reading of these pages, which began with a reference to Dante's Inferno!

"Dante was never in prison. If he had felt the dark vaults of that torment crashing down upon his brain, he would not have invented his Inferno. He would have copied it and thus portrayed it more vividly."

Could anyone have described Cuban suffering more eloquently? This work which he read to his friends was a poem of suffering—and of hope, for "the idea of good prevails over everything and is never suppressed." The understanding listener perceived that something like predestination pervaded the whole poem.

When Martí finished, many eyes were reddened by tears, and the first words uttered came from trembling lips. What could be the meaning of so much sacrifice, except to temper others to the point where they would seek a remedy? It was not his suffering that led Martí to write *El Presidio Político en Cuba*; it was this hope that his revelation would illumine his listeners' souls and strengthen their determination. He did not write a bare relation of what his eyes saw, but rather a poem of lofty religious sentiment, in which an invisible choir intoned words of pardon and love as the heroes tempered their spirits for the great crusade.

That same night it was agreed to publish Martí's essay. He could not afford to pay for the printing, but his friends felt that it was very important to make known this work which contained the unappealable force of an experienced reality, and would help a great deal to further the Cuban cause. At least, thought the most skeptical, it would serve to make life more tolerable for the unfortunate inmates of the Cuban penitentiary.

For a few weeks Martí was very busy reading the proofs of his little book, which was finally printed by the Ramón Ramírez press.

In Spain numerous publications printed harsh comments on the acts of barbarism that the Havana dailies reported without the slightest protest. Some, like *La Discusión*, devoted most of their fervor to the anti-slavery campaign carried on by the Spanish Abolitionist Society, modeled after the English organization. A few days after establishing himself in Madrid, Martí had the opportunity of attending a meeting on February 15 in the Alhambra theatre. The speakers were Carrasco, Revilla, Giner, General Milans del Bosch and Don Gabriel Rodríguez. But the briefest and most eloquent speech was that of General Sickles. Acting not in his capacity of American ambassador in Spain, but simply as a plain soldier, he revealed his body, mutilated in the holy cause of abolition, as he said:

"I may not know how to defend the cause with words, but I have known how to sacrifice my body and shed my blood for it."

Shortly afterwards the English Abolitionist Soiety addressed a message to Don Amadeo de Saboya, asking him to break the chains of the unhappy slave. But the problem of slavery, like the problem of Cuba, was untouchable beneath the cloak of Spanish unity guarded by the Havana volunteers.

Some newspapers analyzed the Cuban case as a matter of humanity.

"Consider the glorious spirits of the aged Domingo Goicuría and Pedro Figueredo; of the Agüero brothers, young men of twenty-two and twenty-four years executed in each other's presence, giving each other a fraternal kiss before ascending to their place of execution; Luis Ayestarán, Rodrigo Tamayo, executed with his son, and that innumerable Cuban cavalry, that puts us to shame, for it has taught us how to die for one's country."

And even *La Cuestión Cubana*, a few days later, pointed out the immense difference between the Spaniards living in Spain and the Spaniards in Cuba. It accused the latter of putting their compatriots to shame through their intransigence and their system of exploitation.

And dealing with specific cases in opposition to a Havana moralist who wrote for a mercenary paper, *La Cuestión Cubana* stated:

"It is immoral and therefore a crime against human dignity and legal rights to erect the gallows before the accused man is tried, as was the case in the aged Don Domingo Goicuría's trial, and it is even more criminal and infamous to have the executioner with his instruments of torture carried on a litter through the streets of the capital of the Antilles, accompanied by that mob thirsty for Cuban blood. How wretched and impotent is the authority of the Island of Cuba!"

And then it added another incident which Martí had made known in Madrid: the case of the little boy Lino Figueredo, who crossed the pages of *El Presidio Político* like a soul in agony.

Directly or indirectly, all the Cubans who truly loved their country collaborated with this press, which was inspired by the justice of the island's cause, the cause of liberty and humanity. Martí could not fail to belong to that group. That worthy press, in which rights were defended sincerely and intelligently, frequently published keen comments on the Spanish dispatches arriving from Cuba and gleefully printed by the obscurantist press. These dispatches concerned the crushing defeat of the Cubans, mass demonstrations and hundreds if not thousands dead or imprisoned, when only a few days before the same newspapers were printing news to the effect that the number of insurrectionists in Cuba was extremely small. "How can such a sudden increase in numbers be possible?" asked the liberal press. With unheard-of impudence *La Época* stated in March that there were only about four hundred insurrectionists on the Island, and shortly afterward an item appeared in its columns to the effect that more than eight thousand men had surrendered and more than seven hundred had died. Doubtless the multiplication of the species took on miraculous proportions in the rebel camp. The debate grew more heated. Mendacious notices in the newspapers controlled by slave traders provided material for commentaries. The latter were also frequently based on communiqués from the North American press. All possible means were utilized in order to expose the dishonorable war being waged against Cuban insurrection, to the shame of the peninsular Spaniards. Helplessly they watched their nation fall into discredit because of the slave-traders who kept an iron grip on their commerce with all the strength of their sinister power.

No stronger comments could be made about Spain and her régime than those appearing in the pro-Cuban newspapers. Did they not publish Céspedes' proclamation denouncing to the world the assassination of the Mola family, the most inhuman, repugnant crime committed against women and children by Spanish soldiers?

And did not nearly all of these papers contain commentaries on the *Libro de Sangre* (Book of Blood) published in New York? This was a record, with dates and places indicated, of 4,478 men shot or garroted and over 150,000 killed in the war.

A more moderate newspaper, *La Constitución,* directed by Nicolás Azcárate, offered this circumspect comment:

"We are hurt and shamed by a fact we wish to bring to the attention of the public and the government: the fact that such actions as are recorded in this book can take place anywhere in the world; therefore we protest once more against the slaughter of the prisoners, and the punishment of political offenses by shooting or by the death sentence. Whenever any one of the scenes described in *El Libro de Sangre* takes place, regardless of the nation in which it occurs, the universal conscience is alarmed and trembles with indignation and pain. The press in all civilized nations has an imperative duty always to champion the cause of humanity and of right, whatever the reason for the war may be. We have an especially strong obligation to do so when we hear and read that this is happening in one of our own provinces."

With the publication of *El Presidio Político* Martí had paid his first sacred debt to his brothers in the quarries; the world then knew the fate of those condemned to prison on the Island for political reasons. He now belonged to the most representative group among the Cubans who were fighting with their ideas for the same liberties which their people sought with weapons in their hands.

Although he lived very simply in Madrid, his financial reserve was dwindling, and he needed some means of support. His popularity and the high esteem in which he was held by his compatriots enabled him to tutor for a decorous sum. He gave lessons at the home of Don Leandro Alvarez Torrijos and the home of the widow of the Spanish general Ravenet. With these classes, plus a few occasional pesos earned by doing extra work, he had enough for his meagre necessities and his great luxuries: books, art museums, and the theatre. He earned a few pesos by translating a contract full of strange technical terms, making use of his precarious English, which had been so important to Don Mariano. His boots needed resoling, but instead of buying shoes he spent his money on reproductions of great paintings.

He began teaching in order to support himself. At the same time, however, mindful of the necessity of forging for himself the best possible weapons for the struggle to come, he carried out his plan to continue his studies, which were interrupted in Havana. Like his teacher Mendive, he too wished to make a reputation for himself in Madrid without sacrificing his patriotic faith. After learning to know this Spanish environment, he realized that the Cuban cause found a sympathetic response in the purest, noblest element among the common people, although it would never find it in the government that represented the people. The government would always be sold to the cause of the profiteers who indulged their own whims in the Island. They had so much influence in the Corte that they could thwart the plans of the best-intentioned governors.

Exiles in Madrid

The school system in Spain was advantageous to Martí because it allowed him to register for and be examined in university courses without having finished his secondary school program. (He was in the third year in Mendive's school when it closed.) Thanks to this anomaly he began his studies in the Universidad Central de Madrid May 31, 1871, four months after his arrival; he registered in the Faculty of Law for first year Roman law, administrative law, and political economy.

But art galleries, theatres, and libraries fascinated him just as much as his studies, and probably more. He could not resist art museums. He spent hours in the Prado before the great paintings of Velásquez, Murillo, or Goya. Here for the first time he met artistic creation in all its power. Goya was the strong father who mastered all difficulties. In the little notebook he always carried with him he recorded his impressions. In the presence of *la Maja* he attempted to decipher the enigma of the great painting, "a brusque and fortunate break with all conventionality." Perhaps this trait and extreme delicacy were the qualities that impressed him most of all in this painter of painters. And concerning the eyes of this clothed Venus, Andalusian, human, feminine, palpable, and real, he wrote: "One never tires of losing oneself in the contemplation of her eyes. In this lay the painter's subtlety: voluptuosity without eroticism."

He also spent many hours in the National Library. There he not only studied and broadened his knowledge by consulting works of reference, he also informed himself about the literature of his day. In Madrid, according to his observations, there was little scientific activity but a great deal of good literary production. The rich Spanish literature, according to Martí, was intimately related with the "Spanish sky, still blue, and the Spanish imagination, not very compatible, indeed, with the grave German speculations. These have been studied, without originality but with great labor and amplitude, by Saenz del Río, and are being studied today by Patricio Azcárate, Mesía, Francisco Giner, and the logical honorable, vigorous Salmerón . . . austere, pure, brilliant spirits, truly legitimate sons of mother science."

Martí

This was the epoch when Krausism was in its plenitude, acquiring a powerful influence represented by those formidable figures whom Martí cited and by others such as Ríos Portillo and Romero Girón. The idea of Germanizing the spirit, of expounding barren theories and abstruse concepts in a muddled style was not at all attractive to Martí. But Krausism was imbued with a high ethical sense which had its effect on the doctrine, and this was congenial to Martí's spirit. It was a vigorous doctrine. Its ideal was to apply theory to daily living. Perhaps the attempt to impregnate reality with that ethical sense was not always successful, but the purpose of the followers of Krause was to act according to noble principles. In general, it can almost be said that it became a sort of sect of honorable men who set a shining example of stoic civic virtues in the midst of the concupiscent spectacle of the September revolution. That revolution, before it prostituted itself, was directed by followers of Krause, men who, inspired by his philosophy, defended freedom of conscience. One who had to move in cultured circles as Martí did could not afford to be ignorant of the doctrine prevailing at that time. But he not only studied it, doubtless he followed it as represented by men like Salmerón or Don Francisco Giner de Los Ríos.

The theatre lured him with an irresistible power. Even as a child he was overjoyed when an old barber, who had discovered his inclination, would ask him to deliver a pair of blond braids for the leading lady or ferocious mustachios for the villain, for thus he had an opportunity to watch the performances from the stage. Later, when he was about fourteen, he was absorbed in the translation of *Hamlet*. And his first work was a dramatic poem which revealed his creative talent.

In the propitious environment of Madrid his old inclination found soil in which to take root. What an enchanting experience a first-night was in one of the theatres of the Corte! For one who placed spiritual values above all else, these displays of talent must have given him hours of the utmost happiness. The women in the orchestra seats all seemed beautiful, like multi-colored flowers, and their red-lipped smiles emanated perfume and charm. Intelligent opinions were exchanged, and words of praise or censure were uttered with sparkling wit. He enjoyed listening to others' opinions more than expounding his own, but his perspicacity and refined taste were already apparent. Nothing that he said was commonplace, and he often expressed himself with such originality that authors and artists took pleasure in listening to him. Thus he met and won the esteem of men like Echegaray, whom he saw frequently in a salon of El Teatro Español, and the rebellious Marcos Zapata, a restless, romantic spirit harrassed by a vulgar reality to which he could not conform. Martí praised such works of Echegaray as *La Esposa del Vengador,* which he credited with an original plot, lofty ideas, and extraordinary merits that outweighed any defects. He congratulated Marcos Zapata for his lofty, vigorous inspiration, especially in *El Castillo de Simancas,* which both enraptured and chilled the audience of the classic playhouse of El Príncipe.

In the Ateneo he found a group of writers with progressive ideas and was received respectfully and shown great consideration. Many famous *salons* were opened to him, like those of the Marqués de San Gregorio, the Marquesa de Vega Armijo, and the Villaurrutias. These salons were frequented by illustrious men of letters, artists, and political figures.

In the affectionate atmosphere of the home of Barbarita Echeverría, the distinguished Cuban widow of General Ravenet, he found an understanding love that tried to alleviate his afflictions. When the intellectual circles accepted him and listened to him with intense interest, Martí felt his faith in Cuba's destiny strengthened. The same person who had left Cuba a few months before unknown and mistreated by a brutal regime was now a human being breathing the air of freedom and tolerance. This was the way he was made free, the way he was made a man, and it could never have been accomplished so fully under the iniquitous regime that dominated his country. That was another grave truth that Spain had taught him.

His precarious state of health, combined with patriotic activities and economic difficulties, hindered his progress in his studies. He suffered from an extremely painful lesion which sometimes obliged him to go to bed and often prevented him from walking—the result of his months of forced labor in the quarries. He underwent two operations to cure this malady, which would always remind him of his prison life, for it was caused by a blow from his chain; but the operations were unsuccessful, and he continued to suffer. Under such circumstances, study was difficult, and he kept postponing it, while his literary and patriotic activities kept increasing. He passed in only two subjects: Roman Law (first course) and Political and Administrative Law. In August he registered for the second course in Roman Law, but he failed both in this subject and in Political Economy.

The polemics between pro-slavery and liberal newspapers were growing more and more bitter, virtually a war without quarter. Faced with the bare facts and with the appeal to humanitarian sentiments made by the defenders of Cuba, the champions of "national unity" countered by wearing out the words pirate, conspirator, insurrectionist.

The execution of Zenea before a firing squad, under mysterious circumstances that reflected on the honor of Spain, was another event of which the press made use in order to accentuate still more the blackness of Cuban reality. Francisco Díaz Quintero, in the midst of a session of Congress, with uncommon straightforwardness, harshly censured the volunteers who were dishonoring Spain and shocking the world with their outrages.

So many voices were raised in condemnation of the "invincible ones," as the volunteers were called in bittter mockery, that the reactionary papers conspired to blame "pirate gold" for everything done or said within Spain in Cuba's defense.

La Época gave an account of a demonstration staged the fourth of October by at least a hundred rebels, it claimed, including some who had been deported by the Cuban authorities.

"These sly birds who are giving vigorous support in their newspapers to Señor Rivero as candidate for the presidency of the Spanish *Cortes,* never cease for a moment to conspire in every possible way against Spain. Rebel gold circulated widely in Madrid yesterday . . . Until there is a campaign against . . . internationalists, and demagogues, the interests of liberty, of society, and of the nation will be in danger."

Exiles in Madrid

With the worst of intentions—that of arousing governmental persecution and thwarting the campaign progress, these denunciations gradually became more insistent. Faced with a reality as obvious to the whole world as the cruelty of Spain's conduct, the reactionaries preferred to unleash prejudice against the righteous clamor of the defenders of the victims, rather than try to prevent the evil.

Every denunciation of injustice, every reproach to the barbarity enthroned in the Island was interpreted as support of revolution. This was the monotonous accusation of the newspapers supporting the cause of national unity.

7. Pain and Duty

Martí was bedridden when the volunteers committed the most tragic of all their crimes: the execution of the students before a firing squad.

The news of the trial spread through Spain. Martí anxiously followed the daily newspaper accounts, which grew steadily more alarming. It seemed so monstrous that those boys, many of whom were his schoolmates in the Institute, could be killed! But although it seemed impossible, his grief-stricken heart was seized with a terrible premonition. If he had already seen so much with his own eyes, why should he not expect even greater atrocities?

Those were terrible hours when a superhuman force seemed to struggle within him as his body rested in a strange bed in another's house, on that somber afternoon when the very air he breathed seemed saturated with blood.

All noble souls were enraged by that monstrous crime. As on previous occasions, honorable Spaniards raised their voices in protest. *El Jurado* published a few words of burning shame:

"The inference of the article in *La Gaceta* is that the monstrous death sentence pronounced against the eight unfortunate students was imposed by certain savages there [in Cuba] who call themselves defenders of Spain. Like blood-thirsty hyenas they surrounded the jail demanding punishment. The summary proceedings and the installation of the court martial were carried out as popular agitation was increasing by the moment and the leaders of those memorable volunteers were assembling their battalions. With these precedents and without the presence of any authority strong

Pain and Duty

enough to subdue the rebellious beasts and make them respect the law, the sentence was pronounced. We decline to transcribe the official report for our readers. We do not wish to grieve them with the realization of how this report will degrade Spain's reputation throughout the world."

Many of Martí's friends were listed among the youths who were executed, among them Anacleto Bermúdez, a classmate. The closest friend he had in Mendive's school, his companion in the celebrated trial for disloyalty, Fermín Valdés Domínguez, was one of those condemned to prison.

Martí recovered from his illness with an aching heart. He was like a shadow, a reflection of all the sadness in the world. They had called him "el viejo," "the old man," in the quarry; now that his suffering had reached incredible limits, he presented an even sadder appearance. The black suit of mourning he wore for his dead friends accentuated still more his somber air.

In those days of increased infamy in Cuba, many of his friends drew closer to him, that he might know that they felt as he did and considered themselves dishonored.

He had a gigantic enterprise before him. He knew it and was not disheartened. On the contrary, every new pain strengthened his faith. He would move the world, he said to himself in his hours of solitude. Later, faced with an apparently invincible reality, he had moments of discouragement. But they were only moments.

The newspapers had printed terrible condemnations of the crime and the criminals. The reactionaries hardly dared to express themselves. But a new blow was aimed at the Cubans: the conservative element published a manifesto, exploiting the nation's patriotic sentiments, in which no less than the Spanish revolution of September was denounced as "filibustería":

"It is painful but necessary to say it now: between the insurrection of Cuba and that of Cádiz there are mysterious connections. The rebels of the Antilles used all available means to incite and further the September revolution, which was favorable to their sinister purposes. The September revolution in turn encourages insurrection among the *filibusteros*."

Martí

With so many crimes being committed in his blood-stained country, Martí grew sadder and found consolation only in his memories. In tender verses he spoke of his sunless solitude, surrounded by a dark sky and black clouds, and he evoked the light of his distant island.

When the year 1872 began, he had not been able to take any examinations. Both his illness and his financial situation were worse; he had to move from his quarters on Desengaño Street to a miserable garret on Lope de Vega Street, number 40. Nevertheless, he did not give up hope of continuing his studies. On May 31 he enrolled in Civil Law. On his registration blank he gave his new address and named the Cuban patriot Francisco S. Ramos, one of his best friends in Madrid, as guarantor.

In that period, which was probably a crucial time for him, the unexpected arrival of Fermín Valdés Domínguez, the schoolmate and friend of the youths who were assassinated on that tragic day, November 27, altered Martí's sad outlook. Fermín had been deported by the island authorities. He could not conceal his surprise at finding Martí so emaciated and melancholy. He thought he was doomed because of his illness.

As the son of a rich family, Fermín had gladly offered to share his means with his friend. But Martí, who always concealed his want and endured his straitened circumstances without complaint, refused to accept his help. Fermín's brotherly insistence finally overcame his objections. They returned to the old house at number 10 Desengaño, where Martí was surrounded by memories and doubtless by affection which did him good.

The days following Fermín's arrival were memorable. Martí was heartened by his presence; the newcomer was more than his friend, he was his brother. They could not find enough hours in the day to tell each other about all their experiences and suffering. Their spiritual kinship was even closer now that both had suffered so deeply for the same cause.

From that moment on Fermín was his inseparable companion. Together they visited the Cuban circles, literary *tertulias,* and salons where Martí was cordially received. They spent some evenings at the theatre. When they were not seen in their seventh heaven—in the orchestra seats of the Teatro Real where they had a season ticket—they could be found in a salon of El Teatro Español, chatting with artists, critics, and authors, or in the *tertulia* of the Café de los Artistas or in a still more pleasant place, their favorite, the Cervecería Inglesa. There they almost always found the genial Aragonese Marcos Zapata, whom Martí liked immensely.

The theatre, *tertulias*, and salons did not occupy all of Martí's time. He spent many of his free evenings at the Armonía lodge and became the orator of this organization. All the Cuban youth of Madrid attended the weekly meetings there, as did noted Spanish authors and journalists. It was the source of frequent aid to the Cuban prisoners in Ceuta and to many persons in need of charity. The lodge founded a night school for poor children; the rector and only teacher was the Spaniard, Don Amelio del Luis y Vela, deported for disloyalty. Members of the lodge frequently visited the school. Martí often did so and spoke inspiring words to the children.

Martí's illness continued to trouble him. The surgeons attending him decided to perform another operation. When they did so they discovered the irremediable defects of the previous operations. Although he was not completely cured (for that prison-acquired lesion troubled him all his life), he improved enough to think about his studies again. Fermín had come to Madrid with the definite intention of continuing his medical career begun in Havana. In August Martí added two new courses to his curriculum: mercantile and penal law. On the thirty-first, the last day for payment of matriculation fees, his illness prevented him from appearing in person, and Fermín paid the fees for him. Martí did not take any examinations at that time.

It was not only his illness and other *contre-temps* that prevented him from devoting himself to his studies. An amorous complication, undoubtedly his first, was another cause for the emotional state in which he had been living for the last few months, and from which he had hardly recovered when Fermín arrived. At some *tertulia*, perhaps by the warmth of a fireplace on winter nights, a deep passion developed. But those lips that spoke to him could not belong to him; they belonged to another, to the generous friend who took him into his home. With firmness he made his loyal decision, not without suffering inner torment.

Then he began to think about writing a work worthy of that great love, nourished by the weak flesh and conquered by a strong spirit. It was to be a dream, an expression of his extremely austere ideas concerning honor and dignity, friendship and love.

In his notebook he recorded the grave incident, the key to the drama he had begun. Because of the vanity of his age, he tells us, he was in danger of committing a grave sin. Then, shocked, he thought of how he would suffer if he were a victim of the crime he had intended to commit against another man. By intuitive understanding he painted a vivid picture. He portrayed that human abyss into which one falls when the arms that one thought to be garlands of roses turn to clay, and one sinks into the hell of suspicion.

His concept of friendship was revealed in the plot, common to almost all dramas, in which the lover is the best friend of the beloved son, or even of the husband himself. Martí asked himself this: pure, terrible question: "Why should there not be loyal friends? And in his notes he continued to reveal his thoughts:

"A friend is the kind of person we all ought to be and a few people are. A lover is a brilliant man acting like an imbecile, which makes the enormity of the guilt even more patent."

All his pent-up, dominated passion leaped forth at every moment from the scenes he was writing. The essence of his drama was real: he had experienced it and was still experiencing it. And the best way to rise above it was to experience it anew through his characters.

Whom else could he have had in mind but Shakespeare when he wrote his drama? True, it may be objected that he had not yet read Shakespeare, for having the presumption to translate *Hamlet* in his grammar-school days was not reading him. But his work has a philosophical message, and the idea of the poet-philosopher who philosophizes in the drama at once suggests Shakespeare.

Martí had no other intention in writing it than to put aside the temptation which pursued him by giving it a new,

Pain and Duty

perennial life in his created work. This work reveals his moral concepts, already formed, and his idea of duty and sacrifice—for it is a sacrifice to cast aside an impetuous love at the height of youth because of a firm concept of friendship. He exchanged the evenings by the fireplace where those red lips offered themselves to him for evenings in his wretched garret where he spent long hours writing, erasing, rereading. Some scenes came to him easily. In others the exact word eluded him, and he erased and rewrote and often remained dissatisfied.

He made his work revolve around four fundamental characters. No minute, precise decoration, no changeable characters, only the real and eternal, the essential. Perhaps they are not such real characters as he had intended; perhaps they are abstractions with universal significance. It is interesting to note that the names he chose for them are not proper nouns, but nouns of symbolic import. And as if that were not sufficient, the names of his characters are German: for the husband Grosserman—tall man; for the wife Fleisch— flesh; for the friend Gutterman—good man; and for the lover Posserman—vile man. What is the explanation of these names? His obvious intention of personifying in each character, a spiritual and moral modality is combined with an attempt to give them a philosophical meaning. And German philosophy, as we have seen, was in vogue in Spain at that time.

He read nothing of what he had written, even to Fermín. His friend knew that he was suffering from this sorrow. And when he saw him writing, he realized that he relieved his suffering by transmitting it into poetry.

The first anniversary of the execution of the students was near at hand. Martí, who was convalescing from his last operation, was writing an elegy dedicated to his brothers who died on that bloody day. In the poem he recalled that eternal, endless day of shadows, lethargy and sadness, when finally his inquietude was transformed into despair over the awful news. He relived those hours of fierce indignation, his vow. And he renewed the vow, for it must never be forgotten, and that pain must tear at his heart forever, reminding him of his promise.

Martí

In addition to his elegy he wrote a page that Fermín had requested of him, recalling the sad fate of the eight young first year medical students.

Martí evoked them courageously and presented them as a synthesis of "that infinite love of country and of glory which is never afraid or downcast or weak; for the bodies of martyrs are the most beautiful altar of honor."

This page did not bear his signature. It was signed by two students sent to prison for the same cause: Pedro J. de la Torre and Fermín Valdés Domínguez. And in the cold dawn of that November 27, like ghosts pronouncing judgment in the silence of sleeping Madrid, on the doors of the palaces and beneath the crosses on the churches, the surviving students fastened the emblem of the nation's shame: a printed sheet commemorating the crime. In the early morning, the people of Madrid stopped to read it. It brought forth just comment from all who had been horrified by the crime and felt ashamed because it was committed by Spaniards.

The speech was yet to be given that evening. The home of Carlos Sauvalle was a center of reunion where the Cubans met to talk about their country's problems or seek some means of helping the needy or defend Cuban rights, by means of newspapers and magazines, from the unjust accusations of groups in the service of the slave-traders or volunteers of Cuba. They met in Sauvalle's house on the night of the first anniversary of that fateful day.

Martí uttered stirring words that night. All the pain pent-up within his soul, his suppressed sorrow and stifled indignation burst forth in his evocation of Cuba, enslaved, trampled, bleeding, and corroded by all the meanness of despotism. All his meditations, his admonitions and biblical apostrophes surged up in his sentences like boiling waves, quickening the fires of indignation and flooding eyes with tears and hearts with anguish.

8. Republican Interlude

The first two weeks in February, 1873, were turbulent days for the *madrileños*. Political unrest grew increasingly more acute until it culminated in the defeat of King Amadeo by the Cortes and by his own government, when the artillery corps was reorganized.

At three o'clock in the afternoon of February 11, the Congress received from the president of the cabinet the monarch's abdication message drawn up by Montero Ríos.

It was a solemn occasion. The Senate was invited to the congressional palace where the two houses met jointly in a Constituent Assembly. Ceremoniously preceded by their mace-bearers, the senators entered the hall as a large group of spectators gathered outside, their curiosity growing. The tension increased until finally one of the assembly members, Estanislao Figueras, stepped to a window facing Floridablanca Street and shouted to the crowd:

"We shall not leave here until the republic is triumphant or we are dead."

Castelar was charged with writing the letter of acknowledgement and farewell to the king. A few moments later the republic was proclaimed, with Don Estanislao Figueras elected President. Castelar, Pi y Margall, Salmerón, and Echegaray had a part in the new government.

From a window of the congressional palace, Figueras announced the good news to the people of Madrid. His words were greeted with thundering acclamation. Shortly afterwards Madrid was filled with the flags of all the countries having a republican form of government.

Martí

On the balcony of an extremely modest home a banner appeared that no one recognized. Finally someone learned that it was the emblem of free Cuba. No one felt indignant or hateful; on the contrary, the people heartily approved of the young Cuban student's way of celebrating the birth of the Spanish republic. The student was José Martí.

A ray of hope shone for the Cubans. How could they help believing that this radical change in government would light the way toward the absolute freedom of Cuba? Figueras was the prototype of impeccable probity and generous sentiments, undoubtedly a republican patterned after their own ideals. Initiated into politics at an early age, he had suffered imprisonment and exile because of his liberal ideas. His government was made up principally of progressive republicans. The time and the circumstances could not have been more propitious.

Nevertheless, from the beginning there were well-founded misgivings for fear that the same men who had theoretically supported the republican ideals of Cuba when they belonged to the opposition party might not put them into practice after getting into power. The man who was to be president of the Assembly—Cristino Martos—gave unmistakable evidence that the nascent republic would not recognize Cuba's right to the same form of government, even though she had earned that right by shedding the blood of her sons for four years. "Viva Cuba española!" he said,—"Long live Cuba under Spain!"—and the assembly repeated his cry.

Without losing a moment Martí began writing a pamphlet in which he demonstrated with irrefutable logic the inconsistency of the new republic's refusal to recognize Cuba's right to the same benefits which Spain had just given herself. In his arguments he pointed out that the triumphant republic would be infamous, mendacious, and insincere if it forgot its own promises, the very foundation of its doctrine. Was not universal freedom the republican ideal? Then "what right had the Spanish republic to destroy those who were pursuing the same goal which she pursued?"

His arguments were like anticipated whip-lashes cracking down upon the new republic, whose attitude by that time was clearly defined. His burning censure was appropriate and timely, for the Republic came into being denying its own reason for existing, when it refused to recognize its double responsibility toward its own ideals and toward those it had supported and admired up to that moment.

It was now apparent that Cuba was a good weapon for the republicans to use against the government when they were the opposition party. This fact made their guilt even more serious. Martí repeated the deserved reproach in every possible form. "I should turn my eyes away in wrath," he wrote, "from the wretched, suicidal republicans who would refuse that outraged, garrotted, oppressed, swindled people the right of insurrection after the Spanish republic had sanctioned so many insurrections."

The Spanish republic had no right to offer anything but absolute recognition of the Cuban republic. Martí underlined his compatriots' firm decision, as if he wanted it made clear that they were not asking for their rights, they were taking them by force. "My country writes her irrevocable decision in blood," he said, and added: "How can a people express their wishes more decisively than by taking up arms?"

El Presidio Político was a fervent poem of blood and pain and apocalyptic rapture. This new piece of writing consisted of the staunch reflections of a statesman. Martí began with duty as his theme, for he was addressing men who had been educated in that tradition, and there was no command superior to the call of duty. "Glory and victory are only a stimulus to the fulfillment of duty" was the rotund phrase with which he opened fire.

He wrote the date, February 15, at the bottom of the pages he had just finished. He read them to his friends in Madrid and received unanimous praise for his valiant, well organized argumentation. A friend undertook to publish them in pamphlet form, and Martí spent a few busy weeks getting them ready for the printer. Shortly afterward his pamphlet was circulating in Madrid and the provinces. "Unaccustomed as the Spaniards are to the idea that Cuba might and should cease to belong to them some day," this article surprised them with its liberal thought and resolute tone. Martí performed his duty by making them realize that if up to that time the war against Cuban liberties "had been infamous, from that point on it would be twice as fratricidal."

His article attracted the attention of the most liberal men and caused comment. *La Cuestión Cubana* of Seville published it in the August 12 edition. It was used to win popular support of the idea of Cuban independence, championed by only one Spanish minister out of the entire cabinet: Salmerón. The Republic was still sending Spaniards to their death, and Cuban republicans were still dying.

In April Martí was still busy circulating copies of his article. On the fifteenth he wrote to a Cuban living in New York, the outstanding figure there among the Cubans who hoped for happier days for their country. Nestor Ponce de León, who had established a bookstore there, was the person who could give his article the widest circulation. All Cuban propaganda reached his bookstore and was, in turn, sent out.

Martí believed that any reform measures the Republic might take would endanger the revolutionary cause and weaken, if not destroy the movement. In order to emphasize his thesis that there was only one solution worthy of the new Republic and acceptable to the Republic in arms—complete recognition—he published in *La Cuestión Cubana,* on April 26, a new article entitled "La solución." In it he gave a vigorous description of his country, industrially backward, commercially poor, incapable of fulfilling its American destiny in a flourishing new world. With frankness he contrasted the Spanish reality with the Cuban ideal. He made the Spaniards recognize the grave responsibility they assumed by keeping the armed republic in their clutches. Spain was condemned to lose her rich colony because she had not known how to administer it properly. The Republic was not responsible for the blunders of the monarchy, but neither should Cuba have to pay for them.

Martí was also deeply concerned over the proposal, which had already received some governmental support, to make Cuba a Spanish province within the federal government. Such a concession would leave his country at the mercy of any change in administration that might take away her rights as a province and return her to the same state of prostration and infamous wealth in which Spanish rule now "held her subjected and oppressed."

A month later in the same Seville newspaper appeared a new article by Martí on the reforms offered, too late, as a solution of the Cuban problem. The reforms were logical, necessary, imperative, when Cuba was still peacefully enduring oppression. The most eminent men in Cuba had worked for them, but not only had Spain always withheld them, she had persecuted, imprisoned, and killed those who dared to ask for them. Cuba must rise up in arms in order to shake off the Spanish yoke. Now no reform could keep her from pursuing her only object: independence. With so many dead bodies lying between the two nations, there were no longer any reforms capable of bridging the abyss which separated them.

Those were days of intense propaganda for Martí, who aroused the pro-Cubans and a large element in the Spanish government to oppose the anti-Cuban conspiracy. It was evident that for the separatist interests, which Martí and many of his contemporaries represented, war in the island with the possibility of a Cuban victory over a greatly weakened nation, was preferable to concessions which might satisfy the group interested in maintaining peace. That could only result in an indefinite postponement of independence, thus eliminating the only course open to Cuba.

The federalists were determined to force from the Cubans a statement that they were willing to join the Spanish federal republic. Martí had already foreseen the consequences of such a situation. A change of administration could put an end to the federation, and Cuba would then return to the same position as an enslaved colony that she had had until then. In the Academy of Jurisprudence the federalists held a meeting in order to obtain the desired declaration. Martí opposed the proposition in a debate that lasted several hours. So powerful and eloquent were his arguments that his listeners all agreed with him, and the federalists' attempt failed.

He was firmly convinced that Cuba would derive no advantage from the change that had taken place in Spain. He had waged a campaign which at least had served to make very clear both the rights of Cuba and the injustice of her opponents. The Cubans realized that Martí was not mistaken in his initial judgment concerning the only course open to Cuba: she must fight her way to freedom.

The experience was painful, moreover, because it had made him see the shallowness of certain men he had thought sincere.

He was overcome by despondency. His idea that nothing could be expected from Spain had been confirmed again. He had to plan, prepare for great future events. But it was becoming difficult to study in Madrid. Moreover, both Fermín and Martí needed a change of climate, for their health had never been good in Madrid. After the hopes they had placed in the republic were shattered, they thought seriously of resuming their studies away from the court. No place appealed to them as strongly as Zaragoza, the ancient city on the banks of the Ebro. Besides, living costs were low there.

Martí had completed many subjects except for taking the examinations. On May 17 he wrote to the Rector of the Universidad Central requesting the transfer of his credits to Zaragoza. The authorization of this change was granted the twenty-third.

9. Flowering Land

At first Zaragoza had a disconcerting effect on Martí. The infinite architectural variety, from the very ancient remains of the Roman and Moorish styles to the typical Aragonese style of the region—evolved from *mudéjar,* plateresque, Renaissance and Churrigueresque—was a constant source of surprise to him. He never tired of looking at the many admirable relics, such as the mosque of La Aljafería, and the churches of El Pilar, La Seo, and San Pablo, or walking along the old Coso, a survival of the time of the walled city.

Until then he had seen nothing like this. It was a completely new emotional experience for him to let his imagination dwell upon the remote ages while he tried, with great curiosity, to read on each ruin, each stone, the millenarian history of the city. Zaragoza—Iberian, Roman, Gothic, Christian, and Moslem—was a composite of the most varied epochs and tastes.

Everything revealed remote splendor, past grandeur. In the old districts he walked along the tortuous streets that led to the Jewish section, or those that wound their serpentine way near San Pablo and La Seo. Façades, marvelous patios, silent stairways, broad, arched galleries, shields on eroded stones. Because he would forget everything in his musings, he often had the sudden sensation that he was exploring, alone, a deserted but enchanted city. When he went on long walks with the little notebook in which he recorded impressions tucked under his arm, he was frequently roused from his oblivion of self and surroundings by the chimes of the Torre Nueva watchtower, ringing out into the pure air.

Martí

One of his favorite walks was along El Coso. He followed it slowly at dusk from the Casa de los Gigantes to the Seminary, stopping in front of the great cross that crowned the Seminary.

He often stopped before the ruins of the Monastery of Santa Engracia. It was a place hallowed by memories for the people of Zaragoza, for there they defended themselves until the French blew it up during the first siege. Its façade, still standing, offered a view of its marble portico, covered with innumerable figures of saints, who remained intact and tranquil as if unaware of the catastrophe that had left them there to keep watch over those ruins. Martí contemplated these scenes where the memory and the deeds of heroes were venerated, places where the people of Aragon defended their freedom with exemplary heroism: El Convento de la Encarnación, the bullet-ridden Puerta del Carmen—the only remaining gate of those that once enclosed the city—, El Arrabal and El Arco de Cineja.

That city seemed sacred to him. It was like the incarnation of the heroic resistence, immortalized in all the people's memories. And now he was in its very heart, wandering through its narrow streets, its plazas and avenues, while in his heart resounded the echoes of the legend. And his imagination transported him to the distant, sunburnt isle where other men, his brothers, also fought for their freedom and, like those Aragonese, embraced death rather than let themselves become prisoners of the enemy.

After a few days everything in Zaragoza was familiar to him. Not only was he deeply devoted to the miraculous city of a hundred temples, so full of surprises for his lively imagination; the environs also offered him an atmosphere of serenity and peace which he needed badly after two years of intense life in Madrid. He would go to the canal of Pignatelli, or stroll along the river bank, or go off alone or accompanied by Fermín to Monte Torrero, to return at dusk. Along the way they would stop to look at the trees, the current of the Ebro, the belfries of the city which rose above the green fields, the cupola of El Pilar and the garden walls overhung with branches and spring flowers. These walks reminded him of his months in Hanábana, long ago, when on just such afternoons he went away into the country, following the river, and his greatest joy was that pure contact with nature. And another more recent memory came to his mind: that of his few weeks on the Isle of Pines, when the idea of deportation obsessed him as his only salvation.

On their arrival in Zaragoza the friends found modest temporary lodging. On the following day, May 23, they went to the ancient building at the end of Sepulcro Street, near the plaza of San Nicolás. There Martí presented his credentials and asked to be admitted to examinations in the University.

Then it was necessary for them to look for more suitable living quarters. This was not difficult because of the desire to be of service which they encountered everywhere as soon as people learned that they were Cubans who had left Madrid in order to establish themselves in Zaragoza.

They found lodging in a boarding house where they felt perfectly at home. The landlord and his beautiful daughters, whom everyone called "little green feet," vied with one another in making the boys' stay a pleasant one. Don Félix Sanz understood the pleasure which Martí took in learning stories about the city and anecdotes which the people told and re-told. Whenever he had a chance he gave free rein to his own accounts. Sometimes he accompanied Martí to show him places of historic interest, and such was the warlike fervor of his words that Martí called him *el patrón valiente,* the valiant landlord. But the greatest surprise in Zaragoza was the discovery of a Cuban Negro, a bootblack who worked in the Arch of Cinejas. Simón had been deported by Lersundi in his first shipment to Fernando Poo on charges of being a *ñáñigo* and an assassin. He managed to make a modest living in Zaragoza, and Martí and Fermín were overjoyed to find him at their own boarding house. Simón represented something very real from their distant Cuba, something which was apparent whenever he spoke in his typical accent.

After the necessary arrangements had been made, the University of Zaragoza received a favorable report on Martí from Don Pedro Alcántara García, Secretary General of the

Universidad Central de Madrid. In June Martí was examined in the subjects he had transferred, passing them all.

He was very anxious to finish his studies rapidly. He was obliged to make a great effort to do so, for he was economically dependent on Fermín and did not wish to be any more of a burden than he could help. Besides, he had one great wish: to study philosophy and letters, his true vocation. And only by finishing the remaining subjects very rapidly could he attempt it.

On August 29 he requested permission to take an examination on eight subjects in the law school. He was examined and passed in six of these in September.

At the same time that he was occupied with these studies he was preparing those required for the *bachillerato,* which degree he needed to have before being granted the degree in law. Don Mariano had already sent him a transcript of his studies in the Havana Institute "with grades indicating his diligence and proficiency."

The spiritual life of Zaragoza also gave Martí a feeling of well-being. Received everywhere with great cordiality, invited by the families of his professors, who treated him as a friend rather than as a pupil, he was touched and won over by this feeling of belonging to a group of friends with understanding hearts. The University was like a greater home, where he spent many hours each day in study, consultation of the books in the excellent library, or delightful conversations with the professors, who appreciated Martí's talents and the personal accent with which he interpreted and treated politics, art, and literature.

This association with kindred spirits strengthened even more his idea that only freedom can make men happy. Would a similar contact with men of this spiritual category be possible some day on his *free* island?

That ancient house in Zaragoza where his triumphs were a cause for rejoicing among his classmates and professors impressed deeply upon his mind the full value of things of the spirit. And spiritual values can live only in an atmosphere of freedom.

Martí came to be so imbued with the soul of the city that instead of studying in the library or the boarding house he preferred to do so on the small, solitary path at the side of the church of El Pilar, or on a bench on the grassy banks of the Ebro. On certain days he could be seen there with an air of profound abstraction, writing zealously in a notebook balanced on his knees. It was his drama, conceived and briefly sketched in Madrid, which he was now finishing in the calm of Zaragoza. When he read Fermín the scenes he had finished, his friend marvelled at the wealth of philosophical concepts and literary beauty. But what impressed him most was his companion's moral temper.

In the mornings on holidays and other days when there were no classes or examinations to prepare for, he went to La Aljafería, which held an extraordinary attraction for him and was, according to legend, the depository of the first gold brought from Cuba by the conquistadors. When he did not go there he looked at the rich collections of tapestries in the churches of El Pilar, La Seo, and San Pablo, souvenirs of the tapestry-weaving of Zaragoza in the sixteenth century. Or he went to see the innumerable Holy Martyrs in the Catacombs underneath Santa Engracia Monastery. In the afternoons he preferred to visit the museums, seeking principally everything pertaining to that rebellious painter who incarnated for Martí the double message of the free man and the artist. Goya, who put lights in the painting of his time, who freed it from shadows and velvets, warriors and magistrates, saturating it with popular life and brilliance, came from that land. Martí was able to admire his portraits of Fernando VII and the Duque de San Carlos, and of that great, life-long friend of Goya's, Martín Zapater.

He often visited the studio of the painter Gonsalvo. There, delightful hours were passed in the exchange of opinions concerning Spanish painting or the painting of the Aragonese school, or in viewing the maestro's works, such as his admirable *Interior de la Catedral de Toledo*. Perhaps there was nothing Martí liked better than to watch silently for a long time while his friend's brush created its world of forms and color.

The Ateneo Científico y Literario on Coso Street and the Casino Artístico, where marvelous works dating from the fourteenth, fifteenth, and sixteenth centuries were preserved,

were places of great *camaraderie*. So were the editorial offices of the Diario de Avisos, where Martí always found a
group of friends who held his writing in high esteem. In
the provincial daily can be found a few articles of his that
reveal the fortunate inspiration of this happy moment.

And he seldom lacked an invitation to spend a day at
the country home of some friend, for example, that of the
notary López Bernuez, where he admired his valuable collection of coins and ceramics.

Martí the art critic was born in Madrid. But it was in
Zaragoza that he acquired a clear understanding of his own
artistic sentiments. He recorded his opinions of monuments
and works of art in his notebook among philosophical reflections, literary criticism, and poetry.

Popular fiestas and celebrations impressed him deeply,
because of their singular combination of seriousness and
ceremony with insouciance and sly humor, so characteristic
of the common people.

One of the most typical processions was that of the
giants and *cabezudos,* or figures representing dwarfs with
enormous heads, a grotesque personification of popular or
historic types. It took place on the eve of the unique, ceremonious *gran fiesta del Pilar.* Over three hundred and fifty
lanterns, richly decorated, representing the mysteries of the
Rosary (even the variations in the size of the lanterns had
a symbolic value), formed the retinue in this monumental
procession of the Rosario. The city glittered, and the fervent
people were on fire with a sort of mystic delirium.

The boys did not cease to cultivate their firmly-rooted
taste for the theatre. On the contrary, the fact that they held
a season ticket to box 13 in the Teatro Principal—the box
no one ever bought—attests to their frequent attendance.
And there, as elsewhere, their friendships were their greatest
source of pleasure.

In addition to all this, Martí had the affection of a
woman with whom he was deeply in love. He had met her in
the home of one of the professors who most admired him,
and whom Martí frequently visited. She was moved by the
gentle, firm timbre of his voice, the fineness of his manners,
the beauty of his words, and the fire of his enthusiasm. The

gallant compliments he paid her seemed unlike any she had ever heard before. Everyone was charmed by his words, and even his host's little boy sat quietly in his chair when the Cuban student came to call, and said that he liked to listen to his stories. The friendship that sprang up between the two young people soon became an impetuous love. Blanca de Montalvo was beautiful and delicate. And he longed so to be loved, he had such need of a little understanding and affection, that he was happier than he had ever been before.

Although he was disappointed in the Republic after having seen close at hand the conduct of its leaders, Martí did not fail on that account to follow the political developments, the subject of long conversations and discussions in the *tertulias* in the offices of the *Diario de Avisos*, the *Ateneo*, and the other places he frequented. Castelar's actions seemed to him the most culpable of all. Ever since that dreadful day, the twentieth of September, one could agree with the upright Don Francisco Pi y Margall that the Republic had died, and that Castelar had been its executioner. The great defender of federalism held the same opinion of Castelar that Martí did: "Voluble as a poet and vain as a woman, from the beginning he let himself be lured by those who, offering him false incense, conspired ruthlessly for the restoration of the monarchy."

And Martí, like Pi y Margall, believed that if Castelar was not a traitor he was at least a man devoid of faith and convictions.

The consequence of the stupid, vacillating policy of continuous transactions with and surrender to the group in favor of the restoration of the monarchy, was the fall of the Republic in the early morning of January 3, 1874, when General Pavía, the military governor, forced the governor to renounce his authority. This brought forth the following exclamation from Pi y Margall:

"We may say that the governor surrendered, not to Pavía, but to Castelar."

This coup provoked Republican uprisings and demonstrations of protest in many cities of Spain. Some were truly sanguinary, and among these was the uprising in Zaragoza.

Martí

The city's few battalions of Republican militia refused to recognize the new government, and the people backed them in their protest. Arms were distributed, barricades were erected in the streets, and the republicans took possession of numerous buildings, from which they considered their movement well defended.

The government troops sent by General Burgos, district commander, opened fire at one o'clock in the afternoon. A battery of ten Krupp cannons fired upon the buildings situated at the corner of the Arco de Cinejas and the Coso, where the *zaragozanos* fired back. The combat was even fiercer at the Mercado, the Puerta del Angel, and the Cuartel de la Magdalena, places which were under incessant fire.

In the early evening the movement was put down. There were several hundred dead and wounded on both sides. As the captain general of Aragon reported in his dispatch, the fight was "brief and rapid, but fierce and terrible."

Fermín and Martí had remained at home during the fighting. They knew very well that it was a heroic but futile gesture and, besides, that the Republic which was succumbing by the moment was hardly worthy of the name. For Cuba it had been a fratricidal republic. They had no obligation or duty to defend it.

Only the Negro Simón had left the house. He had fought until the last minute side by side with the valiant ones entrenched by the Arco de Cineja. When night had fallen and the shooting began to die down, after long hours of hard fighting, with many brave republicans falling at his side, he tried to reach safety. He managed to do so by a clever, roundabout way, and at dawn he reached the door of the boarding house on Manifestación Street. The Cubans were overjoyed on seeing him enter. And when Martí asked him what had happened, the Cuban Negro said:

"*Niño,* it's so cold the words freeze in your mouth."

That same morning, when the city was quiet, Fermín and Martí inspected the places from which the heroic defense had been made, finding pools of blackened blood near all the barricades.

Although Martí had taken no active part in the events of the preceding day, that did not prevent him from being pained by the terrible defeat which the valiant liberals of the beloved city had suffered. And because they knew how he felt and how deeply he loved Zaragoza, the good people asked him to speak at a program organized to alleviate the tragic condition of the widows and orphans. He had also been asked by one who could not be refused: Blanca de Montalvo, who now ruled his heart. There was, moreover, another reason why Martí should be the speaker for such an occasion. His position as a foreigner insured certain neutrality at a time when feelings were still incensed and the authorities were suspicious of the nature of the program.

Martí was intensely pleased to be offered this unique opportunity to express his affection for Zaragoza, for her hospitality, for her concept of true dignity—the dignity of the man who wants above all else to be free and will die for his ideals if necessary. His speech was a complete picture of his own aspirations, his own desires, and a hymn to the men for whom sacrifice was a way of doing their duty. Although he stated very clearly that the Republic had by no means lived up to the ideals of the best republicans, but had been a caricature, a betrayal of the very idea that inspired it, he entoned a hymn to the real Republic, the Republic of respect for all men, for which he was working.

Martí not only was the speaker of the evening, he wrote the verses which Leopoldo Burón, his famous actor-friend from Madrid, read with artistry and enthusiasm.

And thus the Cuban insurgent who had won the admiration and affection of the most worthy people in ancient Zaragoza was twice acclaimed, as a poet and as an orator.

The loss of the Republic was now irremediable. General Pavía's coup was followed by shameful submission and a rapid movement toward restoration of the Bourbon line. There was every indication that before the year was over monarchic absolutism would rule again in Spain. Although Martí certainly had nothing to thank the Republic for as far as Cuba was concerned, he was poignantly hurt by its failure. He dreaded the return of a regime which would make it difficult for him to stay in Spain. He anticipated reactionary measures which would make the atmosphere unendurable.

He devoted himself whole-heartedly to the rapid termination of his studies. Not only did he wish to finish his two careers, the one practical, the other ideal; he also had to prepare for examinations for the *bachillerato*. It would require great effort to finish, as he had planned, before the end of the year, in September.

Many distressing letters came from Doña Leonor, describing the family's pitiful condition. Don Mariano had been without employment for long periods of time, and his attacks of asthma were becoming more frequent. A recent photograph of his father, in which he appeared thin and emaciated, increased Martí's anxiety. His father's old strength and energy were gone; adverse fortune and moral suffering were leaving their mark. It caused Martí great pain to realize that it was the direction of his own life that had caused such hardship for his parents. He must live for them now, make up for the trouble he had caused them. He could not return to Cuba. He must make a new life for himself somewhere, perhaps in Mexico, a hospitable land where he could find work to support the family and devote his life to them. He had already written of this plan to his mother; she was overjoyed at the thought of seeing and embracing him, giving him a new kind of family life. Don Mariano was skeptical. Only one of the American republics seemed to him worthy of admiration: the United States. The others were not worth considering. However, he recalled that he had a few friends in Mexico who had managed to make a living, and he gradually accepted the idea of selling everything and taking his family to Mexico.

On July 30 he took the examination for the law degree, received the grade of *aprobado* (approved), and was granted the title of *Licenciado en Derecho Civil y Canónico*.

Then he was free to concentrate on the courses in philosophy and letters, in which he was keenly interested. July and August were months of hard, uninterrupted study, and on July 31 he registered for all the required subjects except those he had already taken as preparatory study for the law school. In September he was examined successively in Greek language, Classic Greek Literature, Historical Geography, Metaphysics, and Critical Studies of Greek Authors. This left two subjects, Hebrew Language and Spanish History, in which he was examined around the first of October. On the twentieth he asked to have the day set and the committee named for his examination for the degree of *Licenciado en Filosofía y Letras*. The examination was held on the twenty-fourth. Of the three topics drawn, Martí chose number 13: "Roman political and forensic oratory. Cicero as its supreme expression. Speeches analyzed according to his works on rhetoric." After being left alone for three hours, he developed his thesis before the committee, amazing all who heard him by his brilliant original ideas and excellent speech. His examiners questioned him for a half hour. Martí's answers revealed his keen mind and mastery of words. His performance was rewarded with the grade of *sobresaliente* (outstanding).

With his degrees as his only patrimony, without even enough means to pay for the trip, Martí left Zaragoza. Fortunately Fermín was at his side, a comfort and protection in his loneliness.

As he was too poor to pay the necessary fees for his diplomas, he took with him only certificates of his studies. In Madrid, first the Director General of Public Instruction and then the Ministerio de Estado legalized the certificates.

Martí remained in Madrid for a few more days. Some months earlier he had made a hurried trip to the capital and tried in vain to find "intellectual work, translating, any kind of work that would bring him enough income to pay for his matriculation in the faculty of philosophy and letters, which he desired with all his heart." The editor whom he had approached could not give him work, but since then he had added to his law degree that of *Licenciado en Filosofía*. He was now about to begin his career far from Spain, and although he was unable to find employment he again approached the editor this time with a strange proposition. In exchange for the books which he needed, Martí offered the editor "the fruits of an incipient intelligence which hopes some day to produce books." As an example he sent him an article written for the most part on his return to Zaragoza after their first interview. He was willing to give him that article and many others, as many as he might wish, if he considered them worthwhile in exhange for the books that would aid him in his career.

The books that interested him so much were the *Dictionary* by Escriche, the *Commentaries* by Gutiérrez, and, as a more pleasing complement, Azcárate's two philosophical works. Did he acquire them during that brief stay in Madrid? In all probability the strange proposal seemed even stranger to the unknown editor. "Articles of good will in exchange for books of good knowledge. Work in exchange for bases for work; it is, nevertheless, not such a strange agreement"— so Martí thought.

Fermín did not want Martí to leave Europe without visiting some of the great cities. They set out for Paris.

They arrived during the last days of autumn. The city was preparing to return to her magic winter existence. But they still had time to visit the boulevards and the Luxembourg gardens, make an excursion to Versailles, and contemplate the golden countryside and the flight of the leaves borne on the rude winds, before the first snowflakes fell.

The two friends were fortunate to arrive at that time when everything was beginning to revive at the breath of the first winter winds. Those were days of rebirth of mind and body.

The excitement grew. Newspapers reported the struggle of the candidates for the Academy, the number of votes they could count on, their merits, the circumstances that might influence their election. And they recorded the debates in the legislature, true parliamentary battles in which, amid the delirious excitement, there was glowing evidence of the great love with which each delegate desired, in his own way, to serve France.

A day never passed without the appearance of new books in the windows, books written during the summer months "in the shadow of the Italian orange trees, the German linden trees, the white houses of Bongival, or the severe poplars of Argenteuil." The theatres vied with one another in offering new drama, also written during the peaceful days of a vacation in the provinces, a source of revitalizing fecundity.

The gilded Grand Opera hall glittered with a solemn public, the Sorbonne opened its doors to learned dissertations, and in the boulevard cafés conversations were resumed and wit and gaiety sparkled. It was the springtime of the spirit, felt by all. Martí and Fermín wanted to experience everything. They attended performances by Sarah Bernhardt, who made an indelible impression on their minds.

The museums were also enlivened by students from every country who undertook the task of copying the famous pictures. Martí made good use of his time visiting the vast halls of the Louvre and the Luxembourg, drinking in avidly the beauty of the great French paintings. The nudes attracted him especially, and he paused before the firm flesh and opulent forms of Gérome, the provocative *Baigneuse* of Perrault, or Beaumont's slender woman whose flesh was devoid of spirit. He was especially impressed by Lefevre's women of full, exquisite forms and by the inimitable purity of their alluring contours. In Martí's opinion, Lefevre was unquestionably the master of the nude. In his notebook he recorded his impressions. It was not sufficient to carry away the light and color in his memory. He wanted to reduce to formulas the impressions that those masterpieces had left in his mind. *La lune de miel,* a delicate landscape by Leconte du Nours, impressed him by its happy blending of the soul's sentiments with nature.

He had studied French in Spain. It was a language for which he had a natural liking and real aptitude. His desire for knowledge led him to read the works of the thinkers and poets of France in their original tongue before he had mastered it. But thus he had been able to make great progress in a short time. His progress was now apparent, to his pleasure, in his conversations with artists and writers. He met a vigorous intelligent poet of serene character, Auguste Vacquerie, and the two became good friends. Vacquerie asked Martí to translate a beautiful poem of his, which he did while he was in Paris.

Vacquerie gave him one of the happiest moments of his life when he took him into the presence of Victor Hugo, and the great, venerable poet received him with paternal affection. Martí felt as if he were his father and could not contain his admiration.

Martí

The great poet of France had the opportunity to tell the world of his sympathy for the Cuban cause, for "noble, valiant Cuba," and for this sympathy Martí tried to express his deep gratitude. "I have raised my voice in behalf of Cuba, and I shall surely do the same again," said Victor Hugo.

When Vacquerie showed the poet the translation which Martí had just done for him, Victor Hugo placed in Martí's hands a small, recently published book—*Mes Fils*—expressing a desire to see it translated. Martí had a moment of happiness.

Shortly before leaving he spent an afternoon in the cemetery of Père Lachaise. The romantic, passionate boy who had just left his first love behind went to the lovers' tomb, the symbolic tomb of Abelard and Heloise, rich in poetic associations.

"When I arrived there my enamoured gaze wandered in pleasure over the arch. I put my hand on the frozen column, and my living hand was colder.

"For in the shadow of the solemn arches, and upon the marble dais, built from the ruins of a long-vanished nave, Abelard sleeps by the side of Heloise."

Fermín wanted Martí to visit other cities in Europe before embarking for America. They left Paris, and around the middle of January they were in Southampton, where Martí, who was ill when he arrived, was to embark for America. With an embrace the two friends parted in the gloomy port. A disagreeable crossing awaited Martí on the emigrant ship. But he carried with him the grandiloquent pages by the Guernsey exile, which would keep him company and also give him courage for his own tasks.

Fermín, surmising that Martí, in his zeal to take home a little more money to his family, would travel as an emigrant, had paid the difference for a first-class passage. Martí's hours on board began in a filthy place in which hundreds of people were packed, and a suffocating stench made it impossible to breathe. With a dirty plate and a spoon in his hand he stood before a caldron that reminded him of mess at the penitentiary in Havana. In a state of utter depression, as he sought a glimmer of intelligence in the faces that surrounded him, he was suddenly roused from his reflections by a voice.

"Mr. Martí."

A moment later, installed in a comfortable first-class stateroom, he was free from that nightmarish place unfit for human beings.

In New York it was necessary to change boats. As they remained there for only a few hours, he barely managed to see the tall buildings that were almost reflected in the waters of the bay. Four days later they entered the harbor of Havana, again for only a few hours. Without his family, without Mendive, without Fermín, this beloved land of his, bent under the weight of odious slavery, was simply a great hell ruled by men dominated by the most ignoble appetites and the most inhuman passions. Leaning on the rail, he was lost in sorrowful meditations, reviewing the dizzying course of events of his life. Four years ago he had left as an exile, and now he was more of one than ever, now that everything was dispersed. He would have to make a new life. But a day would come . . .

If he had told anyone his thoughts at that instant, an incredulous smile would have been his answer.

On February 8, 1875, the American steamer *City of Mérida* cast anchor in Veracruz, at six-thirty in the afternoon. Martí disembarked and continued his trip by rail from Veracruz to Mexico. On arriving at the Buenavista station he saw Don Mariano, waiting for him, his arms outstretched. Without uttering a single word they clasped each other in a long embrace.

Part III:

Wandering Years

10. Friendly Mexico

Doña Leonor arrived in Mexico with high hopes. At last she could rejoin her son; at last she could enjoy a little rest and economic security.

In Havana the family had supported itself by sewing. Don Mariano had resorted to his old trade as a military tailor during his periods of unemployment, and Doña Leonor helped him. Later, when the girls were old enough to help, they worked harder and on a larger scale.

In Mexico they endured extreme poverty. Installed in a very modest house they earned barely enough to live on with Don Mariano's tailoring jobs. But thanks to an effective recommendation by the Mexican Don Manuel Mercado, whom Don Mariano had met shortly after his arrival, they obtained more customers and did not have to worry about going hungry. As Mercado held a very important position in public administration, his recommendation to the quartermaster, Borrel, brought the family all the work they needed, and Don Mariano, Doña Leonor and the girls worked all day long and well into the night to earn a few pesos more for the bare necessities.

The family was deeply grateful to the generous Mercado. And Mercado liked these good, humble people who dreamed of their son's triumph. Don Mariano showed him what his son had written in Spain, and as Mercado read *El Presidio Político* and the pages addressed to the Spanish Republic, he realized that the youth whom they were awaiting so hopefully was not only a man of great literary talent but a valiant defender of liberal ideas, of Mercado's own ideas, the kind that Mexico believed in and needed.

Gradually his protective attitude turned into consideration and friendship. Señora Mercado, with that inborn, natural courtesy Mexicans have, was glad to receive Doña Leonor and the girls into her comfortable home. Even the close friend of the Mercado family, the painter, Manuel Ocaranza, who had recently arrived from his home in Uruapan and was staying at the Mercado home, became a good friend of the girls. He began to paint a portrait of Ana, who seemed to be the most intelligent of the daughters and always had a trace of sadness in her eyes.

A pleasant friendship which soon became an idyll of love was born in the hearts of Ana and Ocaranza. But the Cuban girl was mortally ill, and in Mexico she had begun to feel worse. She suffered from a heart ailment, and the high altitude of the Mexican plateau was very injurious. She could not endure it, and her heart, now more filled with illusions than ever before, ceased beating. On January 5 she died. Her death crushed Doña Leonor. All her other sorrows were trivial compared to this new one. She recalled that Ana was Martí's favorite sister, the one who understood him best. When she was very small he used to write her verses. Doña Leonor remembered those verses which he wrote when he was fifteen, *Linda Hermanita Mía*, (My Lovely Little Sister), with that impassioned note at the end: "Ana, my dear, forgive me if my verses are poor. I have written them just as they came to me at this moment. I would never correct anything I wrote for you. . . ."

Mercado and Ocaranza offered their sympathy and help to the family during that time of sadness. As Doña Leonor was inconsolable, and everything in the little house reminded her of her daughter, they helped her to look for other lodgings. They moved into a small house on Moneda Street, next door to that of Mercado. Thus they had the comfort of a friend near at hand while they awaited the arrival of their son, already on his way home.

Martí knew nothing of the tragedy that had struck his home while he was on his journey. On the way from the station to their house, Don Mariano told him the sad news in a few halting words. For a moment Martí was speechless, and all his worries about his uncertain future disappeared, leaving only sorrow.

How different was the scene in the little house on Moneda Street from the one he had anticipated. After waiting for him so long, they could not fully enjoy his presence, which was, at the same time, a cause for rejoicing and for deep pain.

Mercado and Ocaranza came later to meet the son, and one of those rare friendships was formed. It was a great comfort at that time to find such understanding people.

Martí spent the first few days after his arrival comforting his mother and talking with Don Mariano who, formerly so reserved and curt, was now eager to hear the details concerning his son's activities. His fatherly pride was evident as he looked at his son and listened to him with careful attention.

Desolation and poverty visited them in the house on Moneda Street. Never had Martí seen more clearly his parents' straitened circumstances or felt his own poverty more keenly.

Always a poet, he had to master his sorrow by putting it into poetry. He had to write a poem that would relieve his heart of the anguish which oppressed it. On one of those desolate nights when everyone was asleep he began to write a poem that had no name because he could not think of an appropriate one. As his gaze lingered on the sights around him, the reality that was closest to him pained him:

"My parents sleep. My sister has died," he began. And another truth, so close to him:

"It is time for thought. It is terrifying to think when one's heart is breaking. Oh, the dreams of the poor, unknown heroes of life, those who find nothing on the endless road but a black sky, a dying sun, and brackish water!"

The Cubans who were living in exile were acquainted with Martí's name through his writings and his prominent political activities. His pages on *El Presidio Político* were sought after and read by all who had heard of that magnificent poem which had made Cuba's suffering known. His pamphlet on the Spanish Republic and the Cuban Revolution had become known all over America. The émigrés in Mexico did not need to be told who José Martí was. And he felt that he had found in them his first protection. He wished only to find work in order to earn a modest living. Law did not appeal to him. He was less inclined every day to devote himself to lawsuits.

Don Pedro Santacilia was the most outstanding of the Cuban émigrés. Martí went to his house with some doubt, but when Santacilia heard his name he shook hands with him enthusiastically. They had a lengthy conversation about the political condition of the country, about what Martí should do and the means of finding suitable work at once. Of course his genuine literary talent would enable him easily to make a place for himself in the Mexican press, which boasted of some of the most prominent figures of the time.

President Lerdo's government was outstanding for its liberalism and its support of intellectual work. Lerdo was carrying on the work of Juárez, the greatest, intellectually, of the Reformers. To Juárez fell the glory of having crowned the work of the Reform. Upon Juárez' death in 1872, General Mejía went personally to Lerdo to announce the death of the *Benemérito*. Lerdo was in his office in the Supreme Court, where he received Mejía. The General gave him the tragic news and greeted him, simply, as the legal head of the Nation and the army. He took him to the body and there reiterated his loyalty. At the same time, Juárez' cabinet greeted Lerdo as the new President. It had been as simple as that. Lerdo, for his part, was governing with justice and firmness. The intellectuals of the nation were on his side, and all progressive elements seconded him in his great zeal to attain the pacification of Mexico. Only the clergy and the conservative elements waged a bitter war against his government. But without faltering in his efforts, he carried out his plan to convert Mexico into a country governed by liberal principles, respecting individual liberties and rights, and characterized by administrative honesty and economic independence.

Martí was enthusiastic over Santacilia's words. To think that there was in America a place like this, where a true republic existed, solicitous of the well-being of the people and the worthy use of their liberties! He was already confident that life here would be a joy. At the close of the interview

Martí felt that he would soon find a means of supporting his family.

He visited the office of the *Revista Universal,* edited by Coronel José Vicente Villada. Now that he was well informed of the political situation and the activities of the liberals who supported the Lerdo government, it would not be difficult for him to put his own pen to the service of a cause which fortunately coincided with his own high ideals. Villada received Martí cordially. Villada's friend, Mercado, had previously spoken to him enthusiastically about Martí, and he had been awaiting his visit. During the conversation they agreed upon a plan for Martí to collaborate with remuneration, by submitting articles. Later, as he became better acquainted with the political situation, he could be on the regular staff.

His first contribution was none other than the poem on his sister's death which he had just finished. The *Revista Universal* published it in its Sunday edition, March 7, with these words:

"Señor Martí is a sincere poet who, as soon as he is known, will win the favor of our literary circles."

The next day Martí's name was mentioned and his presence desired in all the literary groups. In the editorial offices he received the congratulations of many of his companions. But none was so effusive as that of the poet Juan de Dios Peza, a generous, bohemian fellow. They became friends, and Peza introduced him everywhere, putting him in contacts with poets and *tertulias.* Consequently, although he had only recently published his first poem, he received the warmest applause and even heard words of praise from women's lips. One, especially, who was vividly impressed by his poetic gift, urged him to write more verses.

Martí had not discontinued the task of translating *Mes Fils,* which he had begun during the long crossing. He suggested to Villada that he publish it in pamphlet form. The suggestion met with warm response, and on March 12, the printing of the book was begun. The title page bore Martí's name as translator.

Not only was the political situation such that it harmonized with his ideals. The literary environment was the best suited to receive the stimulation which his peculiar art, with its extremely personal accents, needed. All doors were opened to him, all the poets praised him. Martí did not find even the slightest pettiness among those who were already his friends, and even less in the younger group, led by Justo Sierra and Peón Contreras. They were soon truly close friends of his. Literary *soirées* were very popular in Mexico at that time, and were held not only in schools and academies, but in the homes of the outstanding men of the Reform.

The *Liceo Hidalgo,* long a school of distinction, enjoyed the greatest prestige among the literary groups and included the most renowned writers. Toward the end of March the Liceo Hidalgo admitted Martí as a member, thus revealing the high esteem in which he was held by the nation's men of letters even though he had only been in Mexico two months.

One of the favorite *tertulias* was that of the La Peña family, presided over by their beautiful, sensitive daughter, Rosario. Her feminine charms, her intelligence, and the cultured atmosphere, combined to make her salon the most frequently visited by the outstanding figures in philosophy, art, and letters, from Don Gabino Barreda, the representative of positivist philosophy, to Manuel Acuña, the unhappy poet. Unable to endure the pain of his unrequited love, he committed suicide after writing his celebrated *"Nocturno."* His shade almost seemed to wander through the halls and appear behind Rosario. Juan de Dios Peza invited Martí to the *tertulia,* and the latter, eager to meet this woman, gladly accepted. This happened in early March, when his first contribution to the *Revista Universal* had just been read with great interest by the literary public. Rosario was a woman who knew how to captivate but also how to make one suffer.

Martí, like other talented men before him, was ensnared by Rosario's witchery. Ignacio Ramírez, who had cherished a senile passion for some time, sensed that Martí was a dangerous rival and made him the victim of his scathing epigrams. He went to such extremes that Martí even wrote to Rosario: "Ramírez is doing me great harm." Rosario seemed at times to provoke Martí's impetuosity. But she also encouraged her other admirers, without ever giving her heart to any of them, because it belonged entirely to the poet, Manuel M. Flores, the author of *Pasionarias.* Martí was unaware of this. There is no other explanation of his insistence on winning her love, or of the frequency with which he let himself be ruled by his impulses and even let his habitual pride be broken. He told her in a letter:

"I never forgave anyone the wrongs for which I forgive you. I never loved anyone as much as I should like to love you."

In his financial state, barely able to support his family with the income he received from the *Revista Universal,* he was mad to attempt a formal engagement and plan on marrying.

The vehemence of his letters, the ardor of his words when they met, his raging condemnations, frightened Rosario more and more. Her weapon of defense was real or apparent indifference, which would make the mad lover suffer still more.

The *Revista* contained notices concerning the Cuban cause. Antenor Lescano came to the defense of the Cuban revolutionaries, as often as it was necessary to destroy insidious attitudes or utter a word of encouragement.

With Martí on his editorial staff those interests were vigorously defended. After knowing about his life and his writings and hearing him speak of Cuba, no one could possibly expect to confine him to purely literary work without offending his patriotic fervor. Furthermore, did not the writers and editors on the staff of the *Revista* feel as if they themselves were Cubans?

His first signed article concerning the war in Cuba appeared March 21, provoked by a tragic dispatch to the effect that twenty-two Cuban youths had been shot without being granted a trial. The tone of this article was one of moderation. The same was true of the articles which followed, though not so frequently as to abuse the generosity of the editors.

But, although his moderation was evident, he succeeded in annoying the Spaniards with his keen judgments and sharp pen.

Allusions were made to Martí's foreign sympathies and to the fact that his opinions were inopportune. The staff of the *Revista* was extremely partial to Martí and published a commentary which gratified him: "The Cuban cause is an American cause which has the sympathy of all the sons of this Continent and should be defended by the pen, the spoken word, and the efforts of all Americans. The opinions concerning this problem which are printed in the *Revista Universal* represent the views not only of the author, but of the entire staff of the paper, which has supported, and will continue to support them. The *Revista Universal* considers the Cuban question a matter of right, and as such it must defend it with all its strength, it must give to it the same support which it would give to the cause of an oppressed Mexico."

The newspaper *La Iberia* praised Castelar's popularity abroad and alluded to someone who held a different opinion:

"And someone even ventures to say that the eminent orator and writer is no longer popular outside of Spain."

That "someone" was Martí who had observed Castelar's conduct close at hand in Spain. He believed that a man of great talent could fall into disrepute and become unpopular if he ceased to uphold the ideas which brought him to prominence. He wrote: "People today demand consistency and reliability of the men they admire."

In discussing the popularity which Castelar had won in America and then lost through his unreliability, he condemned him for his apostasy, which his great talent made doubly inexcusable.

La Iberia not only defended Castelar, it made a direct reference to a Cuban writer who was "bent on airing the Cuban question in the *Revista*." According to *La Iberia*, the matter had been definitely settled by the Spaniards and Cubans living in Mexico. *La Iberia* wished to give the impression that there was an evil attempt to provoke arguments among the foreigners. Martí stood his ground:

"I know that I am doing what I should, and my conscience is clear."

If *La Iberia*, without any provocation, without being asked to express an opinion, insisted on discussing Cuba, why was Martí not entitled to say what he considered right and just? His associates headed his article with a note praising him for his discretion in treating Cuban affairs:

Friendly Mexico

"*La Revista* stated, a few days ago, that we feel as he does concerning Cuba. In spite of this and in spite of the fact that this newspaper has given him free rein to express his ideas, he expresses them very seldom, and whenever he does so he signs his articles, assuming the responsibility for his comments."

Martí wrote still more severe condemnations of Castelar. He called him an apostate not only because he opposed the plan for gradual abolition which was submitted to him, but also because he had no sooner taken office than he signed the death sentences which Salmerón was too honorable to sign. He had done this after declaiming against the sentences.

The controversy continued, but Martí's ideas were unrefuted and doubtless shared by the Mexicans of highest ideals.

At that time the Liceo Hidalgo was extremely active. When it was not holding literary or scientific meetings attended by the most outstanding intellectuals, it organized discussions of matters of vital, timely interest. Ideas were exchanged, and learning and oratorical skill were displayed. On April 7 a discussion of materialism and spiritualism was begun. The controversial question was whether the spirit exists and if so how it exists in human beings. Martí attended the Liceo that night for the first time. It was also the first time that he spoke in public in Mexico.

There was a strong positivist movement in the country. The most outstanding representative was Gabino Barreda, the man who had modernized the Mexican educational system, transforming it from an archaic, literary system to a scientific one. The revolutionary work of the reformers would have been incomplete without this change, which put the country in step with civilization. The most brilliant Mexican intellects worked with Barreda in an attempt to make their ideals become reality. Their work was a reconstruction of the national spirit which enabled it to receive the impact of contemporary thought. The cult of science and the supremacy of reason were the two essential postulates of the positivist movement.

Martí's words brought forth a murmur of admiration. He defended the thesis of *espiritualismo,* an intermediate theory between materialism and *espiritismo.* He declared his faith in immortality, in the pre-existence and survival of the soul. His words were lyric impulses which failed to convince men who had been educated in the unyielding scientific tradition. They wanted proofs, demonstrations. And when he was accosted by the materialistic arguments of the assembly members, Baz and Pimentel, his reply was applauded by the audience but did not convince the doubters:

"Abstractions are proved by abstractions; I have an immortal spirit because I feel it, because I believe in it, because I want it."

Marti's journalistic interests found ample opportunities for expression in the pages of the *Revista Universal.* After beginning with poetry and literary articles, he turned to unsigned editorials, such as those which were published April 15 and 16, about the war and the national treasury. He also wrote brief editorial notes whenever it was necessary. In Mexico his editorial ability was developed, and he mastered the technique. Making up the paper, filling in blanks in the pages at the last minute so that the pages would be complete and balanced, was a real pleasure. And if it was necessary to write an editorial, a theatre review, or a critical judgment, he did so with amazing speed and sureness, and still the literary beauty and the soundness of his judgments did not suffer.

As a result of these circumstances he joined the editorial staff of Villada's review as a permanent member. He was put in charge of one of the most important sections of the paper, the "bulletins" in which the political, literary, and social events of the time were recorded and interpreted. He adopted the pseudonym, Orestes. By a curious coincidence, his first bulletin was dedicated to the fifth of May, the Mexican national holiday.

He did not intend to offer a mere résumé of events, nor a criticism of them; he used events as bases from which he focused his ideas concerning standards of conduct or ambition. But it was not his purpose to write abstractions which the public could not understand. He tried to draw his public away from mere matters of daily, particular interest to general concepts. Every bulletin was a superior lesson for the understanding, a desire to find reason in all things, however insignificant they might seem.

He did not write to censure; on the contrary he was always quick to praise. But when he did use censure, it was not the kind that pains, but rather the kind that is gratefully accepted. He began to express his ideas of criticism in these bulletins. If it was necessary to censure very harshly, he kept silent, and that was his criticism.

In Mexico he perceived, from the very beginning, the difference between European and American life. He was always ready to praise the spontaneity, the vitality, the originality of American life. He was pained by the imitation, in America, of everything that was old in Europe. Art, life, ideas, forms of government, of wealth, and of social distribution, everything, he thought, like education, should be different in America, for the new man born in a new land.

In Mexico it was easy to see which road America should take. She must cultivate her own sources of originality, examining her own qualities, disdaining all importations which did not conform to the necessities of the new country. Even Mexico's wealth was not as useful as it should be: it was excessive, in some ways, but it did not yield as much as it could.

The excess of practical philosophy which he observed in the youth around him seemed to him a limitation. The imagination also fulfilled a purpose in man's higher life; its influence began where intelligence left off. All dogmatism seemed to him a detriment to the vital aspiration to go beyond the known, beause if we do not succeed, it is not that nothing exists beyond what is known, but that we do not have a way to attain it. Imagination, poetry, the breath of the spirit is what uplifts us. The education of the American man should prepare him to be wholly and consciously American. He continued to live on his legacy instead of living by his own original impulses. Everything in America tended toward a powerful, barbarous vehement rhythm, and yet, deaf to its call, men were living in tune to the echo of Europe, in literary, social, and artistic terms.

Martí

The Indian was a revelation for Martí. He was alarmed to find him standing still on Mexico's road. He raised his voice in warning: you must make him walk, or his weight will be a burden hindering you in your march. His ideas concerning the Indian appeared frequently in his writings. He was inspired both by his vision of the Indian's dormant strength which could be converted into force and life and by his own sorrow over the lamentable state in which the Indian lay. And he praised his discretion, his imagination and intelligence.

The thing that hampered Mexico's progress was the poison which she had not yet been able to purge from her veins. If only she could encourage her strong, industrious element, the life-blood of the nation; if only she could attain the necessary calm to organize her march "awakening from its fear that great sleeping race!"

It was in Mexico that he revealed his journalistic talent. Martí developed, not only as a journalist, but as a man with an American vision, a vision of such an America as he had never before dreamed of.

His bulletins were lessons in Mexicanism and Americanism. Nothing like them was published in the other newspapers. When he included contemporary events in his articles he chose those that could be incorporated into his universal ideas, because every bulletin had some of his thoughts, a bit of his creative urge. He taught the lesson of a man who knew himself: "To be a man is a difficult career that is seldom mastered on this earth."

A few weeks after he began to publish his bulletins, people were eagerly awaiting each new number. Just as his success as a poet and writer was assured after his first compositions appeared, his triumph as a journalist came with his first bulletins.

Thanks to the perfect accord between his own ideas and those that dominated government policy, he could feel that he too was a Mexican, sharing the ideals of the nation's leaders. Those ideals were his, and he could not desire better ones even for his own Cuba. Moreover, when he shared his distress over Cuba, these feelings erased all national differences. He was received so cordially and given such freedom of action that it seemed to him that he was not in a foreign country, but in his own. Even when he expressed himself concerning national affairs, few made him feel that he was a foreigner.

But not only were the Spaniards annoyed by his vigilance concerning Cuban matters, the Mexican opposition party was displeased by his defense of the government, and especially by the moderate tone of his articles, in which he emphasized the stupidity of continuous, bitter criticism. Although he was in a difficult position as a foreigner and a newcomer, he could not be indifferent toward that unjust campaign against the government. He was hurt by the falsehoods that were accumulated in order to combat him, and he was hurt by the systematic opposition which took the place of a reasonable, conscientious examination of the facts. He spoke in terms of a mental and emotional superiority which petty politicians did not recognize, for it would hamper their desire to attack only for the sake of destroying.

From the pages of his bulletins Martí's precepts pointed out the right, natural means of reaching an understanding. He knew very well that the Lerdo government was being attacked without offering useful reforms which could be studied and discussed impartially; it was being attacked with anger, hate, and rancor fanned by ambition. But he did not cease to recommend an opposition party that should not be based on spiteful insults. The mildness of his articles seems candid when one reflects that they were addressed to an enemy who sought only the fall of the government which had taken away their privileges, implanting a program of reforms that reduced the power of the church to purely spiritual matters. But that same moderation, armed by clear arguments, was a powerful weapon for the defense of the government. Hatred does not recognize moderation as an opponent but prefers equal arms, for only thus can it be considered rational.

He saw the country ruled by a civil government that makes possible understanding and harmony in a climate of freedom and respect. He thought of earlier periods of stormy, insecure situations, and he wondered "what the country would become in the hands of a disorderly militarism, without a new system of government, without visible capacity to create it, unsupported until now except by a few individuals, many without authority and almost all ignored and angry." That was not opposition for the sake of ideas, for the defense of oppressed justice, for the highest happiness of the people. It was the opposition of spite and hatred. And when election day came and the opposition did not appear to vote, what disturbing thoughts occurred to him as he guessed the plan which was taking shape in the darkness!

11. Revolution in Mexico

The friendship between Martí and Mercado grew firmer, day by day. Martí appreciated his strong character and good judgment. He visited Mercado's house almost every day and was sincerely missed on the days when he did not appear. Ocaranza also took part in the family gathering. His studio was in the Mercado home; they gathered there to watch him paint, as they commented and Martí spoke of the museums he had seen in Europe. Martí's old love of art and his real aptitude as a critic of painting pleased Ocaranza, who dreamed of perfecting his own art through travel.

Ocaranza was the most independent and original of the new Mexican painters. Martí found some of his pictures on modern subjects as elegant as a landscape by François Coppée, others symbolic and terrible as a tale by Poe. With Ocaranza's guidance he familiarized himself with Mexican art, which was rich in ancient paintings and had a good following of poor but talented students. He discovered the musical, luminous atmosphere of Mexico in the works of Rebull Pina, Cordero, Sagredo, and Ramírez, as well as those of the younger artists such as Obregón, whose Indian scenes were carefully done and colorful; Parra, superior to all the others in the scope and force of his paintings. There was no doubt that the landscape, the light, and the contrasts of Mexico were a perpetual invitation to the artist. Martí himself, as he contemplated the magnificent Mexican plateau and the far-off range of mountains with all their opulent shades of green, the silver line of the distant lakes, and the beautiful city, felt the deep poetry of this incomparable place.

Martí

Aided by influential friends with government positions, Ocaranza went to Europe, hardly three months after Martí's arrival in Mexico. Fortunately, his pictures were left on the walls in Mercado's living room, where Martí could look at them. It was as if the absent friend were present in spirit. And their conversations were continued too, for Ocaranza, a man of extraordinary culture, wielded the pen as deftly as the brush, and he began to publish letters in the *Revista* which abounded in facile, beautiful images and brilliant descriptions of Parisian life.

Don Ramón Guzmán, the owner of the house where Martí's family lived, was one of the friends who occasionally attended Mercado's gatherings. He, too, admired Martí's intelligence and invited him into his home. The Mexicans were very enthusiastic over his talent and were proud to receive him into their homes because of his brilliant conversation and distinguished manners. The Cubans also took pride in calling him their own. Indeed, there was not an emigrant who did not try to win his friendship.

Guzmán had just married one of the daughters of Don Francisco Zayas Bazán, a Cuban, residing in Mexico, next door to the editorial offices of the *Revista Universal*. On his daily trips to the newspaper office Martí had noticed the two beautiful daughters, and he even ventured a respectful greeting when he happened to meet Carmen, the unmarried sister. He was really not a stranger any more by the time he was introduced to her in her house.

Zayas Bazán, a rather unsociable, peevish man, led a secluded life in Mexico after leaving Cuba on account of the revolution there. He lived on the small but well-managed income from his property. He was an inveterate chess player, and he managed to forget the trials of his exile when he was playing. Martí's visits became more and more frequent, after Don Francisco made him his partner at chess. Carmen's beauty was more than worthy of this small sacrifice.

In his bulletins Martí became bolder in his prophecies and stronger in his faith in Mexico. Meanwhile the threat of blind violence was also increasing, the violence that heeds nothing but the order to crush all opposition. The Reforma gave Mexico brilliant days such as it had never known. It was necessary for the darkness to return in order for the reactionary forces to thrive. Dark powers impelled the fanatical throngs, hurling them against the bugbear of Protestantism. It was really nothing but a pretext to accuse the government and stir up a religious conflict among the people without assuming responsibility as a loyal opposition party should. The government was in favor of everything that would raise the cultural level of the people. A printshop was opened in an old monastery, a school in an old convent, a library in the Church of Saint Augustine. Secret gardens and walled cloisters became places where industrious people found means of cultivating their minds.

But the opposition against this new order was implacable. It was already apparent that the once clear atmosphere of Mexico was growing cloudy. In the last few months the interest in literature and art had declined. The zest for intellectual activity was dulled by the threat of disorder and by material difficulties. Unjustly attacked, the government ceased to function smoothly, and its economy was weakened. It gradually became paralyzed. The economic system was unbalanced, and domestic industry could not compete with the foreign products that glutted the market. Things finally reached the point where the people blamed the government for the crisis. In reality, the crisis was the result of incessant agitation on the part of the systematic opposition.

Toward the end of September the newspapers printed comments about the causes of the national troubles and the advantages that foreign industries had over the domestic industry. Untiring in his efforts to encourage reason and good judgment, Martí was happy over this awakening of the national conscience, now ready to face the problems. A thorough understanding of reality was needed, not allegiance to certain foreign economic theories, or the idea that they must be practical in Mexico because they had been applied successfully elsewhere. His Americanism made him uphold this standard against the theorists with foreign ideas: "Servile imitation will lead us astray economically just as it does in literature and politics." And with this consciousness of reality he presented the twofold problem: it was impossible to deprive the masses of the advantage of acquiring an indispensable article at half-price. But it was also impossible to let the Mexican factory workers starve because their products could not compete with foreign products. This special problem demanded specific, concrete solutions, not inflexible measures.

Martí's ideas about Americanism touched upon every kind of intellectual activity. Mexico needed a Mexican literature; Mexico needed her own theatre in order to take another step in her independence; a theatre that would record the people's longings and restore their old enthusiasm, teach them to understand and to love everything that was their own.

"How can a people expect to have a proud new life if it is still copying the decay and nakedness of a jaded way of life that is not its own?"

His articles frequently contained criticism of works by Mexican authors or plans for a Mexican theatre, such as actor Zerecero's project of presenting dramas written by the nation's playwrights.

For the casual observer the theatre is frivolity. Nevertheless, it is a reflection of the people's lives and a portrayal of their character, and how can a nation, having its own way of life, content itself with foreign dramas? Martí censured this indifference on the part of the Mexican theatre. It could so easily present plays by national authors and thus assure even the traveling companies visiting Mexico City publicity and a good audience.

Enrique Guasp de Paris, Lersundi's assistant who gave up the military service for the theatre, was in Mexico City at that time, attempting to encourage the Mexican theatre. Closely united with Martí by their identical ideas on this subject and many others, Guasp had the benefit of Martí's advice and encouragement in his enterprise of developing a theatre group that would present Mexican plays. In the petition which Guasp submitted to the president, Martí found an opportune application of the differential theories of esthetics popularized by the Madrid intellectuals. Martí had a good opportunity to praise an undertaking for which he had long been campaigning in the pages of the *Revista*. He reiterated his ideas and again analyzed the conditions of life in Mexico and the incongruity of not having a national theatre in a nation which had its own society and life. His comments, as always, were intended to arouse that strong original nation's dormant potentialities, especially those of its hesitant or doubting youth, which must rise, through effort and will power, to the heights of its yet unproductive talent. At Guasp's suggestion he synthesized all these ideas in one of his bulletins. None of his previous articles in the *Revista* excelled this one in intellectual force, elevated concepts, and beautiful language.

By September Guasp's plan was approved and about to be put into execution. Martí insisted on the need of strengthening, with works of imagination, the intellectually weak youth which was the product of a systematic practical philosophy. The literature of the time was correspondingly hard and painful, the product of the so-called realistic school which believed that evil can be cured by its exaggerated portrayal. In opposition to realism he formulated his theory that all education must have a superior objective, because "if we need to be better than we are, shall we improve by copying what we are?" Thus the idealist expressed his opinion.

In November the success of the project culminated in the first presentation of works by Mexican authors. Guasp had carried out his purpose and Martí had made a useful contribution to his triumph by his own authority and by influencing his friends such as Mercado and Villada who were directly connected with the government. But Guasp wanted Martí to create something himself. Martí accepted and wrote the play in a few hours.

Several days later Martí attended the try-outs for the parts. Guasp was as excited as if he had written the work, and he recited his lines as if he were the author. It was apparent that Concha Padilla had studied her lines with devotion, and her expression was meaningful and vehement. The truth was that she liked the play very much. In a sense it was written for her, as Martí told her, for he was thinking about how she would interpret it when he wrote it.

His play was presented as the fifth number of the season, the night of September 19, 1875. The Teatro Principal was crowded with people anxiously awaiting the first performance of *Amor con Amor se Paga* (Love Is Repaid with Love), as his play was called, taking its name from a Mexican proverb. The author's name did not appear on the announcements, and this further stimulated curiosity. The critics and men of letters who met in the lobbies and walked up and down the aisles speculated as to the authorship of the play about to be presented.

The lines were surprisingly facile and graceful. Guasp spoke his lines passionately, Concha Padilla with exquisite interpretation. A storm of applause burst from the audience when the last verses were recited. It was prolonged as an insistent call for the author. Finally he appeared between Guasp and Padilla. As the applause continued, Srta. Padilla presented him with a laurel crown in the name of the company.

Martí's triumph was as rotund as it was unexpected. It was, moreover, the most genuine triumph that could be desired because the work, not the author, was applauded.

The newspapers were not sparing in their praise. *El Siglo* could not find words to express its "unreserved love and respect for all that bears the mark of talent and a sensitive nature as exquisite as it is admirable." *La Iberia* considered Martí's work a "beautiful work of art" and commented on the "delightful novelty of the extremely simple plot" and his "graceful verses which seem to belong to our golden age." And Nicolás Azcárate, who had many friends in the country whose hospitality had made him and his fellow Cubans forget that they were expatriates, wrote in his gazette, *El Eco de Ambos Mundos* (The Echo of Both Worlds) an enthusiastic review in which his pride as a compatriot of Martí was evident.

Nevertheless, Martí knew very well that his triumph was one of facile wit. He wished to succeed in higher undertakings of the mind.

The "proverb" was presented twice in the same season and again in subsequent ones. The public always gave it a good reception. Guasp was a resounding success, in spite of the fact that this experimental Mexican theatre was attacked because it was sponsored by the government. Martí wrote a few verses for Guasp's benefit performance on January 26. He praised the power of the actor who transforms and creates and with his genius awakes in his listeners the same emotions which he feels.

Through Guasp's efforts *Amor con Amor Se Paga* was published with the cast of characters of its first performance. On the title page was a statement that it was performed with "extraordinary success."

Guasp's innovating experiment aroused an interest in Mexican works, despite the growing political difficulties. The Spaniards, although they were enemies of Cuban independence, supported Guasp's theatrical experiments and published comments in favor of the Mexican theatre. The purpose of the society was to increase dramatic production, following up Guasp's efforts, for the benefits of his work could not be denied.

Martí took part in many activities at this time and was the recipient of many honors. Indeed his articles indicated as much affection as concern for things Mexican, and he discussed the problems of Mexico with a penetration that is not often found even in the citizens of the nation.

The laborers had noticed that Martí was defending them without flattering them. Consequently, the workers of Chihuahua made him their representative in a labor meeting. The government did not fail to acknowledge the calm reasoning with which he defended his ideals and desired to give him some public recognition. But Martí tactfully refused the office of Secretary to the Governor of the State of Puebla which his friends offered him.

Martí supported all sincere literary and artistic ventures in his zeal to serve the cause which he considered urgent and important: helping skeptical or indifferent youth. Although he had published no bulletins in the *Revista* since November 30, he did publish signed literary articles and critical reviews and an occasional article on Cuba. Perhaps his efforts were more effective that way. Writing bulletins forced him to comment on current affairs, and such topics were becoming more and more controversial as the opposition grew rougher. The moderation which he was obliged as a foreigner to maintain made it difficult to comment because it was not his place to take part in a clash of hatreds which clouded the opponents thinking. He was there to clarify, not to roil, the waters. As long as he could contribute rational advice, his comments on daily events filled a need. There was another serious objection to the bulletin: it appeared without his signature. He wished to stand behind all his ideas. He wished to think for himself and not have his ideas interpreted as a defense of the ideas of the editors for whom he was writing, although they might be one and the same.

He received many distinctions, but he was also frequently attacked. Fortunately the attacks always came from the negative element, the discontented and the envious. A recalcitrant Spaniard, Adolfo Llanos y Alcaraz, the editor and owner of *La Colonia Española,* had made himself conspicuous in Mexico for his anti-American campaigns in an attempt to discredit the free countries, whom he considered more poorly governed than they were in colonial times. In an insulting book, *No Vengáis a América* (Don't Come to America) he gave free rein to his antipathy. With the purpose of ending his stay in a place which he disliked so much, a subscription was taken up in Mexico to cover the cost of his passage to Spain. That was the condition under which he always said that he would leave, whenever anyone suggested that he go. His character can be judged by the fact that he stayed nevertheless.

As was the case with other Spaniards who could not resign themselves to their loss, Llanos concentrated his nationalistic intransigence on comments on the struggle for Cuban independence. He boasted of his journalistic polemics with almost the entire Mexican press, and he never lost an opportunity to attack Cuba.

August 16, 1876, he published an article entitled *La Insurrección Cubana,* in which he transcribed, along with his own peevish phrases, an item from the *New York Sun* concerning the Fourth of July. The *Sun* commented on the complete silence of all the Fourth of July centenary speakers of which it had reports, concerning Cuba's struggle. The New York newspaper expressed its regret that not a single orator, "on praising the heroism of our forbears, had a word of sympathy for poor Cuba."

Revolution in Mexico

Martí was not slow in acting. Three days later his note, *Los Cubanos en el Centenario Americano,* was printed in the *Revista.* He spoke of the genuine enthusiasm with which the Cuban flag was cheered on the night of the great civic parade and mentioned the official invitation which the Cubans received from the parade commission. Using all the newspapers which he could obtain he pointed out the route of the Cuban parade and the ovations it received. Concluding he said:

"One may combat political ideas, but one must admire that which is admirable. This is a law of justice and an obligation."

In answering the *Colonia's* angry reply Martí again set an example of prudence at the same time that he made the truth known. The only *patria* that the Cubans could have until they attained their independence was the record of their history and the moral worth of their men. He showed that the Cubans had taken part in the North American celebration. He quoted numerous accounts from the papers. He was furious when the *Colonia* referred to the *banderita cubana,* the "little Cuban flag," and he replied:

"Not a 'little flag,' a flag! Not an imbecile people supporting the yoke of a nation even more imbecile. A proud nation which inspires in the hearts of brave men, be they friends or enemies, respect, love, and admiration. Flag is a dignified word, worthy of a people that has spent seven heroic years, that has active heroes and errant martyrs and more than enough willing arms to lift the flag on high; a flag that, if more unfortunate than most, will be more respected. If it is late in being unfurled, it will last longer. We honor ourselves by paying honor where it is due."

His vehement article provoked bitter words from the editor of *La Colonia,* words unworthy of an answer. Martí did not take the trouble to reply. But the *Revista* continued to publish notices from United States newspapers supporting evidence for the Cuban's testimony and approval of his inflexible desire that his country be "shown the honor and respect due her" everywhere.

Martí was saddened when blood began to flow in Mexico and he saw how all progress and all prestige which Mexico had gained was destroyed. He had suspended the publication of his bulletins in November, 1875. The burden of writing daily comments would have become more and more irksome as journalistic violence was followed by military violence. Doubtless Lerdo's re-election, which had increased the tension and strengthened the Tuxtepec revolution, did not meet with his approval. But it was impossible not to appreciate the motive for this struggle, or what the government had done to build a sound democracy, with laws to benefit the people, liberal just laws, whose results no one could deny. With his signature Martí had published everything a thinking man could consider it necessary and useful to say in defense of that government. He did what his duty as a liberty-loving man commanded him to do. He could not and ought not to do any more without risking his own integrity.

Although it was sad for him to witness the destruction of a work in which he thought he saw so many of his own ideals realized, his pain at being deserted by many dear friends had no limit. For some time one of the most robust Mexican personalities, Riva Palacio, had belonged to the opposition. At the last minute two of the staunchest supporters of the Lerdo government, Justo Sierra and Guillermo Prieto, who had been so close to Martí in philosophy and in their fight, deserted in order to revile and betray legality, according to the *Revista*. *El Federalista* came to the defense of the accused, calling the editors of Villada's paper blind, biased, and stained with the mud with which they were trying to besmirch the brows of men like Justo Sierra. A more painful moment for Martí can not be imagined. An editorial, evidently by Martí, appeared in the *Revista*. In the part concerning him he said: "As for Martí . . . out of respect for his condition as one not born in Mexico . . . and because of his character, he has not offended nor will he offend those whom he esteems for their intelligence. However, he accepts fully and loyally, the risks of a situation in whose legality, good faith and public benefit he believes. The hour of loyalty must always be the hour of danger."

This was published November 18. The *Revista Universal* published only one more issue, on the nineteenth. Three days earlier the battle on the hills of Tecoac had begun, and

Revolution in Mexico

the government troops were defeated. When Martí wrote his last editorial and declared his affiliation to a cause that had been defeated, he showed how firm his convictions were. He could try to remain in Mexico. In fact, he was asked to do so, doubtless by his friends who had gone over to the winning side. But his decision was made. November 20 President Lerdo left the capital in the company of a few friends, including Villada. On the twenty-third Profirio Díaz entered in triumph, greeted by the ringing of bells, and the shouts of the multitude.

Thanks, no doubt, to the outstanding figures who had gone over to Porfirio Díaz' party at the last minute, there were no reprisals and Martí did not have to give up his journalistic activities. Although it was hard for him to remain in Mexico after this defeat of the American ideal, he needed a few months to orient himself. His family would have to go back to Cuba while he was looking for new opportunities. He certainly had not made a comfortable living in Mexico. The fifty pesos which he earned as a writer on the *Revista* staff was the regular salary paid to all the writers, and it barely enabled him to eke out a living and support his family.

For several months he had been on intimate terms with the Zayas family. His friendship with Carmen had become a tender, serene love. Although Don Francisco's opposition had not been entirely overcome, Guzmán, who had been a good friend from the beginning, softened the future father-in-law's pride.

In regard to his political activities he had nothing to regret. He had defended what he thought was right. But he had carried his convictions to dangerous extremes, not out of loyalty to a political idea or a regime, but out of loyalty to his concept of man, the human concept. He sought no refuge. On the contrary, risking his very life in the face of a hostile regime, at a time when the most fundamental laws were sure to be forgotten, he took up his pen in anger to flay the flayer of men, the man who degraded his brothers.

Even though he had done what his conscience commanded, he still was not satisfied. At that dangerous moment

115

his indignation impelled him to shout his convictions, and he did so. He published several signed articles culminating in *La situación*. In his final article, entitled *Extranjero* (Foreigner), a compendium and synthesis of his ideas, throbbed his virile reply to those who had harbored evil sentiments in their hearts. To those who might ask, "And why are you writing this? You are a foreigner," he replied with an analysis of the process of thought. He who prevents the expression of ideas, he wrote, breaks the laws of nature. He based his conduct on his concept of humanity. He exalted the power of righteous wrath, a powerful force which was his source of strength. None of his other works of this period equalled this one in vigor, beauty, and profundity. Beneath the philosophical concepts and lyric flights one could detect the purpose: that of defending himself from vulgar accusations. Some may have defended the fallen regime for the sake of personal advantage; he never desired or received any such advantage.

His righteous indignation, which he poured forth impetuously, made him blush for others' shame at that time when peoples' wills were crushed, conscience was forgotten, laws were suspended, free men were flagellated, and their ideas suffered outrage. His blood "curdled at the sight of the satisfied smile of a happy victor."

He did not ask for Mexican citizenship when he could have made use of it as a means of flattering the man in power, nor did he speak of his love of Mexico at a time when his gratitude might be taken for servile flattery. Now, as he was leaving, he declared his loyalty to the wounded men and his love for those who had suffered such a misfortune. He did so at the very time when he was in danger and he had nothing to gain by saying these things, for he was going away.

He spent some thoughtful days when it was not easy for him to chart his course. Where would he go, what would become of his home? Domínguez Cowan was an intimate friend and a great help in this difficult hour. Through him he also received a generous offer from the father of Carmen to whom he was at that time engaged. He could not accept financial aid from one without accepting aid from the other. Resigned to his straitened circumstances, and happy because it revealed such fine natures to him, he refused both offers at that critical time. On December 30 he left Mexico for Veracruz. *El Federalista* bade him farewell in an editorial published the same day, to the effect that he was going to Guatemala: "Fortunately he will not be gone long. He will be far away from us for a few months, but perhaps in June we shall see him again."

January 1, 1877, he arrived in Veracruz. He could not forget his cares. Not even his close friends like Domínguez Cowan to whom he wrote from Veracruz, could guess his bitterness because they had never realized how silent pain could crush his spirit. His plan to go to St. Thomas was infeasible; he was not granted the concession which he had been expecting. A new idea came to him. He would go to Havana with legal papers all in perfect order and under an assumed name, to disorient anyone who might have kept track of him thus far in his journey. He knew that it was an imprudent plan, but it was necessary. He told his friend, "Take a look at my home, and you will find the reason for everything." Why was he taking this dangerous trip to Havana? He had to find work for his father there, something "in keeping with his advanced years and his sick mind." After he had succeeded in that—and he intended to succeed even if he was imprisoned—all other dangers would seem petty to him. He could not stop worrying about his family. His future wife was also beginning to worry. He encharged his friend with one supreme trust, which Martí knew he would fulfill like a command: "look after my family."

He left Veracruz January 2, on the steamer *Ebro*, bound for Havana, as Julián Pérez—his second Christian name and his mother's surname.

On January 6 Julián Pérez reached the harbor of Havana. As soon as he set foot on Cuban soil he went to the Valdés Domínguez home, his best protection. Fermín was back in Havana, having earned the degree of M.D. at the University of Zaragoza. Fermín found Martí stronger and more cheerful.

Martí

He had considered going to Guatemala during his last days in Mexico when he scanned the American panorama in search of a place where he could find shelter for his beliefs, begin a new life, and found a home. During that period of prosperity Guatemala was governed by General José Rufino Barrios who had done a great deal to further education. It was widely known that a Cuban who had fought in the revolution, José María Izaguirre, had been invited to found the Normal School of Guatemala and to serve as president of that institution. Martí had spoken of him to the Cubans living in Mexico. They were aware of Izaguirre's excellent qualities. His Normal School was known throughout the Central American countries. Everyone knew that it was not only an educational center but the literary and cultural center of Guatemala at that time. It was also known that President Barrios was giving his complete support to Izaguirre's work, and that Marco Aurelio Soto, a renowned statesman in charge of public education, had a very high opinion of the Cuban. Martí had both the qualifications and the diplomas that he needed to apply for a position as a teacher in that flourishing school.

Fermín's father, a Guatemalan, encouraged him. He not only had classmates and friends in influential positions, President Barrios himself had been a pupil of his. Fermín's father gave Martí letters of introduction for all of his friends, including a very hearty one for the chief executive. He also gave him a thousand pesos and assured him that he would help him find work for Don Mariano. Everything was arranged under such propitious signs that he had no desire to tempt the prison gates by being seen in Havana any more than was necessary. He stayed in Fermín's house until all arrangements were made and then purchased his return ticket.

He was able to observe the progress of the revolution close at hand. Reports were not encouraging. After nine years of fighting, fatigue was becoming evident, and the revolution kept losing force. Martí had the impression that this cruel struggle had been prolonged too long and was sapping all the Cubans' strength. The successful war would have to be brief but decisive.

Revolution in Mexico

Martí remained in Havana a little over a month. He left for Veracruz February 24 under the same name which he had used on leaving Mexico, Julián Pérez. He left with high hopes and with the means to facilitate his family's return to Havana. In a few days everything was ready. Before he set out for Guatemala, Don Francisco Zayas Bazán consented to the marriage between Martí and his daughter. From the opulent fields of Yucatan he set out for Belize, the Capital of British Honduras, and leaving behind him that charming, populous land of the Caribs called Livingstone, he entered Guatemala by the mouth of the Río Dulce.

12. Guatemala Days

With the chill of exile in his heart Martí entered Guatemala from the Atlantic coast. He crossed the land of Isabal, a land of lofty volcanoes, fertile hills, and wide rivers, on his way to Guatemala City. He was dazzled by the golden corn and wheat. The aromatic coffee was spread out in wide zones, and the slopes of the mountains were covered with a great diversity of fruit trees. The luxuriant Atlantic coast was covered with an extraordinary flora.

His curiosity was no less intense than his surprise. Man was surrounded on all sides by a benign, useful exuberance. As he contemplated the new scene, spontaneous lines came to him, and when he stopped to rest he composed a hymn to this land of happy abundance.

On his way he stopped at a little village called El Jícaro, to watch the passing of the beautiful equestrian wedding procession of a smiling boy and girl. He dismounted in front of the home of an Indian who was "talkative, boastful, lettered, and blind in one eye," which latter characteristic, Martí wrote in his notes, was more important than most people realized. Martí struck up a conversation with the Indian while the latter fried some eggs for him. The Indian recited, for Martí's benefit, though rather badly, a local fable. The first stanza made Martí look up; the second impressed him. He was struck by the originality of the verses, their grace, animation, presentation of nature, wise observations, and American quality. He thought of how trite most fables were. Who was the author? The author was a Guatemalan, and Martí was impressed by this humble, industrious rustic's admiration of the city man who had interpreted his intimate feelings, taking the inspiration for his work from nature.

A few days later Martí entered the white city of Guatemala. It all seemed to him like a presage of good fortune and happy hours. The graceful Indian woman had welcomed him to her country; nature pierced his sensibility with its prodigious beauty. And now, as he faced the institution of higher learning he thought that all he needed in order to make a new life was a humble teaching position.

Shortly afterward he reached the doors of the Normal School. Izaguirre was favorably impressed by the newcomer's experience.

"I am a Cuban. I have come from Mexico. My name is José Martí. My qualifications for teaching—"

"José Martí!" Izaguirre interrupted. No other introduction was necessary. He had read Martí's pamphlet on the Cuban penitentiary. His nationality and his merits were sufficient titles to win everyone's sympathy. Immediately he offered him a position in the school. Martí preferred to teach history or literature. Izaguirre gave him the latter, plus the composition course, for which there was no instructor at that time.

Izaguirre took him to his home and gave him lodging there. It would be necessary later to arrange for a visit to President Barrios, and he would also take charge of that.

The President's sympathies for the Cuban cause had long been well known..His bold act of recognition of Cuba as a belligerent nation had caused him serious diplomatic trouble. Martí impressed him very favorably, and the President felt inclined to give him a chance to develop his talents in Guatemala. He had arrived just when the Faculty of Philosophy and Letters was being created, and there he would find the opportunity to teach the subjects he liked. Meanwhile, the classes Izaguirre offered him would tide him over.

Martí devoted himself with loving enthusiasm to his new professorial tasks. He had never been happier, had never felt more creative than he felt now that he was becoming a teacher. His truly original mind, his study and his conscientious application combined to make his classes stimulating. His classes were always popular.

Martí

After presenting Martí to the highest authority in the Republic, Izaguirre introduced him to the man who had been president before him, General Miguel García Granados, leader of the revolution of 1871, a man of great national prestige, as important as the President himself.

General García Granados' house was a meeting place for national figures of culture and distinction. Martí was given a cordial reception there and met the Guatemalan elite. A pleasant friendship soon developed between Martí and Don Miguel's five daughters: Adela, María, Cristina, Leonor, and Luz. This placid family life was a pleasant contrast to the bitterness of his last days in Mexico.

The Normal School had an excellent reputation. Some of the nation's most competent professors taught there. Izaguirre also had the benefit of the guidance of a friend and former classmate of his, the famed Cuban educator, Luis Felipe Mantilla. Nevertheless, the school had many enemies among the religious fanatics because it occupied a building that had belonged to the Paulist congregation. To overcome this hostility he made the School a popular center, organizing frequent literary meetings. He also encouraged the development of one of the best gardens in Central America, in which the nation took great pride. In this way he won cooperation and good will toward the School.

Under these circumstances, Martí's presence naturally helped Izaguirre's cause.

At the first meeting which Martí attended, two of the speakers were members of Barrios' cabinet, Martín Barrundia and Lorenzo Montúfar, both experienced orators. When the orators were through, Martí requested permission to say a few words. Izaguirre granted his request with natural misgivings, for although he considered Martí a discreet young man, he knew nothing of his oratorical ability. Martí's opening paragraphs captured his listeners' attention. He spoke on literature in relation with politics, always a delicate subject, but he presented it so skillfully that he avoided all difficulties. He was heartily applauded, especially by General Barrios' secretaries. From that night on Martí's reputation in Guatemala as an orator was established. For days his speech was commented on as a great event. Because of his impetuosity and exuberance he was nicknamed "Doctor Torrent." One critic, who praised his fecund imagination and facile expression, said that "as in young, thick forests, there is a great deal of excessive foliage in what he says."

Soon Martí was one of the most frequent visitors to the home of General García Granados. His inspired words and his fertile imagination exercised a sort of witchery over the young girls. One of the sisters was singularly impressed by his personality. This was María, no more beautiful than her sisters, but possessing finer sensibilities. She had a graceful figure, and her face reflected her inner sweetness. Silky black curls framed her white face. Long lashes veiled the dreams in her melancholy dark eyes. Her melancholy beauty and her tender, caressing voice filled Martí's imagination with dreams and fantasies. He felt attracted to her. He singled her out from among her sisters and appreciated her spiritual superiority. With her twenty years and her sad beauty, she charmed Martí.

Martí would have liked to "weave for her a garland of loving thoughts." His engagement with Carmen bound him. It would be cruel to encourage this love; he must erase it from the girl's mind.

Martí's presence changed the course of her life. Little by little the sadness already apparent in her glance and her voice was accentuated. Did she know about his engagement, or had she guessed it? She could not overcome the feeling which possessed her. Wrapped in her own thoughts, she became sadder and more silent. Perhaps no one understood what she suffered. Only Martí knew the secret, and he also suffered, powerless to remedy the situation.

The peace of the first months in Guatemala was turning to deep suffering not only on his own account but on account of the harm he was causing. He realized that only by his gradual withdrawal could María's pure sentiment be diverted, for it was so ingenuous that it had taken on alarming force. His visits became less frequent. His courtesy was unchanged but his attentions diminished.

Martí

Martí's presence aroused great interest after his speech at the Normal School. Another one of General Barrios' ministers, Joaquín Macal, Minister of Foreign Relations, became interested in his writing and asked his opinion of the new code of laws which were just going into effect. Martí answered him on April 11. His letter was a fervent eulogy of the new, native forces of Guatemala, praise of her eagerness to find her own guiding theories in herself, and of her way of putting the useful theories into effect. If he had been of some service before, he said, he had no recollection of it; what he wanted was to serve more.

His article on *Los Códigos Nuevos* (The New Codes of Law) gave him an opportunity to develop and amplify his ideas following the historical process of American civilization. It was a hymn to the new idea expressed by the new law, the American spirit.

General Barrios kept his promise. On May 29 Martí was notified of his appointment as a professor of French, English, Italian, and German literature in the recently established Faculty of Philosophy and Letters. Montúfar, Minister of Education, confirmed the appointment. Montúfar doubtless had some influence on Martí's nomination, for he had mentioned Martí's speech to the President and praised it highly.

It was a time of growing activity. *La Revista de la Universidad* (The University Review) requested articles from him. His pupils wanted a text for the history of philosophy. He had copious notes of everything he had seen, and he intended to use them at some happier time. For the *Revista de la Universidad* he would write about his teaching and matters of general interest. He was beginning to organize his notes for those articles, in which he tried to breathe new life and meaning into the doctrines of the philosophers.

Besides devoting himself with growing love to his chair in the University, he helped Izaguirre with his literary gatherings at the Normal School. Early in July at one of the meetings he gave an address with which he surpassed his previous fame as an orator. His subject was the influence of oratory. His insistence on proving its influence seemed unnecessary to all who heard him; it was enough to hear him to be convinced. He revealed his knowledge of history and philosophy and was lavish with his eloquence. In *El Progreso*, a Guatemalan daily paper, a review of the meeting appeared. Martí's speech was very highly acclaimed.

Later he collaborated in an effort in which all Guatemalans interested in raising intellectual standards took part. The society *El Porvenir* elected him vice-president, and Martí put all of his intelligence and efforts at the service of those who were disinterestedly and lovingly working for the spiritual redemption of man.

September 15, Guatemalan Independence Day, was near. The government had given a real impulse to the cultural movement of the country and wanted the commemorative program to be outstanding. Martí's triumph in the few months which he had spent in Guatemala had been so apparent and so complete, that he was given one of the most important parts of the program.

For the author who had triumphed in Mexico with *Amor con Amor se Paga*, it would not be difficult to write a dramatic work for the commemoration. The government assignment reached him through one of his most admired friends, Antonio Batres, and he could not refuse. In two weeks he had written a drama concerning Guatemalan independence.

But of all the articles he was working on during those months he was most interested in the one in which he recorded his impressions of Guatemala. Love and gratitude were the words with which he began. With the loving care of a silversmith he fashioned that book in which he captured all the colors of the foliage and trees, like butterflies caught and fastened to the pages, all the lights of the Guatemalan sky, all the beauties of her nature and her people. He traced the routes of the generous land of Guatemala and portrayed the Indians. He sang of the simple, natural gifts of this hospitable land, honorable family life, work which made man free. Throughout his descriptions of Guatemala he proclaimed his avid love of American grandeur. With sonorous epithets he spoke of ancient Antigua, lively Quezaltenango, growing Cobán, Escuintla, the sugar-producer, volcanic Amatitlán, warm Salamá, and charming Huehuetenango. For every place he had a precise word, a phrase of understanding.

Martí

He believed in the religion of an ardent, generous America. With the eyes of a sick man and a poet, he looked upon the virginal land. Out of his sufferings as a lover he wished to make this great offer. There was a woman who incarnated all the beauty of this land of pensive lakes and majestic volcanoes, a woman who had turned her thoughts toward him and who lived in the depths of his heart. For her this book was written. As he could not show the love which she had inspired in him, he offered it to her in this form, this living offering of all the beauties of this land which he loved because it was hers and because it had her tenderness, softness, and delicacy. Pouring out his silent, repressed love in this great poem helped him to recover a little of his lost peace.

He did not limit himself to the description of the natural beauties of the country. Across his pages passed the men who had offered the vigor of their ideas. He mentioned the happiness of the people, the courteous manners of the Indians, who were more beautiful here because their living conditions were more humane and better suited to their needs. He offered a fecund program: cultivate, work, distribute, following a plan of useful distribution of wealth. "Teach, destroy oligarchic centralization, restore to men their damaged or undiscovered personalities."

He had just finished his book. He was happy and at peace with himself, as if he were beginning to pay a debt. He had worked intensely during the last few days, for he was preparing for his trip to Mexico. Izaguirre had agreed when he hired him to give him a leave so that he could be married in Mexico.

At the end of the second week of December, 1877, Martí arrived in Mexico City. On the morning of the twentieth, he was married in the church, La Parroquia del Sagrario Metropolitano. The same afternoon the civil marriage was performed. The ceremony was followed by a fiesta attended by their old friends, among them Martí's poet friends, Juan de Dios Peza, Agustín F. Cuenca and Peón Contreras and the journalists who, a year ago, had been his co-workers and even opponents, such as the esteemed Anselmo de la Portilla. They all wrote compliments or verses in Carmen's album. There was music and recital of poetry.

Although their friends insisted that they stay longer, Martí was determined to keep his promise to Izaguirre. He left the manuscript of his essay on Guatemala, which was to be published, in the hands of the Guatemalan Uriarte. He began his return trip with his wife without even having time for a honeymoon. The long days spent traveling over almost impassable roads in an uncomfortable coach made it necessary for them to rest frequently at the Indians' huts. The journey, although uncomfortable and annoying in some ways, had its charms. It was a constant surprise to Carmen, although it grated on her aristocratic temperament

Martí had planned his trip so precisely that they arrived at Izaguirre's house on the day when the month's leave was up.

He resumed his teaching and became definitely established. But he did not dare visit General García Granados' home. Circumstances had forced him to make this terrible decision which caused him unutterable suffering. To avoid meeting María he isolated himself and devoted himself to his classes as much as possible. He inquired of Izaguirre and learned that she was languid and absorbed in her thoughts. Perhaps his decision had served only to make matters worse. She seemed to be failing by the moment, and seemed doomed to an early death.

María's languor became real illness. A slow fever consumed her. No one could cheer her or rouse her from that silence which cast its gloom on everyone around her. A few days later she died, without uttering a word of complaint.

All Guatemala City mourned her death. Everyone was touched by the death of such a young girl, and one so well loved. She was as simple and modest as she was lovable. An enormous crowd attended her solemn, moving funeral services. The coffin was covered with white satin and adorned with white wreaths. She was borne on the shoulders of her friends to her final resting place, followed by a silent, deeply moved retinue. Izaguirre, Martí, and the Cuban poet, José Joaquín Palma walked together in sorrow. They stayed, alone, in front of the vault as the mason finally laid the stone in place. They walked away together, with hurried steps, when the first stars appeared in the deep blue evening sky. As they walked back, some tender, new verses, of penetrating popular flavor, began to take shape in Martí's mind.*

In Carmen he found the comfort he needed. Her beauty fascinated him and inspired him to write verses. She gave him the strength to win, a love that made him feel strong and triumphant.

He went back to his classes and planned to do more publishing. His book, *Guatemala,* recently published in Mexico, was highly praised by those who had had the opportunity to read a few fragments in Guatemala and by those who read the book in Mexico. "This is the kind of book America needs, that her nations may know one another better," said the Guatemalan Uriarte. The idea suggested others to Martí. He thought of editing a review that would bear the name of the land that had received him lovingly. By March he had made up his mind and published a broadside, a prospectus of the *Revista Guatemalteca,* which he circulated among his friends. The program was ambitious: to inform the readers of artistic, scientific, and literary progress in Europe and the amazing machines that North America was producing, to review every worthwhile book that might come from the European presses and at the same time to reveal to Europe the beauty and the wealth of America and everything that was admirable in her men and in her art. The spirit behind his program is well expressed in these words:

"I know Europe; I have studied her spirit. I know America and her spirit. We have more natural resources, in these lands from the fierce Río Grande to the southernmost tip of Chile, than in any land on earth. But we have fewer civilizing elements, for we are much younger historically, we do not have so many centuries behind us, and we Latin Americans have been less fortunate in regard to education than many other people."

The prestige of the Normal School grew every day. But in the same proportion the number of its enemies increased.

* The author refers to the poem *La Niña de Guatemala,* one of Martí's most popular. (Ed.)

especially among the presidents of *colegios* whose enrollment suffered because of the increasing registration in the Normal School. A silent war was carried on against Izaguirre, and every opportunity to discredit him with the government was seized.

March 19 was Izaguirre's saint's day, and his friends and colleagues gave a party in his honor, one of those gatherings that had contributed so much to the school's prestige. The program, in which the most noted artists of Guatemala took part, was widely commented. A rumor reached the President to the effect that Izaguirre was making use of the school for his own personal benefit. This was the way the program was interpreted. Izaguirre was summoned, and the President expressed his disapproval and his intention of dismissing him. Izaguirre resigned at once.

Martí's resignation was not long in coming. Izaguirre's arguments could not dissuade him.

"I shall resign even if my wife and I starve. I would rather do that than be an accomplice in an act of injustice."

On April 6 he received notice that his resignation had been accepted.

The news of the Peace of Zanjón* reached Guatemala around the middle of February. Many doubts crossed Martí's mind. His first intention was to go to New York, but Carmen dissuaded him. Her father was going back to Cuba, and they might as well do the same. Many Cubans were returning. He also considered going to Peru and had the Peruvian consul in Guatemala approve his certificate of studies from Zaragoza. But they stayed in Guatemala a few months longer. He had written many articles which he intended to publish in the *Revista Guatemalteca*. Now he could not realize his ambition. One of his articles was entitled, "Preliminary Comments on the Reports of the Government Leaders at the Conferences in May, 1878." Guatemalan law provided for annual meeting in May of the poilitical leaders, with the idea of "discussing the major problems of the nation, the necessity

* Ending the Cuban War of 1868-1878. (Ed.)

of racial assimilation, and means of providing honorable work, strengthening public institutions, and increasing the nation's wealth by developing her educational facilities." In anticipation of this meeting he had written a study of Guatemala's main problems, agriculture, education, and the indigenous race. In the book he had written a few months previously he had recorded many useful suggestions. Now he summed them up and tried to formulate practical solutions. But the government had been unjust to the men who served the nation's best interests. His article remained among his unpublished manuscripts.

Since 1876 Dr. Marco Aurelio Soto, a friend of many Cubans and a sympathizer with their cause, had been President of Honduras. José Joaquín Palma had gone to Honduras. Before leaving, he left a book of his verses which he wished to publish with Martí. Martí returned it to him with a letter that was an inspired eulogy of poetry and the poet's genius. Not only did he praise Palma for being, indisputably, a poet, he praised him still more for being a Cuban poet and one whose country inspired his verses.

Palma knew about his resignation, and he imagined the difficulties he must be having. On behalf of Marco Aurelio Soto, who greatly admired Martí's talent, he invited him to come to Honduras before leaving Central America. Martí accepted and began making preparations for the trip. He remained in Guatemala until July 27. He had decided definitely to return to Cuba, but he was very pleased with Palma's invitation, not only because he wanted to know as many American nations as possible, but also because it gave him a chance to delay his return to Cuba. No matter how ardently he might wish to go back, under such circumstances, the return would hurt him like an insult.

He spent barely three weeks in Honduras, not only sightseeing, but doing what was always of foremost importance to him—meeting men, especially the humble country people, guardians of the original, rich heritage of the people. And indeed, of all the admirable things he saw, he was most surprised and delighted by the "harmonious language of the shepherds of Honduras, who speak a Spanish of bygone centuries with a grace and fluency that would make the best orators take notice."

Around the middle of August, José Joaquín Palma said good-by to Martí and his wife as they left for Cuba.

13. Visit to Cuba

September 3, 1878, Martí and Carmen entered the harbor of Havana. In the months following the peace declaration, especially after the extinction of the last hope that had glowed in Maceo's protest at Mangos de Baraguá, Cubans from all over the world returned to live again under the bright sky of their native land after years of absence or deportation. Those were days of intense activity in the harbor. The lists of new arrivals, published in the newspapers, contained many distinguished names.

What were Martí's plans? Personal circumstances had determined his return. Carmen was soon to have a child, and she longed to be near her family. Also Martí wanted to take advantage of the opportunity to live in his own country for a few months, near his parents and sisters. But there were political factors involved too: he wanted firsthand information from the men who had fought and from the common people in general about the real reasons why the war was lost. He was convinced that the struggle had not been in vain, for the Cubans had been able to keep fighting for ten years, thus proving that they could fight. Diverse causes, mostly internal, first retarded their victory and finally made it impossible. If those causes were removed, or the errors corrected, it would be possible to wage a successful war. A prolonged struggle results in victory to those who are best equipped to hold out, that is, those who are constantly receiving supplies and reinforcements. If the Cubans were to win, they would have to fight a short war provided at the outset with all the necessary means of winning.

It was evident that after that ten years' struggle the Cubans had won a respect which they had never been shown before. Even the peace terms of the Zanjón Treaty constituted a recognition of Cuban rights and personality which they had not previously enjoyed. Possibly Martínez Campos' promises would not be kept, but it was undeniable that the Cubans had earned a new consideration. For Martí, who had spent eight years away from Cuba, this fact was evident, and it bolstered his own convictions. The men who had learned on the field of battle to live a life of freedom would want to preserve that freedom, and when they realized that there was only one way to do so they would take up arms again. He was eager to know the attitude of the soldiers. Had they come out of the war conquered by their own lack of faith, or did the fire of freedom still burn in their hearts?

In order to meet his increasing domestic obligations, Martí had to find work immediately. Writing for the newspapers was out of the question. He could never agree with the circumstantial politics of some liberals, who were working to establish a Partido Autonomista, or Autonomist Party. That kind of political action was necessary for the time being and could carry on, in a way, the old struggle for Cuban independence. But Martí could not take part in what he considered an impossible settlement.

Among the compatriots he found in Havana was Nicolás Azcárate, his old friend from Madrid and Mexico. Azcárate had opened up his law office and was beginning to resume his old practice. They talked over Martí's prospects for finding work, and Azcárate asked Martí to work with him. Although his practice was not yet really established, there might possibly be enough work for both of them. Martí gladly accepted. There were very few ways for him to make a living in Cuba. However, his certificate showing that he had completed his course of study in the University of Zaragoza did not entitle him to practice law. He was legally required to have the diploma. September 16 he applied for permission to practice law on condition that he would obtain his title within a certain time limit. His petition was refused because the court had no authority to grant it. Consequently he had to occupy a subordinate position in Azcárate's office, serving as assistant, although his generous friend tried not to make him feel inferior. Nevertheless, Azcárate's practice could not offer him the remuneration he needed, especially after the birth of his son on November 12, which of course incurred additional expense.

Martí's friendship with Azcárate became closer. Every day they discussed Cuban problems in his office. The reformist who was so badly treated in Spain in spite of his moderation continued to be faithful to his ideals and was an enthusiastic supporter of the newly organized Liberal Autonomist Party. Azcárate tried to convince Martí that this party's program was the only one which, supported by national unity, could obtain for the Cubans the rights which they claimed and needed. He sincerely believed that the Cubans were not prepared for self-government. But Martí had felt for a long time that the only freedom the Cubans would ever have was that which they acquired by force of arms. A friend of Azcárate's, Juan Gualberto Gómez, a Cuban who was in Mexico when the Zanjón Armistice was declared, frequently joined these conversations. Gómez and Azcárate had met in Mexico. Although Azcárate was no separatist, the two were drawn together by their love of democratic principles, their hatred of despotism, and their reformist ideals which had been responsible for their exile. Juan Gualberto Gómez shared many of Azcárate's ideas, but Martí's arguments won him over completely. Before long the three were really sharing each other's ideals and thinking alike. If Cuba was to obtain her independence, and to that end there was only one path to follow—revolution—, the Treaty was nothing but a truce. Many other Cubans held the same view. Martí was its fervent supporter wherever he had a chance to express himself.

Every afternoon after this work was done, the three friends met in Azcárate's office to talk, not only about politics, but about literature as well, a subject which Azcárate found more pleasing. He wanted to revive the old literary gatherings such as he used to have in his own home, attended by the most distinguished Cuban intellectuals. The time seemed ripe. The *Liceo de Guanabacoa* had asked him to preside over its literature section. Azcárate felt that his ideas could be expressed better in a literary discussion than in a political one. Martí in turn believed that any kind of exchange of ideas always helped the cause of freedom.

In the Valdés Domínguez home on the Prado a group of men of letters and science began to meet. Many of them were active in politics. Mendive, the beloved maestro, ill and broken in spirit, attended the gatherings. He had completely lost faith. When Martí spoke to him eagerly of new revolutionary projects and tried to convince him that the Cubans stopped fighting not because they were tired but because they needed to pause in order that they might take up the fight again with renewed strength and better weapons, Mendive shook his head, saying:

"Do you think that if there were any hope for us even within the next ten years, I would be here now?"

The meetings were attended by Carlos Navarrete y Romay, a man of letters and science; Anselmo Suárez Romero, sweet singer of the Cuban countryside and soul; Vidal Morales, a former student in Mendive's school who used to visit the Valdés Domínguez home in the old days; and many other schoolmates and comrades in exile. Martí's former teachers and classmates, now his admirers, were delighted to hear him speak. He had not disappointed them. They had seen in him the promise of the man he would some day become. It was a pleasure to hear him tell of his life in Spain, Mexico, and Guatemala. He read many of his articles written in Spain and Mexico and hitherto unknown in Havana. One night his friends met to hear him read his drama, *Adúltera,* upon which the learned Carlos Navarrete y Romay made sound comments.

On his arrival in Cuba Martí had gone to live in an unpretentious boarding house, Number 15 Industria Street. Some officers of the Spanish army were living there, and Martí talked to them at mealtime, always defending Cuba's right to independence. He emphasized the point that his attitude had nothing to do with hatred of the Spaniards. To hate them would be to hate his own parents. But Cuba's right to self-government signified, not hatred, but the practice of a true doctrine of fraternity between the two countries. He cited his years in Spain as proof that it was possible for a Cuban to live in Spain and be treated as an equal and have his ideas respected even when publicly expressed. In Cuba the Cubans had never been able to live as they had in Spain. No matter how violently his Spanish listeners might object to these views, the war had accustomed them to the idea that the freedom of Cuba might be possible some day. And their intransigence was gradually being softened.

Martí did not work very long with Azcárate, whose practice did not bring the results which the latter had hoped for. Azcárate obtained a high government position. Martí, less successful, and not really interested in a career as a lawyer, preferred to teach. He had not only his certificate of studies of philosophy and letters from the University of Zaragoza but his documents confirming his appointment as a professor in Guatemala. He obtained a position in the Hernández y Plasencia primary and secondary school. But without the proper authorization it was impossible for him to teach in Cuba, and in order to obtain it he needed his diploma. In a letter dated January 29, 1879, he requested permission to exercise the rights of a *Licenciado en Filosofía y Letras* on condition that he would later obtain the title. But neither his certificate of university studies nor the fact that a foreign country had honored the certificate by offering him a chair in philosophy convinced the Cuban government. Without his diplomas, involving thousands of *pesetas* for the Spanish treasury, which he could not pay, all his studies were completely worthless. On February 6, he was given three months in which to obtain his diploma. Thanks to this concession he had a breathing spell during which he could support himself and his family by teaching.

The Liceo of Guanabacoa called a meeting to vote for a new board of directors. January 12, 1879, was election day. Nicolás Azcárate was elected president of the literature section and Martí secretary.

At the same time the Ateneo de la Habana announced a series of lectures like the ones held at the Liceo de Guanabacoa, and Sunday noon discussions of literature and fine arts.

The Liceo at Regla was not idle either. In a meeting held on January 29 Martí was appointed as a member of the teaching staff. In that school Martí found an old friend he had known at the time of his imprisonment and deportation,

Pedro Coyula, persecuted because of his political activities. They resumed the old friendship. Coyula was living in Regla and visited the Liceo with Martí.

Unquestionably it was a period of teeming ideas. Every academic rostrum was crowded with intellectuals eager to bring light after the long night of the ten years' war. Literary activity was becoming more and more intense. All meetings were very well attended, and there was a veritable longing for intellectual satisfaction.

Besides these gatherings, which had brought the Liceo great prestige some twelve years previous, a series of scientific and literary discus.ions was organized under Azcárate's direction. The topic of the first series of discussions was Realism and Idealism in Dramatic Literature. The participants were Cortina, Martí, Madan, and Azcárate, the moderator. The learned Don José Ramón Leal opened the meeting. On the night of March 7, when the first debates were to be held, the auditorium of the Liceo was packed with a distinguished audience including some of the most beautiful Cuban women. This sudden revival of intellectual activity was widely commented.

Leal opened the meeting and read a paper in defense of realism in art. Martí followed, presenting the opposition. The poet, Diego Vicente Tejera, who wrote unsigned criticism for *El Triunfo,* called Martí's address superb, "full of sentiment, erudition, profound ideas and brilliant images, now captivating, now enrapturing the audience with the beauty of his language or the sonorousness of his magnificent periods."

Another newspaper, *La Patria,* claimed to be the first to have hailed Martí-as a promising orator. He was precise in his thinking, he knew how to synthesize. He fascinated, moved, surprised, his audience. He held their interest with his facile eloquence, his bold, original idiom, his changing images.

As a journalist Martí had less freedom in Cuba than elsewhere. As an orator he had constant opportunities to express himself, and he did so enthusiastically. Since he had spent his whole adult life outside of Cuba, he was known only by a group of friends. He wanted to be known by all, not because of vanity, but because in order to pursue an idea one must know it first, and he was the incarnation of that idea which must pervade Cuba and the consciences of all her sons.

Prominent figures in the liberal party gave a banquet for the journalist, Adolfo Márquez Sterling on April 21. Martí attended. Several after-dinner speeches were given. The party leaders were surprised when some of the guests insisted that Martí speak. Martí was not on the program. But it was natural that he should be asked to speak, for he was being proclaimed as one of the glories of Cuban oratory. The shouts for Martí persisted. And Martí spoke. The autonomists exchanged uneasy glances, but they could not prevent it. Martí's literary speeches were nothing compared to the impetuous ardor of this improvised political speech. It seemed that he was referring to the program of the new party when he said that rights are to be taken, not requested, seized, not begged for. And he spoke of the incomplete freedom which had been conquered, not received from anyone.

He contrasted two kinds of political creeds: first the kind that feels, speaks, and makes demands without ever renouncing its only true glory (that which comes from its heroes). That was his kind, and he drank a toast to it, to its pride, dignity, and energy. He smashed his glass rather than drink to the other political creed, the creed of those who accepted inadequate solutions, did not heed their country's voice, and silenced their hearts in order that the truth might not rise to their lips and escape.

This speech had extraordinary repercussions. How insignificant the doctrinaire politicians felt, those who based their entire theory on conformity! But others had felt his inner light illumine their hearts. The unexpected toast echoed throughout the city.

The programs of the Liceo of Guanabacoa continued, with Martí almost always taking part. The celebrated Cuban violinist, Rafael Díaz Albertini, was to give a contest at one o'clock in the afternoon, Sunday, April 27. Martí was to give an address in honor of the artist.

General Ramón Blanco, the Captain General, had heard about Martí's oratory, and had begun to suspect that it was dangerous. But what they told him about the Monday night toast was more serious and really worried him. Azcárate, out of courtesy, had often invited him to the programs at the Liceo. That Sunday in April he decided to find out some things for himself.

Martí spoke. His words were still spellbinding. Each new address seemed better than the previous ones, so intense was their emotional effect. But could anyone doubt that many paragraphs of this speech were a hymn to Cuban heroism and the survival of the sacred fire of freedom in the people's hearts? All the Havana elite attended this program in honor of an artist whom they considered their own. On the platform the Captain General squirmed in his seat, his face livid with surprise. What was Martí trying to accomplish with his speech? Perhaps the presence of authority had precipitated him into the field of dangerous truths, for danger was his element. He evoked the ten years' war, sketched the ideals of independence, referred to the peace treaty as a lying transaction, and concluded by predicting the birth of freedom. The fire of the revolution burned in his words and illumined the future.

Blanco had not been misinformed. Everything they had told him paled into insignificance in comparison with what he had seen and heard. Had he not perceived clearly a throb of sympathy between the speaker and his audience? At the first burst of applause he rose and approached Azcárate. Standing near him was Miguel Viondi, another one of the Liceo orators who had become a friend of Martí. Viondi heard General Blanco's words very distinctly:

"I do not want to remember what I have heard, what I did not think anyone would ever say in front of me, a representative of the Spanish government. I am going to conclude that Martí is a madman . . . but a dangerous madman."

The editors of a Havana newspaper, doubtless jealous of the brilliance of these displays of Cuban intellectual accomplishments, opened a campaign against the Liceo. They also circulated an exposé called the "Exposé of the Seventy," signed by a group of women, protesting against the activities of the Liceo as an attack on popular ideas and beliefs. Far from producing the desired effect, it was proven that the Liceo's activities had the support of all lovers of the higher manifestations of thought and art, for a large, select audience filled the hall the following evening. The occasion was propitious, and Azcárate took advantage of it.

He opened the session with a brief address in which he alluded to the fanatics who were trying to wage a ridiculous war against the Liceo meetings, for those meetings dealt with something which obscurantism will always hate: scientific reasoning. He declared that the Liceo was open to all those who wished to maintain a creed or an idea, whatever it might be. That was the standard of the Liceo. Then he gave the floor to Martí. The latter spoke of the dramas of Echegaray. He described him as he remembered him, the first time he saw him entering the Teatro Español:

"A quick resolute man with a nervous walk that was ill-suited to the ceremonious pace of the theatre, a man of lively, nervous speech, brief, simple gestures, short beard, pale color, and a slightly protruding chin, as though he were accustomed to delve into the unknown. He wore glasses which shone, not with the reflection of the light, but with the fire of his lively glance. His brow was prominent and high. Such was the man."

He pointed out the mission of the modern theatre, which should not be a worthless copy of domestic troubles but the presentation of noble aspirations and sacrifices, which would uplift and strengthen the people's spirit. In a concise and brilliant analysis of Echegaray's dramas he pointed out their beauties and their moral. This speech was Martí's greatest success.

Martí's classes in the *colegio* of Plasencia barely enabled him to support his family. After the June examinations there was very little activity at the school, and Martí's financial embarrassment was even greater. This means of support was entirely eliminated when the Governor General, on July 26, had his permission to teach in the secondary schools annulled because he had not obtained his degree in the three months' time which he was granted.

He would have been in a very unpleasant position if his friend, Miguel Viondi, had not lent a helping hand. Viondi had one of the most prosperous law offices in Havana. Many young lawyers worked there, and he invited Martí to join his practice. Martí refused. He did not consider himself useful enough. Besides, he lacked the professional experience. Furthermore, he had again requested in March, although without success, permission to practice law, in the same manner in which he had requested permission to teach. But the report of the Audiencia confirmed the previous decision.

Tactfully, Viondi insisted until he finally persuaded Martí to enter his office. Martí performed his professional tasks with enthusiasm and optimism and his peculiar way of gravely pondering events and men. It was not long before his companions admired and esteemed him. Viondi was amazed at his knowledge of legal theory. He had already observed his knowledge of this subject in the lawyers' gatherings which were held every week in the home of Juan Francisco Ramos.

In the long summer afternoons the day's work was concluded early enough to leave time for a good conversation. Viondi, like many of the eminent lawyers of Cuba, was a man who enjoyed and cultivated the art of conversation. His office had an adjoining terrace where they sat in rocking chairs every afternoon. From the fatigue of the day's work they went out to enjoy a view of the ocean and the cool breeze. Since Martí had begun working in the office, the afternoon conversations were eagerly anticipated. Martí always had something stimulating to say, whether he related an episode concerning his travels or presented with fervent eloquence his dreams of Cuba's future. Viondi, like Azcárate and all the most advanced intellectuals, was an autonomist. There were very few separatists, and most of these were men of action who had left Cuba after the peace without enjoying that intellecual equanimity which Martí found and which enabled him to appreciate Cuba's deceptive condition. To him the real men were those who had gone from the battlefields of Cuba to exile in lands of freedom. The solution was not to be found in long waiting and in expecting a gift that would never be given. The only solution lay in independence.

There were many other Cubans who thought as he did, and they met to strengthen and carry out their ideal. Juan Gualberto Gómez was a member of one recently founded revolutionary club, and Martí belonged to another.

Juan Gualberto Gómez visited the office daily, and Viondi was beginning to suspect that plans for a conspiracy were discussed in conversations with Martí. Could it be possible that there was a conspiracy so few months after the Zanjón treaty?

"You are the only conspirators in Cuba," he would tell them with a touch of irony.

When Martí and Juan Gualberto joined their friends on the terrace and the conversation turned to politics, even to the formulation of plans, there was a meaningful exchange of smiles. Martí was good in literary matters, but too much of a dreamer in politics, according to the tolerant judgment of his friends.

As the conversations between Martí and Gómez became more frequent, and Viondi detected a slight nervousness on their part when clients arrived, he offered them a room which no one used, in the rear of the house, where they could be more at ease. They were grateful for this tactful favor.

Neither Viondi nor the other friends knew that a new revolutionary movement was being prepared, and that these very friends of theirs were among the leaders.

In Oriente province leaders such as José Maceo and Guillermo Moncada were making preparations. In Las Villas, Emilio Núñez and Serafín Sánchez raised the new flag. Contact was maintained with the clubs in Havana and in other provinces, and agents had been sent out to visit the leaders of the old revolution, now dispersed throughout different countries in America. Calixto García, a prisoner in Spain when the Zanjón treaty was signed, was now in the United States. Antonio Maceo, the nonconformist of Baraguá, was at that time in Jamaica. These were the two leaders of the conspiracy.

In his modest house Martí received frequent visits from members of the revolutionary clubs. Juan Gualberto Gómez joined him on the afternoons when the arrangements were not all completed in Viondi's office or when they had interviews with other agents. They also met almost every day with Betancourt in his jewelry store. In an upper room of the house they met with Pancho Peralta, Salvador Rosado, Pedro Freire and others. Martí's activities were increasing, but they were also arousing suspicions. He made frequent visits to towns near the capital, and once when he went to Artemisa and San Antonio de los Baños to interview persons interested in his plans, he was followed.

Martí was right in thinking that the Cubans' desire for independence had not died out and that they were ready to fight for it. This was proved by the armed uprising in Oriente, August 26, 1879. The fighting broke out with extraordinary vigor in Oriente, led by José Maceo and Guillermo Moncada, supported by Belisario Peralta, Angel Guerra, Limbano Sánchez, Jesús Rabí, and other distinguished leaders and followed by thousands of men. Las Villas also responded under Brigadier Ramos, Emilio Núñez, Serafín Sánchez and Francisco Carrillo.

The Havana clubs must redouble their efforts in order to give more effective aid and extend the movement. To that end a meeting of the club presidents and secretaries was held in Regla, and a central committee was named, with Martí as president. Enthusiasm grew, as did the contributions, intended especially for the rebels in Las Villas and for the preparation of a similar uprising in the province of Havana.

The government was alarmed by the growth of the revolutionary movement, which had begun so vigorously. But General Blanco would depend on the services of some Cubans who had fought in the last war, especially a lieutenant colonel whom the conspirators would never suspect and who, nevertheless, betrayed them. If Martí as an agitator was a significant figure, now that he was president of the central committee in Havana he was undeniably dangerous. The authorities were soon notified of his new activities.

It was September 17. Around noon Martí arrived at his home, accompanied by Juan Gualberto Gómez. They had been hard at work on revolutionary plans all morning. Martí asked him to stay for lunch, for they still had matters to settle. They were seated at the table when there was a knock at the door. Someone was asking for Martí. He waited for him in the living room. Martí went in to receive the stranger, spoke with him a few minutes, and went back to the dining room. Calmly, he asked for his coffee, for he had to leave at once. He entered the bedroom followed by Carmen. A moment later he reappeared, shook hands with Gómez, and said:

Martí

"Take your time over your coffee, and make yourself at home. Please excuse me. I have a very urgent matter to take care of."

As soon as they left, Carmen, with tears in her eyes, told Gómez what had happened:

"They're taking Pepe away. That man is a police officer. Try your best to find out where they're taking him, and notify Nicolás Azcárate."

Juan Gualberto went out hurriedly. On the corner he saw Martí and his companion getting into a carriage. He followed them in another and saw them get out in front of the police station. A few minutes later he talked to Azcárate. Martí was immediately declared incommunicado, but the rule was waived for Azcárate, who had strong influence with the government. Through Azcárate, Gómez received instructions from Martí and was asked to pick up the papers which Martí had been keeping in Viondi's office. He sent Viondi a letter asking him to look after his family.

Always in favor of proceeding carefully, Blanco heeded Azcárate's plea and decided to deport Martí. On the twenty-fourth he was issued a passport "to go to the Peninsula at the disposition of the Civil Governor of Santander." The following day he sailed from Havana, on the *Alfonso XII*.

14. They or We

Doctor Lebredo, an office partner of Viondi, and other friends had recommended Martí to the purser of the Alfonso XII. He was a great-hearted man, understanding and tolerant. In a few days he had begun to feel affection and admiration for Martí. Thus the trip was less lonely than he might have expected. So completely did they understand each other that when the boat touched at Santander where Martí disembarked, they had already sealed a deep friendship.

He enjoyed momentary happiness in Santander when he visited the consul Agustín Lozano, in whose home he met the poet, Juan de Dios Peza, the dear friend of his days in Mexico. Peza had just arrived from Madrid and was passing through Santander on his way to Mexico.

His passport was viséed on October 22 by the Governor of Santander, providing for his passage directly to Madrid with the specific obligation of presenting himself before the Governor of that province, which he did on the twenty-ninth.

One of the most important matters being negotiated in Viondi's office had to do with the will of Don Bartolomé Mitjans. Viondi was representing Mitjans' widow, Doña Dolores Alvarez. Martí had intervened in this matter. The arbitrary decisions of the court, favoring the opposing party, forced them to turn to the higher authorities in Spain. Viondi took advantage of Martí's deportation in order to have him negotiate with the lawyers in Spain and see that justice was done. Martí's first letters gave Viondi a minute account of his interviews with Ríos Portilla and Romero Girón, lawyers connected with the case, and an account of the procedures they were planning in order to combat the abuses of the judge and court of appeal, determined to auction off the rich estate. They could attempt no proceedings, Martí explained to them, that had not already been considered by Viondi. For him it was a question of judicial morality, "influence to dominate, or at least to balance, the contrary influence." Thus he had presented the problem and thus he would present it painstakingly to Martos.

He was crushed by worries—the poverty of his wife and son, the lack of news from them, his pending debts, among them the debt he owed on the furniture he had bought on credit for his house, with Viondi vouching for him. He finally took to his bed. In a brief interlude to calm his anxiety he made a trip to Granada, where his spirit was soothed a little by the contact with nature.

He had all his hopes for a just settlement of Doña Dolores' suit placed in Martos. Just as he himself saw the problem, as a case of judicial morality, so he would present it to Martos carefully. Martos at that time was the "skillful eloquent unifier of liberal efforts." And at that very moment debates on matters affecting the Island were going on in Congress. What disorder, what discouraging ignorance, what erroneous judgments, how many deeprooted prejudices existed even in the best intentioned minds, in the most favorable concepts

He found very little to admire there either in theatres or athenaeums, and the debased state of politics only made one want to look the other way. Therefore he made use of his time in casting off that which could be of no use to him and strengthening his good points. He studied English with tenacity and gathered all the information that might be useful to him in the work he had dreamed of for so many years.

With a friend he went to keep the appointment Martos had made with him. The interview lasted for three hours, and he barely managed to bring the conversation around to its only object: Viondi's suit. Cristino Martos wanted to hear about Cuba. From Martí's lips he wished to hear the truth, only the truth. Everything was a revelation for Martos. He had suspected nothing of what Martí told him: "the deception of the truce, the revolution that triumphed in the hearts, the iniquity with which the Cuban Negro is incited to rise against the white, the prison of Santander, filled with unknown, wounded prisoners, secretly exiled after Zanjón." And not only did he examine external realities, but the intimate composition of the Cuban and the Spaniard, the contrary aspirations of the two groups, the struggle of ideals. Martos, to whom all this was new, listened intently to Martí's words. And the greatest surprise of all was that of hearing such truths spoken with astonishing eloquence and with very clear, serene judgment. So deep was his impression that in a letter to Viondi he wrote these words: "Martí has impressed me so much that I believe he is the most talented man I have ever known."

Martí's curiosity took him to the session on the following day. It was a famous day in the Cortes. The sessions were suspended in homage to María Cristina, who was about to be married. The entire cabinet attended with Martínez Campos presiding. Sagasta, forgetting the politics of the hour, delivered a speech full of flowery phrases in homage to the king's betrothed. Martos made a speech full of dark prophecies. And suddenly, to Martí's surprise, he made a valiant speech, a Cuban address, that was entirely denunciatory, ending with an appeal for mercy for the unfortunate island.

It cannot be said that Martí participated in the festivities held in connection with the royal wedding. In his uneasy state he could only wait doggedly. But such pomp and futile, bizantine luxury aroused many comments. He saw clearly the absurd attempt to prolong the existence of dead epochs in living bodies. Without comment he pointed out the reverence with which the same people who had deposed Isabel from her throne in 1869 now kissed her hand.

The first letter which he received from Carmen caused him intense suffering. The destitute state which she and their child had reached took the form of an accusation. Why could he not devote himself to them, like other men who put wellbeing above all else? Why had he made his life unnecessarily complicated when everyone in Cuba was devoting himself to a quiet life in the shelter of the home with the fewest possible cares after so many years of suffering and misery? Carmen was justified, but she was measuring Martí by the usual standards. That was her great mistake. In his despair Martí exclaimed:

"A hundred daggers thrust into my breast would not pain me as much as this first letter."

Powerless to help his wife, he pondered countless plans, without being able, in his poverty and growing insecurity, to adopt any. He realized that at that time the greater his freedom the better it would be for them, and he would have left her with his father if the latter were not so poor. But that could not be. The problems that he had acquired only he could solve. His wife and child should be with him. He would fight for them. This decision led him to think of leaving Europe rapidly, for there he could find no way of making a living. But first it would be necessary to go to France, going from there to the United States, where he had possibilities of obtaining work. With his letter to Viondi dated December 8 in Madrid he mentioned his intention of leaving for Paris. On the eighteenth he attended the *fiesta del Hipódrome,* the Paris-Murcia benefit festival given to aid the people affected by the flood in Murcia. On this occasion he was able once more to see and admire Sarah Bernhardt.

' He wished to take advantage of the few days when he was to remain in Paris to meet poets and artists. His friend Vacquerie had received him cordially. From Mexico he received the numbers of the *Revista Universal* in which his translation of *Mes Fils* appeared. Victor Hugo applauded it warmly. With Vacquerie Martí attended one of Sarah Bernhardt's receptions. In her salon he perceived "a potency in her thought, a virility in her purpose, an eager restlessness that reflected well the rather tempestuous spirit of the mistress of the house and of her century." He also visited other salons, like that of the writer Julie Lambert, frequented by the writers most in vogue at the time. There, in spite of the good conversations, he did not find the very human atmosphere which even at a distance he thought he perceived in the salons of Sarah and the great Victor Hugo.

As five years ago, he again visited the cemetery of Père Lachaise. He did not wish to leave Paris without visiting the cemetery, which at times seemed to him like a sumptuous boulevard where, however, one's meditations became more intimate and the spirit took on a religious calm. He wandered through the place peopled with memories. He stopped before the tomb of Musset, shaded by the tree planted by his friends. He reflected a moment before the tomb of Rousseau.

The year came to an end, and he said good-bye to Paris. In Le Havre he took a boat to New York.

15. Interpretation of New York

New York received him with a spring sky on a winter day. It was January 3. Lodging in keeping with his resources was what he needed for the moment, and it was easy to find. It was made available to him in the home of Manuel Mantilla, Number 51 Twenty-ninth Street, on the east side of the city. Like so many other compatriots, Mantilla supported himself as an emigrant partly by providing comfortable economical lodging to the Spanish Americans passing through the great city. When Martí arrived he was received by Mantilla's wife, Carmita, a Venezuelan, not a Cuban, she informed him with a charming smile illuminated by the deep glow of a pair of black eyes. Then in order to soften the effect of her remark and reply to a compliment of his, she added that she felt Cuban at heart. And they began telling each other their life stories.

Hospitality offered by such a pleasant, cordial woman seemed excellent to him, and he decided at once to stay there. He needed nothing so much in his sadness at that time as a bit of feminine understanding. And Carmita had such beautiful eyes!

The situation of his wife, who was living in Camagüey in her father's house, was a deep humiliation for him at that moment. He would have liked to have her and their son stay in Havana with his family to wait for word from him. Carmen had not endured for long the straitened circumstances of Don Mariano's home, and it seemed more natural to her to live with her own family in her own home where her presence would not be a burden. From Camagüey she had written him a letter like a live coal which burned his dignity. Since then he had thought only of ways of having her join him.

Only five days had passed since his arrival when he was already writing to Viondi, sending him the money for her ticket. How great his bitterness must have been in order for him, in such a condition, even before finding work or feeling assured that he would find it, to make such an effort with his flat purse. And against his usual custom he asked Viondi for money so that his wife could make the trip to Havana and take the boat.

Ever since his days in Mexico Martí had been considered a man of letters. An opinion to that effect was circulating in the *Almanaque* of that country for 1879, which had recently appeared. He could be and had already been everything from a proofreader to an author of books. He could write truly interesting books, like the one on Guatemala published in Mexico. Biographical, historical, artistic books, books that were pleasant and extremely useful for the reciprocal knowledge of the countries of America. He thought about this and about the support he might have from a friendly press like that of the Cuban, Néstor Ponce de León. But his first and most legitimate hopes failed him. He thought of other sources of help: the Appleton Company, but Appleton was in France, and the Asturian who received him was unsociable and distrustful. Frank Leslie's staff was also unable to help him. He did not become discouraged. He was seeking, and he would find new paths.

His first impression of New York was that of being in a country where everyone is master of his fate, of his liberty. One breathed an atmosphere of confidence and optimism. And all groups seemed to enjoy equal liberty.

The spectacle of this natural, free exercise of a people's own strength in such a natural, free environment seemed to him a thing of surprising grandeur, doubtless unique in the world in contrast to the conventionalisms of decayed Europe.

Men who were their own masters moved unceasingly in all directions, filled the streets, hotels, and places of entertainment, and were perpetually concerned with their well-being. Here a man was his own king, and if another force moved him it was the desire to improve by his efforts what was everyone's patrimony, the surroundings in which he lived, making it a symbol of his power and his reign.

Never had he been surprised by any other countries he had visited in the world. Here he felt surprised. That endless zeal which was observed everywhere, that continuous movement, that restlessness, doors that were never closed, men who passed by rapidly with hardly time to look each other in the face, or to look up at the sky, this was something that bore no resemblance to the static, lazy, useless life of the European countries. But at the same time that these thoughts came to his mind and he wrote them down in his picturesque English written with Spanish words, other ideas complemented his thoughts. Was not this devotion to business excessive? Was not the cultivation of ideas and the noble longing of the soul neglected? Serious doubts occurred to him, suggesting the possibility that some day this immense nation would be confronted by periods of distress. If they did not strengthen their spirit, if they did not dignify their lives "by the ardent love of intellectual pleasure," if noble passions did not also take shelter in their hearts, how could money alone be expected to give them the greater happiness, the only enduring kind? A life based upon material wellbeing does not provide the consolations which intelligence needs.

And he resolved to study this original nation from its roots to the point in its development at which he found it, to follow it, in the family, the school, in its recreation, and clubs and on the dazzling avenues, in the sermons from the pulpit and those from the political rostrum. He would study its potent origin, the greatness of its liberty, and at the same time the servility of its tastes, given over to imitation of things across the seas—the superstitious admiration of everything French, of costly, loud exoticism, instead of the work of art of pure, sober beauty.

On many a spring afternoon he mingled with the crowd on Broadway. Everything attracted him and compelled his admiration in this feverish life, in which his powers of penetration immediately perceived that dualism of a nation marvelously adult in practical things and puerile in the intellectual order.

He wished to know the women better, and he found them increasingly harder to understand. A display of coldness, of indifference to everything but immoderate luxury, the desire for wealth dominated them. The one thing he was sure of was that these New York women disconcerted him. And he made a curious confession. Everywhere, from Southampton to the Atlantic coast of Guatemala, there had been a woman's soul to comfort him. But the weeks went by in New York, and he did not find his beloved pair of eyes. During many sunny afternoons he strolled among the crowds along fourteenth and twenty-third streets where the beautiful women of New York displayed their rich clothing. He visited conversed and dined with American women. They had translated his verses, they had adorned his suit with boutonnieres, he had attended gay gatherings, and he still could not understand them.

Carried away by his thoughts, he examined the future possibilities of that country which astounded him, and he asked himself if it contained the necessary forces on which the foundations of a new era for mankind could be built. What else if not this would be the transcendental significance of the United States? And he even formulated a much more important question: was America going to Europe or was Europe coming to America? In all that he observed and scrutinized he kept finding answers to the infinite questions that were being formulated in his mind. He suspected that he was not in this country merely in passing but that it was to be the seat of his future life. What other place could offer him a similar panorama of work and respect as well as contact with such ideas as were now teeming in his brain?

On this free country, which received men from everywhere who sought liberty through work, he had based his hopes. He always had conceived of it as the only place where it would be necessary to strengthen the will and the efforts of the Cubans when the definitive hour of redemption should draw near. He had arrived and had found it to be what he had dreamed: an immense country where a man who has an idea or a project to offer finds an outstretched hand. That must be the law of labor: certain compensation in exchange for honest work. And that law reigned here.

In the gatherings in the living room of the boarding house which Carmita Mantilla warmed with her presence and charm, Martí had the opportunity to meet the Cuban painter, Tomás Collazo, with whom he talked a great deal of his impressions of European museums. Collazo recognized in Martí a highly original critic with a vigor and a style of his own. Their conversations concerning art became animated and frequent.

One day he had found Collazo waiting for him with surprising news. He had an opportunity for Martí to work and earn a good salary. He explained that a weekly of great aspirations had just begun publication in New York. It attempted to reflect the vital problems of the nation and at the same time devote competent attention to the literary and artistic currents in the world. Tiblain and Murphy, principal writers for *The Hour,* as the weekly was called, had asked him to recommend an art critic to them. Who could be a better one than Martí?

Martí's surprise was enormous. What ever made them expect him to write a column on art in English? Collazo would not take "no" for an answer. The things Martí was telling him, translated into English, would cause a sensation. He knew what he had to say, and he would make himself understood.

One thing was certain: he knew about painting, and it was no time for hesitation. He was to say in English what he thought, translating word for word if necessary.

With his permit to visit museums he went to see the Stebbins collection. He spent a magnificent afternoon in the company of the great masters. And in his barbarous English, as he called it, he wrote his art review with fear and trembling. He commented on Fortuny's technique as hyperrefined, Meissonier's lacking in inventiveness, Detaille's negligent and light, Bourguerau's rosy and silken.

His articles were picturesque. His vivid imagination, retained in the English language, as if he had written in Spanish with English words, startled and yet pleased his readers. The fire of his phrases, the impetuosity of his opinions, a certain unfamiliar air of intrepidity and rebelliousness were a curious attraction in the pages of *The Hour*. On February 21 the art section published an article of his on the painter, Madrazo, whose studio he had visited a few months before in Madrid.

This first opportunity, so unexpected and unusual, afforded him much useful knowledge and the esteem of men like Charles Dana, the editor of the *Sun*, who asked him to write for his paper.

Martí's part in Havana in the preparations for the new conspiracy gave him an important position among the revolutionaries in New York, who continued to support the movement initiated in August of the preceding year.

But Martí noticed that there was not enough enthusiasm at a time when the war which had broken out in Cuba was in danger of failing without the outside help it needed. He was distressed by the lot of the many men who were risking their lives at that time on the insurgent side. They had been unable to prepare a single one of the expeditions which the insurgents had counted on. That of Calixto García, the leader of the movement, met with all sorts of difficulties, and its delay endangered the movement. His arrival at the coast of Cuba, on the other hand, would be a new encouragement for the revolution.

In his meetings with the men who composed the Revolutionary Committee Martí expressed his idea that it was necessary to support the insurrection with steady, adequate aid. His voice reached faint hearts and appealed to consciences. Their effort must be worthy of the efforts of the fighters. They must hasten to save from danger those who were offering their lives on the field of battle.

The Cuban Committee, at Martí's suggestion, prepared a program for January 24. The exiles gathered eagerly in Steck Hall. They were curious to hear him, for many who had heard him a few months before in Havana had praised him as an orator. Martí disappointed them a little. He gave them a reading, not a speech. He had preferred to read in order to organize his thoughts better and to avoid emotionalism as much as possible.

Soberly he began to read his pages. The audience listened to him intently. With flawless, energetic words he uttered his first sentence:

"One should do one's duty simply and naturally."

His paper was an enumeration and synthesis, a program of ardent patriotism. The lessons of the ten years' war and evocations of the heroic life flashed like lightning through his lines. He examined the different elements of the population in Cuba and analyzed the Spanish policy and the falseness of its promises. He portrayed the intolerable position of the Cuban, which sooner or later would make the struggle inevitable. He commented on the undeniable fact of the war which was raging in Cuba, the price they would have to pay for liberty if they really wanted to.

His paper was long. That night no one left the hall without pressing Martí's hand and promising himself to contribute with his efforts to the work already in progress.

The Committee, by the sheer influence of his enthusiasm, entered a phase of unaccustomed activity. There was no club on the Island or outside that did not receive a steady stream of messages of encouragement, suggestions concerning new contacts, words of praise. The old leaders were exhorted to come to the fore in this growing, developing war. "Those who are dying for us have a right to our incessant aid."

Martí's words and example aroused enthusiasm. Efforts were made that had never been made before, and they began to glimpse the possibility of sending out the expeditions which they had not heretofore been able to organize. Martí became such a guiding spirit of their work that he was named provisional president of the committee.

March came to an end. When he was completely absorbed in the revolutionary work, Carmen arrived with their son. Thanks to his collaboration in the *Hour* and a few articles on literature which he published in English translation in the *Sun*, he had enough to meet his modest needs. But that would no longer be sufficient. And how could he abandon his revolutionary project now that he had just acquired the new responsibility of the position conferred upon him? Carmen's presence was a vigorous call to reality. Furthermore, Mantilla's house was now like his own. Growing affection had warmed his heart there in his loneliness. As there were no other possibilities at the time, Martí had Carmen and their child stay there.

April was the month of culmination of all their many efforts. On the thirteenth General Carlos Roloff and Colonel José María Aguirre, carrying out the orders of General Calixto García, sailed from New York for Jamaica. From Jamaica they would go to Cuba. They would continue the labor of General Bonachea, working in absolute unity, according to instructions, for their duties were all equally necessary and patriotic, all part of the same task. The number of circulars sent to clubs multiplied, and Martí did not forget to send such a brave warrior as General Emilio Núñez "warm congratulations for the magnificent campaign you are carrying out."

On the twenty-eighth all the clubs and important people received a circular stressing the need for rapid decisions.

"Honorable men have no need to debate for long a deed of honor. There is no room for doubt when we must choose between aiding those whose triumph will benefit us or abandoning them at the moment when they are dying for us."

In his first letter to Viondi after Carmen's arrival he hinted that success was near at hand:

"The impossible is possible. We madmen are sane . . ."

The cause of his enthusiasm was the departure of the expedition commanded by General García, who, everyone hoped, would give the movement a decisive impulse. Indeed, the expedition left the first week in May and reached Cuba the thirteenth. On that very date in New York a proclamation was circulated, signed by Martí, in order to announce that fact. A few days later another proclamation of the Revolutionary Committee commented on the importance of this achievement and pointed out the duty to help.

"Simultaneously and energetically we must wage the war here and there. Those who abandon the cause will be guilty."

He inserted the names of the men in the expedition and concluded by publishing the proclamations issued by General García to the Cuban people and army, proclamations previously written by Martí at General García's request.

Martí

The leader of the revolution reached Cuba when the country was almost wholly defeated. Many forces were isolated and dispersed, others decimated, and all hope was lost of resisting while waiting for aid that did not come. Consequently, many leaders accepted the peace offers which General Blanco made them through representatives of the Liberal Party and surrendered their arms. General García disembarked near Santiago de Cuba. From the very first moment he was pursued in order to prevent any possibility of joining the inner groups.

There was little political activity in the months that followed. Efforts were vain when everyone knew about what little success General García's expedition had had. The number of patriots arriving in New York from the battlefields of Cuba to tell a heart-breaking story was growing by the moment. Thanks to the policy of General Blanco, many lives were saved. Polavieja, on the other hand, carried persecution in the province of Oriente to the point of blood and fire in his zeal to exterminate the revolutionists.

In August even General Calixto García was forced to capitulate too, and he agreed to go to Spain. On the Cuban battlefields there was now only one insurgent general whose conscience troubled him and would not let him capitulate without first hearing Martí's opinion. This valiant young man was Emilio Núñez, and he expressed well his respect for Martí's opinion in a letter written in Los Egidos camp on September 20. When all the other leaders, even Calixto García, had capitulated he still resisted and did not want to surrender his arms without first hearing Martí's advice.

Martí received his letter of October 13. He was not a professional instigator, a demagogue capable of asking him for futile sacrifice. Even if Núñez had not asked his opinion, he was already moved to ire by the criminal way in which the country deserted its defenders. He had to restrain himself from pouring forth all his feelings on paper, for they could be put to an evil use by the enemy. But the liberty which his land needed and would attain some day must be conquered by great effort. It was not reasonable to expect to do at once what other leaders had not done in the past year of fighting. Renewing the fight would not solve Cuba's grave, general problems. With his absolute honesty he advised Núñez "as a revolutionist, as a man who admired his energy, and as an affectionate friend, not to remain futilely on the battlefield to which those whom he was defending were powerless to send aid."

His letter was an admission of defeat. But it contained many lessons that might some day be useful to him. In the ten years' war indefinite prolongation, internal dissension, and regionalisms were vicious circles which the insurgents could not break through. Similarly in this new experience the lack of coordination, the shortage of adequate, well organized material, and the exclusion of leaders like Máximo Gómez and Antonio Maceo were obvious causes of confusion and failure.

Almost completely occupied by the incessant work of the Committee, he had hardly been able to do anything else except to write his art criticism for the *Hour* and a few articles which the editor of the *Sun* received with great cordiality. The *Hour* also printed some of his "impressions of America" which he had been meditating about and writing down ever since his arrival. Every day he had jotted down curious notes in the moments of surprise which the life and customs of this nation afforded him.

These "impressions" in which hard truth and just tribute were expressed with equal directness and frankness, must have seemed a bit sensational. Who could ever imagine that this writer who signed his impressions "a very fresh Spaniard" was José Martí? Even his confessions concerning his own life were disconcerting. But he was in a new country, and he sought eagerly new ways of life. The direct and the vivid were the impressive thing, and people liked what revealed a personality.

With his articles he managed to live. He was encouraged by his faith in the success of Cuba's new efforts to shake off the domination that was strangling her. What was left for him now? His trip to the United States was motivated chiefly by one great purpose: to have contact with the supporters of the war.

But that stage was already past. It was impossible for him to stay there without adequate resources, especially in those painful months of the end of the war. Carmen's arrival aggravated his difficulties. On the other hand, during those first months of loneliness Martí had not lacked for tenderness. The idea of leaving him in freedom took possession of his wife. She could certainly not be happy there. Toward the end of November she went back to Cuba with their child. On the twentieth of that same month Carmita Mantilla gave birth to a little girl on whom Martí lavished the tenderest affection.

During those restless times Martí decided to go to Venezuela. With his articles he earned enough money to undertake the trip. Charles Dana had been so kind that Martí ventured to ask him for aid in exchange for articles for the *Sun*. Martí would never forget the one who, when the crucial time came, helped him to keep a firm grip on the reins of his life.

Some Venezuelan friends whom Martí had met at Carmita's house had tried to dissuade him from taking the trip. Nicanor Bolet was one of them. He foresaw that Martí, with his revolutionary aureole, would find in the Venezuela governed by Guzmán Blanco an atmosphere hostile to his activities. In February he sailed for La Guaira.

16. The Shade of Bolívar

One enters the land of Bolívar, on the journey from la Guaira to Caracas, by a hazardous route filled with surprises, making the trip in a coach, among mountain peaks and crests, or skirting the edge of an abyss. At times one touches the clouds and it is dizzying to look down.

"How does one go to the statue of Bolívar?" was the question he asked when he reached Caracas in March, 1881.

In the solitary plaza the great trees were the only witnesses to this wordless dialogue in which a traveler dreaming of the freedom of his distant land looked for inspiration to the liberator of nations, and felt that he received encouragement.

What Bolívar did with a nation following him was what Martí would do when the time came for his people, tired of being slaves, to understand clearly the price of liberty. For a long time still he meditated upon freedom, the destiny of America.

Venezuela was going through a period of prosperity and intellectual unrest. Many new names were appearing and the zeal for renovation seemed to be the watchword. Out of the classroom came young men eager to excel. Venezuela had a great literary tradition represented by a man venerated for his humble wisdom and his unyielding dignity: Cecilio Acosta.

The austere home where the sage lived in retirement was the place which Martí immediately sought. The room

161

Martí

where Acosta received his friends was very modest. There were a very few books in one corner of his bedroom. His vast reading was all precisely classified in his mind. Acosta's conversations were not displays of erudition but the sober utterance of his thoughts.

Cecilio Acosta seemed to Martí an anticipator. He found that the Venezuelan's ideas were the same as his own. He felt captivated and moved when he discovered what advanced opinions Acosta held. The latter was a defender of the poor, not a flatterer of the powerful. He had meditated upon the destiny of America and ways to inject into its veins rich new blood which would give it a life of its own and free it from European ties. From his lips Martí learned of the tragedy which was then unfolding its wings over Venezuela.

Cecilio Acosta alienated the friendship of Guzmán Blanco, then in command in Venezuela, because he was not a man to ingratiate himself with the powerful. His dispassionate attitude of censure was his reply to dictatorial, capricious measures. Official annoyance made itself felt. The punishment of excommunication weighed upon the learned man. Only students and men of independent judgment gathered staunchly around the persecuted man.

Martí's name was not unknown in Venezuela. Here some were familiar with his articles in the *Revista Universal* of Mexico; others had read his book on Guatemala; and many had heard of his remarkable oratory. But everyone knew of his devotion to the idea of freeing his country, an idea which had always had the sympathy of the Venezuelan people.

Shortly after his arrival a program was organized in his honor. Caracas wished to satisfy its curiosity. The Commercial Club celebrated its opening with this first cultural meeting. Men of letters, young people of the university, and great crowds attended the meeting. Martí spoke from one of the balconies. What should be the subject of his speech in the cradle of American liberty? Bolívar inspired him.

"The poem of 1810 is unfinished, and I wished to write the last stanza."

The Shade of Bolívar

Never before had he developed his ideas so fully. The freedom of Cuba was the freedom of America, for America would not be free as long as any part of it was not. His address was also a song to the destiny of America. He had never before expressed so clearly and profoundly his American sentiments. In Venezuela there was a propitious atmosphere in which old glories would be reborn under a new light. His voice took on rich accents when he demanded for the American nations a life of their own, not an America extended like a carpet to be trodden upon by foreign nations.

The Colegio de Santa María, a school reputed to be one of the best, offered him a means of livelihood—some classes in French language and literature. But the young people around him wanted a stronger, more vital kind of instruction. Venezuelan youth at that time felt an overwhelming urge to lift up their faith, sustaining it by high principles. Although Martí's oratorical gifts had aroused the youth of Caracas, it was not mere classes in oratory that they desired of him.

Dr. Guillermo Tell Villegas, the illustrious director of a *colegio* of excellent reputation, offered the young enthusiasts the main hall of his school. Several nights every week from eight to ten the spontaneous group of pupils met with Martí. When he finished speaking of liberty or science, when he defined his idea of poetry or of heroes, when he let his impressions or his sorrows be glimpsed as between parentheses, they were all full of admiration.

It is no exaggeration to say that for a while the literary life of Caracas centered around Martí. It was not enough to hear him. Everyone wanted to read his works, give him an opportunity to write and publish the many things that should not merely be said before an audience and then lost. He had often thought of publishing a magazine. He had tried to do so months ago in New York, but Ponce de León was not interested in publications at the time. This moment in Venezuela was one of such enthusiasm that the idea might take root and prosper.

Just as it was fitting that the review he founded in Guatemala should bear the name of the land that inspired it, he now had equally good reason to choose the title of *Revista Venezolana*. It would be a work of collaboration, a means of drawing near to the youth and stimulating their thinking. He invited them to collaborate, not as a mere courtesy, but out of the need to realize the ambitions which he saw rising all around him. Some students brought him their pages. Martí read them and always found something to praise in them. But he thought that some weak paragraphs could be strengthened with more direct expressions, or that certain words would be better than the ones employed. He consulted with and asked opinions of those who had come to consult him. He made them feel at ease and express their ideas spontaneously. And little by little the tone of the articles was elevated and the superfluous disappeared.

Until then circumstances had prevented his enjoyment of the repose and calm which Venezuela offered him. He spent most of his time preparing the first issue of the review.

The house where he lived was across from the little plaza of Altagracia. He was never alone there. There was always some friend who sought his company, some youth who wished to consult him about a problem. During those days when he was preparing the *Revista Venezolana* visits were frequent.

Fausto Teodoro de Aldrey, editor of *La Opinión Nacional,* belonged to Martí's group of new friends. He was one of those who encouraged Martí to publish the *Revista Venezolana,* and on Aldrey's presses the first number was printed. It appeared June 1, 1881. Martí began with a page bearing a statement of his purpose. Here there were gifted men—men to be proud of. His purpose was to sing their praises, "to make my humble contribution to the national fervor, to push onward the powerful American wave, to aid in the creation of new leaders, to quell all ideas of minimizing the greatness of our past."

The serene tone of his review would not be perturbed by philosophical partiality or exclusive criteria. He intended to settle minor disputes in order to devote himself to the task of creation. The truth could be seen from many angles. All men believed themselves to be contemplating it in its pure state. But, "Are they not all seekers after the truth with lamps of different colors?"

The Shade of Bolívar

He had a warm place in his heart for the just man who labored for integrity as well as for ideas. He devoted his greatest efforts to the making of men. Above the peaks of human greatness rose the figure of Cecilio Acosta as eulogized by Martí. The vigorous outlines of the man were flooded with light. And in the magic evocation of the inner life of the poet and the sage one could see Martí's thoughts emerging.

For months Martí had longed to have his wife and child come to Venezuela. As soon as he knew that it would be possible to establish himself he wanted to have them at his side. Carmen had not decided. They had stayed in Havana for several months in the comfortable home of Manuel García, one of Martí's brothers-in-law. Reports from their friends concerning living conditions in Venezuela were certainly not the kind to encourage their going. Even Azcárate advised them to wait until Martí was more certain of being able to support them. Martí did not know of this delay, and when he thought that they must be on their way, Carmen and their child had left for her father's home in Camagüey.

After a slight delay the second issue of the *Revista Venezolana* began to circulate. His study of Cecilio Acosta was read avidly. He who had suffered persecution and hostility for the sake of his ideas was honored as only the just can be honored. Thus Martí paid the debt of gratitude of all the Venezuelans who felt, as Martí did, the outrage committed against the man who dignified the country by the *caudillo* who was dishonoring it with his mad ranting and his ridiculous pomp. News of Martí's interpretation spread. People discussed the article by that Cuban Martí who was teaching a course in freedom in Venezuela.

It was dangerous to talk very much about freedom in a tyrannized nation, as Martí soon learned. A few days after his article appeared, Guzmán Blanco summoned him into his presence. By means of flattery he wished to win Martí over to his cheap, glittering politics. Martí's refusal was answered by threats, and the interview ended in an argument.

Martí

Martí left this interview with the "illustrious American," as he had himself called by his subordinates, with instructions to leave the country without delay. How many dreams cherished during these few months in Venezuela came crashing to earth!

He had barely enough time to take the boat to New York. He wrote to his mother and to Carmen, who might already be on her way. This thought worried him a great deal. But his friends relieved him of worry. They would see that his wife and child, on arrival, continued their journey. One of his friends, Arístides Rojas, lent him a small sum of money to cover the cost of his passage. Sadly he said good-by to the friends who had received him affectionately. He felt both loved and respected, and he had almost forgotten his old sorrows there, where his spirit, his mind, and his faith all lived fully. It seemed to Eloy Escobar and his family that their house would have no light after Martí was gone.

The last evening before his departure he wrote a farewell letter. He addressed it to Aldrey, but it was intended for all the friends to whom he had not had time to say good-by personally. There was nothing in the letter to reveal the real reason for his hasty departure. It was, rather, his most rotund, concrete reiteration of his faith in America:

"I am a son of America, and I belong to her. I consecrate myself to the building, the revealing, and the arousing of this America, of which Venezuela is the cradle. Here there is no bitter cup for sweet lips, nor does the asp bite manly hearts, nor do loyal sons and daughters renounce their cradle. Let Venezuela give me a way to serve her, and she will find in me a son."

He could not have found a more succinct form of expressing his philosophy, his pride, and his generosity. Those who knew how to interpret the signs of the times could read in those lines the hidden motive which deprived them of this unsurpassed friend.

The next day, July 28, when his letter appeared in *La Opinión Nacional*, Martí was on board the *Claudius*, bound for New York. A few friends had stayed with him until the last minute. One of these was Fausto Teodoro Aldrey, the editor of *La Opinión Nacional*.

Part IV:

Years of Fusion

17. Servitude and Grandeur of the Pen

The people of Caracas were surprised by Martí's unexpected departure. He had won their love, and so completely had the progressive young men, in their zeal for reform, shared his ideas that during those months there he had become an integral part of their lives and ideals. On August 10, Aldrey, assuming that he had reached New York, wrote him an account of the sorrow his departure had caused.

At the same time that Martí had to leave Venezuela, news was circulating concerning a daily which was soon to be published. It was thought to be backed by Guzmán Blanco. Fausto Teodoro Aldrey and his son, Juan Luis, were concerned about the forthcoming rival of *La Opinión Nacional*, and before Martí left they made certain, not only that he would collaborate on their paper, but that he would act as their representative in obtaining advertising from North American firms. With their first letter to him they sent him a few issues of *El Monitor,* which did not turn out to be such a dangerous rival as they had feared. They also reminded him of the instructions they had given him as their correspondent. He was to follow them out "to the letter."

When summer came the Mantillas had gone to live in Brooklyn, and there Martí found lodging with them once more. As soon as he reached New York he wrote to Carmen, thinking she might still be in Havana. Then he began thinking of a way to keep his agreement with the Aldreys. That would afford him some measure of economic security and yet not prevent his accepting other work.

169

Martí

The topic of the day when he reached New York was the attack on President Garfield, an event which completely held the interest of the public. Many other outstanding events were taking place during those days, but that one was so vivid that the rest seemed to be eclipsed. He could find no more appropriate subject for his first news letter. The daily papers were full of interesting news concerning that subject, and while Garfield's condition became more critical, political rivalries were stirred up by the possibility of the President's death. Feverishly Martí began work on his first article. But he sent more than that. He had agreed to send the Aldreys news from everywhere in order to enliven the pages of their daily. Martí wished to keep his agreement as fully as possible. He prepared a vivid review of the latest news from Spain and France, enlivening it with his singular imagination and his ample knowledge of European conditions. The steamer, *Claudius,* which left on the twentieth, carried two extensive reports of his. Even at the last minute, when the *Claudius* was on the point of sailing he added some "last-minute news" simply as a concession to the wishes of the editors. In the letter which accompanied his articles Martí revealed his hopes of prospering and making a place for himself.

As soon as his reports reached Caracas they were published. On September 5 his account on Garfield appeared. The mail was delivered at two o'clock in the afternoon, and at four *La Opinión* was going to press with ten galleys filled with Martí's work. The next day his letter on Spain and France was published. Aldrey was completely satisfied with Martí's competence and activity and began to fulfill his part of the agreement by sending him the first payments. They were even disposed to increase the amount if Martí would send more correspondence and reviews of general interest.

The articles caused a sensation. According to his agreement with Aldrey, Martí's name was withheld, and no one knew the identity of "M. de Z.," the initials which he used. They aroused lively curiosity. Someone wrote to New York in an attempt to investigate. It was not to the advantage of the newspaper for Martí's identity to be known at that time, and he was advised to be very cautious. Among his first letters was one that was not published, a commentary containing an allusion to the Pope, in a vein which would not further the interests of the newspaper. The editors felt, however, that they should concern themselves with happenings in Rome. Therefore it would be well, they wrote in a letter dated September 22, for Martí to write something with an *ultramontane* flavor, in accordance with the circumstances prevailing in Venezuela. This might avoid clashes and polemics in which the victory would finally be won by "the fanaticism reigning among even the men of highest standing." In order to convince him, as if his conscience could be silenced by arguments of expediency which went against his own ideas, they made use of the argument that no one knew who "M. de Z." was.

Doña Leonor was very surprised to receive the letter Martí wrote on leaving Venezuela. Through listening to Don Mariano's opinions she had grown accustomed to the idea that Martí would stay for only a short time in those countries that were in a continual state of revolution. However, the had never expected him to leave so abruptly. What had happened in Venezuela should be a lesson to him. She reminded him of what she had been telling him ever since he was a child: "Anyone who tries to be a redeemer is crucified." Her letters were full of complaints because he did not write, because he had left her, because he was far away.

"What a useless sacrifice you are making, my dear son, of your own peace and that of all who love you. There is not a single person who is grateful for it. Most people attribute your sacrifice to a desire for fame, others, to expedience, and no one appreciates its true value."

The details she told about the family were touching. His father suffered from frequent attacks of asthma; his sisters were anemic. They had been subjected, almost since their childhood years, to hard work in order to eke out a wretched existence. His letters to his mother increased her sorrow, not because he told her his troubles but because he omitted them, and she guessed them.

Doña Leonor's letters kept coming. They were all filled with bad news and complaints concerning his silence. Was that due perhaps to his inability to send her the twenty pesos a month that he had promised? She wanted to know the truth. Whatever troubles he might be suffering, she said, would be easier for her to bear if she knew about them, for when she did not know, she imagined them to be even greater than they were.

It was a torment for Martí to be unable to give his parents the aid that he would like to give them and that they needed and had a right to expect from him. He had never been able to take care of them regularly, effectively. His life had been in a continual turmoil.

Carmita Mantilla's home was a Venezuelan house. Martí loved Venezuela because he never recalled the troubles and bitter experiences he had there. He remembered, on the contrary, the many kindnesses, the friendly hands, and generous hearts. His leisure hours were Venezuelan hours, shared with Pérez Bonalde and Gutiérrez Coll. They encouraged him to publish the little book which he wrote in Caracas and read before a gathering of friends.

Pérez Bonalde had written a poem to the Niagara which Martí enjoyed. One night when the poem was read before a group of Venezuelans in a house in Brooklyn, Martí expressed such admiration that it was suggested that he write an article about it that would serve as a prologue. In it he would also comment on the author. As if he had the poet by the hand he approached his pages, pouring forth his idealism, his regard for the new men and new times, the age of broken barriers, in which men crossed the earth inspired by sentiments of humanity, love, and pardon, returning to the true Christ. It was the optimistic song of an energetic epoch when man, on his way upward, rose from his knees to stand as tall as the hills. All of Martí's dispersed credo took shape in this prose, which was perhaps too exalted but revealed great thoughts.

Martí's mysticism in regard to this poem proceeded from meditation to action. He had seen man on the threshhold of a new world, ready for the leap that would make him the master of himself and of his future greatness. He was the missionary of that new religion which would bring men back to themselves, help them in their own reconquest. He had always been a missionary, and now more than ever before. His doctrine could be reduced to a few words: "Only the genuine is fruitful." That was the lesson he had learned in Mexico when he preached his ideas about discarding European imitation in favor of what is one's own, in the theatre as in everything, and spoke of Mexico's unknown and un-utilized riches; in Guatemala when he wrote an Arcadian poem to fecund nature there and to the country's serene, pure beauty; in Venezuela when he found emotions seething and about to burst and saw men who bore within themselves all the wisdom of the land and the intuition of the future which he himself cherished,—there was his American mysticism. He did not dream, as Bolívar did, of federations of nations, but of federations of souls, of purposes, in a religious zeal for true liberty. Useful wealth which gives nations sovereignty and does not lead them to sloth-producing opulence; the wealth which comes from work and is conducive to human dignity; the work which elevates nations and wins them respect.

"No! Human life is not the only life! The tomb is a road, not a terminal. . . . Death is joy, renunciation, a new task. Human life would be a barbarous invention if it were limited to life on earth."

As a child he had believed these ideas. As a man he confirmed his belief in them.

His correspondence with *La Opinión Nacional* continued to be his most important task, and he gave himself over to it fervently. He sent no less than eight letters to Caracas every month. At times as many as five of these letters were dated the same day. They throbbed with the vibrations of the most important events in the world. What was happening in France, Italy, Russia, Germany, Spain was recorded on his hastily written pages. But not as a dead relation of events, but rather a vivid swarm of actions which escaped the printed letters to acquire the vigor of reality. Rising above the dead words, his descriptions of landscapes, of men, and events acquired depth and movement. Men were individuals with sentiments. Places were not mere names, they came alive in his descriptions that were not loaded with details but were composed of a few essential strokes. Nothing worth including was omitted: parliaments, academic receptions, the deaths of illustrious men, interviews with kings, Paris salons, new books, political rivalries, figures whose names dominated an epoch or a moment. Across the pages of his articles passed the people whose presence enlivened the contemporary scene. Some were beginning, some ending their careers. And the United States? Everything, excitement, celebrations, things insignificant or portentous, heroism, ingenuousness, brutality, grandeur, the vigor of new men, the lives of the millionaires and laborers, exhibits, politics, movements of ideas, a whole dizzy world came pouring forth from his full, abundant pages.

His reports aroused curiosity in all the American countries. In Colombia some of his articles were reprinted, and the unknown author was highly praised for his style.

The Aldreys, despite the good reception Martí's articles were given, harassed Martí with instructions as to how to write them. Rather than his large, lively syntheses they wanted separate news items, mere notations of events, an unsubstantial accumulation of news. They justified their exigencies as a desire to satisfy their readers' tastes. Martí was very irritated by this curtailment of his talent. He was attracted by the great, and if he erred it was always on the side of the ideal and the lofty, as he broke the ties that bound him to the commonplace. He felt wretched when he was deprived of flight.

After four months of incognito the editors of the newspaper decided to publish the name of their New York correspondent. Not only did they print his name at the end of his account of Christmas, published January 1, 1882; they revealed his identity in an accompanying note of greeting and praise of his work. The Aldreys were already worried for fear that others might guess the anonymous correspondent's identity and print his name before they did. They wished to have that privilege, which would give them certain importance.

But that was not sufficient reason to make them change their tactics. Sometimes Aldrey, sometimes his son Juan Luis, vexed Martí with requests for "abundant separate news items." But as Martí continued to send them his marvelous pictures full of movement and color, their reprimands became more constant and annoying. Out of consideration for his friends, Martí made no reference to their remarks and tried to satisfy them by adding occasionally, at the end of his reports, a bare relation of events.

In one letter their observation took more specific form: "I must inform you that our public is complaining about the length of your latest reviews of Darwin, Emerson, etc. Furthermore the paragraphs are very long. I wish to continue this section, but it must have short paragraphs." A few days later, as if they were trying to frighten Martí, they informed him that many of his articles were not published, some for lack of space, others because they did not conform to the newspaper's policy, "such as the articles on the Peruvian question." As if that were not enough, they tried again to express the readers' wishes, in regard to the type of correspondence and also made a more substantial recommendation: "that you try in your criticism not to deal harshly with the customs of the North American people."

This last letter was dated May 3. When Martí received it his correspondence for that month, dated the twenty-third, was already in the mail. He made an immediate decision not to write any more for *La Opinión*. These letters to Caracas which friendly hands were already compiling in book form had become something very close to his heart. But he could see that the Aldreys were no longer showing him their old consideration. He was not hurt by their telling him the truth, but because of their friendship he had grown accustomed to expect kindness and consideration.

He made no reply to the brusque letters. His silence was his response. But he opened his heart to a loyal friend from Caracas, the gentlemanly Diego Jugo Ramírez, and he even sent him a letter to the Aldreys, a letter written in anticipation of the possibility that the truth might be distorted. It was to be sent to its destination only in case the need should arise.

Martí

He realized how ingenuously he had received the first words of encouragement from the editors of *La Opinión*. He understood that naturally it was of great advantage to them to have him writing for their paper at a time when a rival, whom they thought to be a formidable one, was appearing, "I have just enough time to tell you briefly," he wrote to his friend, "that from the very instant that *El Monitor* disappeared, the letters from Aldrey and Luis, that had been so grateful and vehement in their expressions of consideration and affection, became, in my opinion at least, negligent and a bit indifferent. I,—ingenuous!—received their letters as a natural response to the great affection I felt toward them." The suspension of Martí's letters, without any explanation, might cause comment, and perhaps the editors would invent stories censuring Martí.

It pained him to have lost a beloved rostrum, especially since he wrote those articles with his friends in Caracas, who would read them, in mind. However, he received offers of similar opportunities from Buenos Aires and Mexico.

By April *Ismaelillo* was published. That was the title he gave to a poem to his son he wrote in Caracas in a rare moment of repose. His friends had encouraged him to publish it. Now that the book was published, it seemed to him a simple, inconsequential thing, and he was ashamed to see it in print. He wondered if he had succeeded in giving artistic form to the throng of winged visions that fluttered within his brain when he thought of his son. There was such simplicity and tenderness in these verses, in which, forgetting everything else he played and talked with his son—with the image of his son,—that he was surprised when he emerged again into the world and was wounded by reality.

The verses of *Ismaelillo* were composed in hours when he was at peace. They came from his soul during an interlude of hope. The prolonged wait during that winter in 1880 in New York brought something else between him and his wife besides a feeling of indifference. It brought the love of another woman who in that bitter hour of his life sweetened his sadness. And he strayed from the straight path which he had wanted his life to follow.

Servitude and Grandeur of the Pen

Ever since that time his thoughts cut like a knife. His verses were born amid that confusion of thoughts which surrounded him. The idea of anticipated death, a death he bore within himself, presided over his visions. In his *Canto de Otoño* (Autumn Song) he said:

"Oh life, farewell! He who is going to die has already died!"

His decision, which brought forth such protest from Doña Leonor, to establish himself definitely in New York, required his looking for some kind of permanent work, no matter how unsuited it might be to his interests. He knew that there was little demand for Spanish letters, and he did not wish to profess to be an authority in that field. There were innumerable commercial offices where it was possible to find work if he would only subject himself to the accepted working habits of the city. Finding work was simply a question of time and the opportunity to look for it, and he set about looking. The newspaper frequently carried advertisements requesting employees speaking English and Spanish. He answered the advertisements in an attempt to find the most suitable position possible. In July an important firm decided to give him a chance in its offices for one month at the end of which time permanent arrangements might be made. The office hours would begin at nine a.m. and last until the day's work was done. On the following day Martí arrived on time at the office of Lyon and Company, 31 East Thirty-Third Street, Broadway, and he began work. The month of trial proved satisfactory. His work was almost mechanical, "but my soul is at peace, and my eyes see no other kinds of ignominy than those most common to human nature." It was not agreeable, of course, to leave a warm bed on cold mornings, go out to earn his living, and come back after the sun had set. And it required a great deal of will power to take part in that herd-like life led by city workers here. "They are, however, a herd of kings."

Other occasional work fell to him during his months of unemployment, especially the assignments which the Appleton Company gave him. For this company he was translating Marrafi's *Tresor de Vertu* into Spanish under the title *Antigüedades Griegas*. He spent many days on that difficult

177

task, and even after he found a permanent position he continued working until late at night, determined to finish the translation. He turned it in in September, receiving a hundred dollars in payment.

He knew now that it would be possible for him to live, although at the expense of everything that was his true vocation.

On his return to New York Martí had found the Cubans' morale very low. It was not the proper time to think of political activities only a few months after the loss of the *guerra chiquita*, the "little war." But he lost no chances to go to programs attended by Cubans, or to expound his uncompromising ideas whenever the opportunity arose.

During his months in Venezuela he had thought a great deal about the organization of the war which should free Cuba decisively from her oppressors. It could not be an improvised undertaking. A long period of time must be spent in making convictions take root, creating faith, and developing a system of aid that could provide Cuba with everything necessary for victory.

What should be done? The results of previous attempts still weighed too heavily on the people's spirit, and without faith it was impossible to advance in the undertaking. It was necessary to create a cult of freedom. It must first be an idea in people's hearts, that it might, later, be the impulse behind their arms. Martí had never been idle at that task. Since his return to New York he had devoted himself to the organization of several groups that were dispersed. It was necessary to arouse some, to calm the impatience of others.

Around the beginning of 1882 Flor Crombet was very close to Martí, and together they made plans, with a new surge of enthusiasm. The task of utilizing and directing the new forces, without which nothing could be accomplished, would require the efforts of the men who had earned respect and admiration by their valor and loyalty. They must show their country a united front without the divisions of the previous wars. If they would stand together, capable of restraining their impatience until the probability of victory called for action, when the time was ripe the word could be exchanged for the sword.

Flor Crombet left for Honduras. He carried a letter from Martí in which the latter presented his ideas to General Máximo Gómez and gave him an account of the preparations already under way. Flor Crombet was to ask him, in the name of the men of judgment in Havana and Camagüey, in the name of Don Salvador Cisneros, and in Martí's as well, if he did not believe that these ideas which Martí had written to him should not be the basis for the organization of a new revolutionary movement.

Flor Crombet also bore a letter to General Maceo. In it Martí outlined the movement which was being initiated. It included the active revolutionists, those who had been revolutionists and changed their minds, and those who thought the revolution unnecessary. The existing unrest was revealed in his letter. But he did not consider either legal or powerful "any revolutionary manifestation which is not assented to and directed by the men who have acquired this special right by their merits."

During the days when Martí was writing those letters there was great unrest in Cuba. Ruin seemed imminent, and the feeling of uneasiness was so great that the idea of the revolution was winning converts among the Cubans in the interior of the island. Even the liberal press pointed out what ruinous prospects the country had to face, and for this the Spanish administration was to blame. In their longing the Cubans all thought of two names: Gómez and Maceo.

General Gómez' ideas, which he presented to Martí in a brief letter dated October 8, were to a certain extent an encouragement for his own ideas: the nation which had exhausted itself in the long struggle must once more endure the same ordeal. Then, when the old element was amalgamated with the new, the opportune moment would arrive. "Meanwhile we must make all preparations calmly, without any ostentation, and above all let us try to preserve our prestige in order that we may count on the confidence of those who in their desperation might turn to anyone." Prudence told them that it was necessary to work without stopping, but without precipitating events.

No practical results were obtained. Prudence at that time was a major virtue, and these men who lived through the war and knew its difficult hours had not lost enthusiasm, but they must safeguard their reputation. They must wait for the opportune time to meet. In Honduras Flor Crombet had long conversations with Eusebio Hernández, who was very closely connected with General Maceo and seemed to exercise great influence upon him. Martí's enthusiasm, of which Crombet spoke to the General, did not arouse the latter's. On November 3 Hernández wrote to Maceo, after praising Crombet's character highly, these words laden with significance:

"He is dignified without being arrogant and sufficiently intelligent not to be used, under any circumstances, as *the instrument of another's Machiavellism.*"

Martí would not allow the sacred fire of the *patria* to go out among the exiles, even though he might not offer definite aid to the several insufficient, personal attempts that followed in close succession. He was looking further ahead. The very attitude of Gómez and Maceo, safeguarding their own reputation until the real hour should come, was a warning.

Martí was not mistaken when he said that his correspondence to *La Opinión Nacional* had circulated all over America. In all the South American countries his articles in the Caracas newspaper were noticed. His reports were commented upon and reproduced, and the editors of *La Nación* of Buenos Aires considered him a perfect correspondent for their paper.

Martí was not satisfied to lead the life of a mere office worker or translator. Such tasks did not prevent him from writing for the newspapers of his America. And so it was that in a conversation with the Argentine consul in New York, it was suggested that he begin his collaboration on the staff of the great newspaper of Buenos Aires. Martí accepted. On July 15, 1882 he mailed his first letter, of rather somber hues, perhaps, because the month had begun in the shadow of the scaffold on which Guiteau* paid for his evil deed of vengeance against humanity. There were comments on

* President Garfield's assassin. (Ed.)

other events of the month: a freighters' strike, the latest debates in Congress, schools of Christian philosophies, congresses of educators. At the end of some reflections on the bitter quarrels between the Democratic and Republican parties there were words that seemed like a reply to the Aldreys' concept of the press:

"The press cannot be, in these creative times, a mere vehicle for news or a mere slave to interests, or an outlet for an exuberant, flowery imagination."

On September 13 the article was published under the general title, *Letters from the United States*. A few days later Bartolomé Mitre, of the editorial staff of the paper, wrote Martí an extensive letter in which he informed him that for a long time they had desired and needed a competent United States correspondent. They believed they had found the right person in Martí. His first letter, Mitre went on to say, was read in Argentina and the neighboring countries with marked interest.

Then he went into detail in order to justify the omission of a part of Martí's correspondence which might give the impression, because of its extremely radical conclusions concerning the political and social organization and the progress of the United States, that a campaign was being opened against that nation as a political body, as a social entity, and as an economic center. The article made no mention, on the other hand, of the great lessons which it offered to mankind. The editors believed—and in Martí's earlier articles they had found reason for their opinion—that he was doing full justice to the great, the noble, and the beautiful in the United States. Mitre's letter was most considerate. He reasoned with Martí in a convincing manner about his motive for omitting part of his letter:

"Your letter would have been all shadows if it had been printed just as it was, and I should have run the risk, had I published it in its entirety, of giving the impression of prejudice."

This reasoning carried weight. Martí was not a man who was trying to darken the picture, putting into it nothing but shadows when there was also a great deal of light. On December 19 he wrote his reply to that letter, "equalled in its logic only by its generosity." Mitre was right in making the omission. It was fitting to emphasize in its full strength the splendid struggle of men which the north exemplified, in contrast to the bad attempt to go back to the stagnant old times which was being favored in certain American countries beneath the literary standard of poetic love of tradition.

During those December days when he was writing his letter to the editors of *La Nación,* Carmen had come with their child. After not seeing them for two years they had come, in the middle of the very severe winter, to cheer him in his loneliness. These were days full of small attentions directed toward the reestablishment of their home life. He did not have, at that time, the inspiration or the necessary quiet to undertake the pleasant task of writing his letters regularly. But every month, beginning in January, he assured the editors, in accordance with their wishes, his letter would be sent directly by steamer. He would try to make each letter "varied, profound and animated." "The picturesque will relieve the serious element, and the literary comments will form a pleasant contrast to the political items."

With his mind calm and his life in order he began the new year, 1883, in the new little home in Brooklyn. During his leisure moments he wrote his letter, opening with the New Year celebrations which he described with light phrases interspersed with serious comments.

Nor did he abandon his translation of the book on logic, which he considered a very fine work in spite of the fact that he thought so many puerile rules were useless. The earnings from the translation would permit him to realize one of his greatest desires: to bring his father to his side. Don Mariano had never cared for the countries of Spanish America. On the other hand, he considered the United States a marvelous country, and he had always cherished a secret hope of visiting it.

His sister Amelia's marriage was an event that made Martí rejoice, for he sensed her happiness in reading her letter. He felt so happy that he went visiting, sang a little, and talked more than usual.

A smiling panorama of the future made him happy. Nothing had disturbed him as much as the thought of the suffering of his father and his family. Now he was prospering, and while they rested he did all the work. And he played with the idea of having Don Mariano come to see him and enjoy a rest as soon as the cold weather was over, around March or the beginning of April.

In 1882 a magazine entitled *La América* began publication in New York. It was mainly commercial in character, for its object was to find markets in Latin America for everything pertaining to agriculture, industry and commerce which was produced in the United States. A Cuban who had been established in New York for some time and knew Martí, E. Valiente, was the publisher. Martí became a collaborator in March, 1883. His literary reputation was already well known in the Spanish American nations, and his appointment as correspondent for *La Nación* must have been the determining factor influencing the editors of *La América*. The greater the reputation of the collaborators, the more a periodical of this type would be in demand.

One could say that the March number was written almost entirely by Martí. Articles of real importance concerning commercial problems or opinions on matters of economics were combined with information about new inventions and exhibits and comments on books related directly or indirectly to the character of the magazine.

In June Martí was a contributor, and in a note to the readers he informed them that beginning with that issue he would take a more direct part in the work of the newspaper.

Month after month he continued to write his full share. Even many of the advertisements revealed his pen. He had had the opportunity, in his travels through Mexico, Guatemala, and Venezuela, to observe and learn to know close at hand the peculiarities of agricultural, commercial, and industrial wealth. He let fall in his writings hints and useful advice. He saw from a distance the whole spectacle of the unknown or hidden forces which were struggling to spring up from the American earth and would bring to it, if properly utilized, along with economic independence, the well-being and respect which it needed in order to subsist.

In his articles he insisted upon the things that were essential for the transformation of the character of the sons of that America. Only through a scientific education would they be able to take advantage of the changed rhythm which was occurring in the north and had given the United States its growing economic potentiality. Martí believed that an exclusively literary education was harmful to Latin America's growth because it created nations of useless men of letters with an excess of Greek and Latin and absolute neglect of the knowledge that drives nations and makes them free and happy.

In October his name appeared as editor. Such had been the importance and significance of his labors. And the review circulated throughout the nations from Mexico to Argentina, arousing admiration everywhere.

It was no longer simply a matter of correspondence filled with picturesque, vivid descriptions of literary fantasy. The real man, the clear-sighted American was in those orienting articles which summed up the future and the greatness of a continent.

The Spanish Americans in New York organized a Bolívar centenary celebration. At Delmonico's the most brilliant representatives of the nations liberated by Bolívar met on July 24. Never was there a more animated, vehement celebration, for all felt they shared in the glory that Bolívar had won with his sword. It was the call of liberty. A hundred men of America sat down at the sumptuous table which filled the room. There was no country that was not represented by men of merit. Flags and music floated through the air, presiding over the gaiety. Among the poets the most outstanding were Peón de Contreras from Mexico, Pérez Bonalde from Venezuela and José Joaquín Palma from Cuba. When it was time for a toast it was remarked that from the Río Grande to the Río de la Plata there was only one people. Three Cubans raised their glasses there. Antonio Zambrana drank a toast to the improvement of the republican institutions in America. José Joaquín Palma improvised some admirable *décimas,* and Martí had something to say when he was asked to reply to the toast "to the free peoples." His words were the only ones that carried an undertone of bitterness, for he could not forget that Cuba could not sit down to the banquet table of the free peoples.

Servitude and Grandeur of the Pen

Martí organized his daily life around his correspondence, the editorship of *La America* and his translations. Now there was to be no lack of anything in the bright little Brooklyn home. He was able to carry out his proposal to have Don Mariano come. He had been able to do so little for him; he wanted him at least to have a few months of rest and happiness at his side. Doña Leonor was worried about the trip, for her husband's health was not good, in spite of his good spirits. But her son would not be convinced, and he sent home the money for the passage and additional money for clothes for the trip.

In September Don Mariano was in New York. Martí was touched by the serene courage of his father, a man of integrity who never complained; his strong spirit never bowed to adversity.

Proudly he took his arm and walked with him, talking to him about his projects and hopes. As they walked along Don Mariano contemplated everything avidly. This nation in which everything had gigantic proportions was bigger than he had thought. He measured its greatness by its size. His son confided in him. Carmen was not happy with the simple life they were leading. Her wealthy family had been the obstacle and always would be. Disagreements between them reached such an extreme and became so apparent that Don Mariano announced that he was going back to Havana. But Carmen decided to leave first, and Don Mariano stayed on for some time in order not to leave his son alone then, although the winter was hard on him, and he had to spend whole months next to the fireplace. Those were days of great intimacy and understanding. His son made grave confessions to him: his life was following two paths. It was too late to change. Don Mariano understood and was saddened by this other sorrow of his son's. But he now felt a singular affection for Carmita Mantilla, and like a grandfather he held her little daughter, María, on his lap.

La América had changed ownership. The company that took it over proposed to intensify the activities of the review, and Martí continued as editor. The success of the publication was his own success, for each number was written almost exclusively by him. Zambrana felt that the magazine was at least what he had dreamed of, and Martí's articles had the air of a tale by Cervantes or a Georgic, and they made one think of a garden next to a workshop. No less of an admirer was Charles Dana, who had read *La América* carefully and thought that it possessed the necessary elements for great prosperity and influence. In his letter he took advantage of the opportunity to express his regret that Martí's offer to collaborate on the *Sun* had not been accepted:

"If only you had the gift of writing in English in the same animated, eloquent, picturesque style of your articles in Spanish, your collaboration would be truly invaluable. Even in translation, with the difficulty of reproducing satisfactorily your eloquence and effect, it is always a pleasure to read a manuscript of yours and try to put it into English."

Baldomero Sanín Cano in Colombia was looking for issues of *La América,* that he might enjoy the articles on commercial subjects. He learned later that the author was Martí, and he decided to look for everything he wrote. He never tired of reading "that prose, both solid and elastic, developed in noble, architectonic periods, adorned with Hellenic sobriety and elegance, laden with sincere emotion in a continual recurrence of images."

From Caracas, where his good friends did not forget him and always regretted the bitter hours he was made to endure there, he received, around the end of January in 1884, a diploma. It was from the society of the Friends of Knowledge, who made him their correspondent in New York.

Around the middle of June Don Mariano had sailed for Havana. Martí had learned to understand and love his father. What a deep impression of his son Don Mariano carried away with him!

18. An Altar, Not a Pedestal

Relations between Martí and Flor Crombet had cooled since the plans formed in 1882 had not materialized and had terminated in the indifference with which Martí's letters were received by Gómez and Maceo. It was easy for Martí to see how Flor's own enthusiasm was counteracted by hostile forces, and he suspected intrigue.

Two years had passed. Flor wrote to Martí from La Paz, Honduras, notifying him of General Maceo's trip. His letter was written in May, 1884. There were symptoms of a more difficult situation in Cuba, and the patriots believed that the time was ripe. Maceo set out on a tour of the exile colonies and was to count on Martí as his main support in New York. Flor Crombet and his friends hoped that Martí would support him with his "prestige and well deserved influence."

After meeting in New Orleans, Gómez, Maceo, Crombet, and Eusebio Hernández set out by separate routes on trips of propaganda. They met in the summer in New York. Martí joined the group with fervent enthusiasm, preparing to abandon all his usual duties in order to devote himself to the organization of the movement.

On October 10, the anniversary of Yara,* a meeting was held in Tammany Hall. There was unaccustomed enthusiasm. Martí gave an eloquent address, and everything seemed to point toward successful, effective organization.

A few days later, Maceo and Martí met with Máximo Gómez in the latter's hotel. They had informed Martí of the plans which they had formulated in Honduras. General

* _Grito de Yara_, beginning of the Cuban War of 1868-1878. (Ed.)

Martí

Gómez had arranged for Maceo to leave for Mexico accompanied by Martí. Maceo was entrusted with a delicate mission.

The lack of funds obliged them to delay the trip until money could be collected from the revolutionary groups. Meanwhile the meetings in Gómez' room continued. In the heat of his enthusiasm Martí made suggestions which General Gómez began to find annoying and out of place. He was the one who had been intrusted with the direction of the preparations. One day Martí anticipated what he was to do in Mexico and spoke of the result of the commission. Gómez did not let him finish. In a harsh tone he interrupted him:

"Look, Martí, limit yourself to what the instructions tell you, and as for the rest, General Maceo will do everything that needs to be done."

A courteous good-by and a decision to abandon the task were the consequence. Two days later, October 20, in order that his resolution might not be the result of temporary clouded judgment, Martí wrote to General Gómez of his decision and his ideas. Not only was he determined to consecrate his whole life to the undertaking, he was equally determined not to contribute one iota to the establishment in his country of "a regime of personal despotism which would be more shameful and tragic than the political despotism which it now endures."

Not only that inopportune fit of anger, but also the opinion that General Maceo expressed later, giving him to understand that the Cuban war should be considered the exclusive property of General Gómez, raised an indignant protest from Martí:

"No! God forbid that you should try to suppress thought, even before finding yourselves, as you will tomorrow, in front of an enthusiastic, grateful people, with all the splendor of victory. The fatherland does not belong to anyone."

Martí knew very well, for they had already informed him, that there was intrigue in Honduras against General Gómez, and that without the latter's realizing it he was being prejudiced against Martí. But Martí was a man who had neither the desire nor the patience to try to ferret out or undo intrigues.

An Altar, Not a Pedestal

Some friends of Martí, among them Enrique Trujillo, saw the letter before it was sent. Martí read it to those whom he considered capable of understanding his ideas and judging them, to those who had been thinking about Cuban affairs for a long time and ought to know the truth concerning his decision. Martí was horrified at the thought that people were so ignorant of the republican, democratic spirit with which the war must be waged and the republic must be founded. In order to preserve that spirit it was necessary to fight.

Preparations continued but with no results. The promises of aid on which General Gómez was counting, some of them sufficient to cover the expenditure of the war, were not fulfilled. Martí took refuge in his work and writing. But the break was evident, and comments began. Through the colony of emigrants ran a dull, subterranean rumor against Martí. He was judged ambitious or unpatriotic by those who did not know the reason for his behavior. An attitude of censure took shape and kept growing. Martí decided to face the calumny. His opportunity presented itself on June 13, 1885, when a meeting was held to elect the officers of the Cuban Relief Association. At the meeting certain allusions were made to him with the intention of attacking his political conduct.

Upright and courageous in his attitude, he printed a sheet which he distributed on June 23. He saw to it that it reached all those whom he considered interested in Cuban affairs. He took up the confused rumors censuring his political actions which had reached him. He considered these opinions erroneous, and he wanted to explain his conduct. "My compatriots are my masters," he said. "All my life has been employed and will continue to be employed, in the service of their best interests. I owe them an account of all my actions, even the most personal. Every man is obliged to honor his country with his private as well as his public conduct. On Thursday night, the twenty-fifth, beginning at 7:30, I shall be at Clarendon Hall to answer to whatever charges my fellow citizens may choose to make against me."

A large audience answered the invitation. Curiosity led persons not in the habit of frequenting political meetings to attend in order to watch the strange bout.

Martí

Martí asked for accusations. A man named Rico said a few words in a tone of censure but soon began to stammer and could not continue. Then Martí spoke. He did not make a show of accusing anyone, nor did he criticize. On the contrary he expressed his deep respect for those who cherished the love of their country. His patriotic attitude won him a round of applause.

The next day Trujillo wrote to Maceo:

"It was an immense satisfaction for me to know that in that meeting not a word was said which might hinder the forward progress of the revolution or give our enemies an opportunity to present us as divided among ourselves and hating each other. I did not expect anything else of Martí's profound political and patriotic tact."

A few days later Martí sent Trujillo, for publication in *El Avisador Cubano,* an "open letter" in which this sentence stood out:

"The only friends of the fatherland are those who know how to discard for its sake their anger and their temptations. The only one who serves the fatherland is he who obeys it."

And so he lived, waiting anxiously, without hindering the progress of those who thought differently, but without helping any undertakings which in his opinion imperiled the success of the revolution.

He had lived for a whole year in this sad silence, he told the patriot, Lucena, in his letter of October 9, 1885, when he declined the invitation of the emigrants in Florida to participate in their observance of October 10.

He believed, as he said in his letter, that the tenth of October could not be separated at that time from the political character which it was given by the projects being carried on. His presence might appear to indicate approval of what he really condemned. Or if he participated in it he would have to explain his personal position, "which would be out of keeping with the purpose of the meeting."

Thanks to his pen his reputation grew, and his fame was extended throughout the countries of America. His letters to *La Nación* reached the most remote places in America, and there were those who found new messages in them. It was in that newspaper that Rubén Darío, from his little village in

An Altar, Not a Pedestal

Nicaragua, formed his concept of style, and Martí's prose style figured among those which made the greatest impression on him. Darío knew Martí through the "formidable, lyrical ccrrespondence" which he sent to *La Opinión Nacional,* but he followed him especially in *La Nación,* studying his "profuse prose, full of vitality and color, plasticity and music." He thought he saw revealed in Martí's writings "the cultivation of the Spanish classics and an acquaintance with all ancient and modern literatures; and above all, the spirit of a great, marvelous poet."

Heraclio de la Guardia, a Venezuelan poet, published his poem *Al Centenario de Bolívar* (To the Centenary of Bolívar) with this dedication:

"To José Martí. You love Venezuela, sir, as a son."

Men of the stature of the Chilean Vicuña Mackenna or the Argentine Sarmiento expressed their admiration in terms of spontaneous eulogy. "I am amazed at Martí!" wrote Vicuña Mackenna. "What a manner of conceiving and expressing his ideas! He manipulates a pen as Gustave Doré played with the crayon!" And the great Sarmiento, in spite of other discrepancies caused by his enthusiasm for the United States, was on fire when he finished reading Martí's letter on the Statue of Liberty and was moved to write an extremely long letter to Paul Groussac.

Sarmiento was not even sure that Martí was a Cuban. "A Cuban, I believe," he wrote in his letter to Groussac. But he considered Martí worthy of his admiration for his descriptive talent and his style reminiscent of Goya. And the opinion which Sarmiento formed of Martí in his letter is of great value because of the highly personal form in which he expressed it:

"There is nothing in Spanish which resembles Martí's roaring style. After Victor Hugo, France has nothing to offer to equal this metallic resonance."

Martí wrote and translated ceaselessly during those dark months while his fame was growing great in the countries of America. His correspondence with *La Nación* was uninterrupted. Doubtless that was the pleasantest of his tasks.

A newspaper entitled *El Latino Americano* was published in New York. In it appeared articles that were pleasant reading, and poems by Spanish Americans. Adelaida Baralt, a very good friend of Martí, worked as a translator for the newspaper. Inspired by her conversation with Martí and by the memories he evoked when he spoke of his life and his travels, Adelaida encouraged him to write a novel with autobiographical elements. Martí excused himself for declining, saying that he had never cultivated this *genre*, but his objections were soon overcome. It was not necessary that his name appear in print. When he began trying to think of a pseudonym, Martí took it from his friend's name: Adelaida Ral.

El Latino Americano published *Amistad Funesta* (Ill-Fated Friendship) as Martí called the novel, in several installments. He received fifty-five dollars in payment.

Writing the life of Juan Jerez, the protagonist of *Amistad Funesta,* at a time when his keen ethical sense had kept him aloof from the *caudillos'* plans for the sake of his ideal, relieved him of his sufferings.

He had an opportunity to unburden his soul in writing these pages, which contain innumerable confessions of his own sentiments. He endowed Juan Jerez with those excellent qualities which he always praised and which were an inherent part of his character: "He belonged to the select race of those who work not for success, but against it."

"I am living in a sort of spiritual fear which does not even leave me the strength to write to those whom I love the most," he said in a letter to Domínguez Cowan by way of justifying his prolonged silence. And he would not listen to the argument that he did write and translate for daily papers, for "that is earning my bread." Nevertheless, he was completely given over to that activity. At the same time that he was writing *Amistad Funesta* he prepared himself for his correspondence by reading and taking notes and continued translating for Appleton.

He thought out his entire study of Grant, and wrote it without rest as he leaned on the railing of the ship in which he commuted daily between Brooklyn and New York.

Did he not wish, with this study of General Grant's character, to confirm through a great, well-known experience, his own ideas concerning the spirit which must inspire the war in Cuba? "Wars must be seen from the clouds," he wrote in his masterly essay, and he developed his ideas and showed his profound knowledge of man's nature and of the facts of warfare.

He was not a warrior, but he knew what the warriors of freedom and victory should be like. And he knew how Grant, who gave orders during the war without tolerating any contradiction—which gave him authority and victory—rejected counsel in peace-time, surrendering only to those who flattered him and giving everything to those who pretended to believe in him. Thus he lost his majesty "because he compromised the majesty of the laws."

In December, 1885, he finished his translation of the novel, *Called Back,* by Hugh Conway, which he entitled *Misterio.* He wrote a brief prologue to the first edition, which appeared at the beginning of the year 1886. His aspiration as a translator was that the book might be read at one sitting, as one can read the English original. At least a friend in Mexico had read it to his family.

His work was his cure for his ever-present sorrows. He was also writing for *La República* of Honduras. His correspondence with *La Nación* continued, and through it he refined and tempered his concepts concerning the politics of the United States. His state of mind was receptive to this subject, for he wanted to clarify indirectly, through tangible realities, his own ideas on political, economic and social matters.

It was not mere chance that he frequently devoted entire letters, or a good part of them, to sketches of the lives of generals or politicians. One must use all possible means of facing the tragic errors which it would be necessary to avoid in the future. The development of the strength of this nation provided him not only an opportunity to write his letters but an opportunity to express his ideas concerning what should be done and the dangers to be avoided.

During this epoch in his life Martí never wrote without having before him the vision of his country's future. If he praised something it was because he wanted it for his country even if he did not say so. If he censured something he considered it harmful for his country.

Martí

In August, 1886, the Gómez-Maceo revolutionary plans were a failure. They found only obstacles in their path, doubtless because of the lack of a real organizer capable of extraordinary sacrifices to draw together the diverse and even contradictory elements. They had spent two years in the undertaking. The expeditions which were organized had disastrous results. General Gómez printed a circular letter *To the Cubans* in which he gave a vivid account of their efforts and the ineffectiveness and concluded with this generous offer:

"Cuba can always count on our poor efforts as long as she is enslaved."

The emigrants became discouraged. From Cuba came a rumor of benefits obtained, thanks to the autonomist party's propaganda. And the accounts of the meetings organized by the Party revealed the enthusiasm with which their orators were acclaimed by the towns they visited.

Revolutionary propaganda in New York had come to a standstill. But Martí knew, as did other patriots, that autonomist ideas would never take root in Cuba because they could not solve the serious Cuban problem, which was more a problem of American harmony.

In January, 1887, Don Mariano began to feel worse. By the end of the month his condition was serious. A letter from Martí's brother-in-law, José García, informed him of his father's condition. He died on February 2.

For many years he had had no news of Fermín. Now Don Mariano's death brought them together again spiritually. At that very time Fermín had just obtained indemnity for the accusations made against him and his companions who were executed.* He had worked without rest to obtain the public declaration that the tomb of Castañón had not been profaned. The testimony of his son, Fernando Castañón, and Don José F. Triay, published in *La Lucha* on January 19, 1887, crowned his efforts. In Martí's sorrow, the courage of his friend was a comfort to him. For Fermín's triumph was the

* The students executed by the Spaniards in Havana, November 27, 1871. (See Chapter 7. Ed.)

triumph of moderation and justice. With it he had given Cuba in one of her saddest episodes, the incalculable strength of the victims. "By obtaining without anger a confession of their crime from the murderers, you have sown for the future. You are happier than those that encourage unfounded hopes or pronounce threats that cannot be carried out."

Several times since Don Mariano had visited him Martí had expressed the wish that his mother live with him for a few months. Now that Doña Leonor was alone and had gone to live with one of her daughters, the idea came to him again. Doña Leonor resisted, arguing that her years would not permit her to make the trip. But her son's wishes gradually persuaded her, and finally in one of her letters, dated June, 1887, she wrote: "In regard to what you said about your plans for my trip this summer, I don't deny that it would have been a great pleasure for me . . ." This assent was decisive for Martí, and that same summer Doña Leonor embarked for the north.

Since Carmen returned to Havana with their son, Martí had established himself in Carmita Mantilla's house. María now was a real daughter, his care and his consolation. His responsibility was more than that of a father. He lavished attention on her.

Doña Leonor was treated like a mother in that home where her son had found tenderness. Every effort was made so that she could enjoy the few months that she was to spend with them. But she had left her heart in Havana with her grandchildren. She talked about them constantly, telling of their little ways and their charms. Her life, always devoted to her family, could not leave its old channel. She would not be happy until she went back home.

Enrique Trujillo, their good friend, decided to have a reception in honor of Doña Leonor.

On December 26 the gathering was held in New York. Recitations, dialogues, songs sung by children in English and Spanish composed the first part of the program. The second part included a reading of *Ismaelillo* by Enrique Trujillo, compositions by Tejera, Francisco Sellén and Rafael C. Palomino, recited by the authors, and musical numbers.

Martí

Shortly afterward, before the winter grew severe, Doña Leonor returned to Havana.

On April 16, 1887, through the intervention of the Uruguayan, Enrique Estrázulas, who maintained with Martí a firm friendship, Martí was named Consul of Uruguay in New York. The consulate was at Number 120 Front Street. Martí went there daily and established his office. A few months later, Estrázulas left for Europe, and Martí was left alone at the Consulate with his secretary. That office became the center of his activities. He began to be surrounded by books on all sides—shelves on the walls, a revolving stand near his table, volumes piled in the corners.

"For two dollars and a half," he wrote Estrázulas, "I have bought thirty-three volumes of French drama, and the entire parliamentary history of the revolution, bound in fine leather, for three dollars and a half. If you could see the Consulate!"

His work continued. He translated the novel *Ramona* and wrote for *El Economista Americano,* which Ponce de León had begun to publish. Martí could not contribute much because he was given very little space. At that time his friend, Colonel José Vicente Villada, was the editor of *El Partido Liberal* of Mexico, and he asked Martí to contribute. He was very glad indeed to grant the request of the former editor of the *Revista Universal,* where Martí got his start as a journalist. He was also engaged in the pleasant task of translating Moore's *Lalla Rookh.* He planned to have it printed with magnificent illustrations and a few pages by Bonalde and Tejera. This work compensated for other translations which required spending "months at a stretch combing other books," as he thought when he prepared to translate *John Halifax, Gentleman.* And as if that were not enough, he again took up the idea, after pondering it for a year and a half, of publishing a monthly. He might call it *El Mes* (The Month) . He would write it all himself, and it would be complete in each issue; "a current history and resumé both expository and critical of important events in politics, the theatre, national movements, contemporary science, and books; covering events wherever people really live."

The tenth of October was drawing near again. Martí was once more in contact with the enthusiastic patriots of New York in order to continue revolutionary propaganda. They had no newspaper or club at that time. Several of them shared the expense of publishing a sheet written by Martí, an invitation to all the Cubans to observe the memorable anniversary together.

The salon of the Masonic Temple on the corner of Twenty-Third Street and Sixth Avenue was filled by a brilliant audience. Tomás Estrada Palma, who had recently arrived from Central Valley with the aureole of a patriot and teacher, presided. The speakers were Enrique Trujillo, Rafael de C. Palomino, Serafín Bello and Colonel Emilio Núñez. Amid affectionate applause Martí stepped to the rostrum. "Prudence may restrain, but fire can not die." This explained his reappearance. He stressed the meaning of the date and the significance of the meeting as a meeting of hearts which must be united for the decisive hour. The vision of the fatherland which had been taking shape in his mind and growing stronger with experience and the clash of many contrary ideas and passions, was conjured up by his words. The republic would not be incomplete, partial in its methods, or purposes, but "the sincere fatherland where even our oppressors may live in peace if they learn to respect the rights which their sons have known how to conquer for themselves." In order that this republic be founded, certain obstacles must be overcome, such as "the interests of the war profiteer, the passion of the race-obsessed man, the pride of the lettered, the shamelessness of the political intriguer." And while they awaited the failure of the Cubans who hoped to obtain from Spain the rights which the Island needed in order to make life endurable, it was preferable to keep the banner furled—until it could lead them to victory.

The newspaper, *El Pueblo* (The People), published in Key West by Martín Morúa Delgado, printed an anonymous letter written in New York. It was an account of the October 10 meeting. Martí was accused of having declared himself an autonomist or expressed himself in terms contrary to the revolution. On October 26 he replied: "To think that after attending that meeting I could read such an account of it and not know who should be punished for it!" Fortunately the speeches made by the orators that night were ready for publication. They would bear out the truth of everything Martí said. But it pained him to think that all his efforts "to make it possible to establish in Cuba a government that would not have a place for all its elements and classes" could be judged even momentarily as favoring the creation of a "republic representing one group, a guilty, sterile republic."

Martí's attitude in withdrawing from the Gómez-Maceo plans had started the rumors consciously or unconsciously being spread against him. Even Trujillo noted a certain evolutionist flavor in some of Martí's correspondence around the beginning of the year 1887. Martí had previously attempted to deny or explain certain ideas which Señor Ricardo Rodríguez Otero had attributed to him in his book, *Impressions and Memoirs of My Trip to the States of New York, New Jersey and Pennsylvania.* According to this book, Martí was willing to accept whatever solution Spain might offer for Cuba's problems if the majority of Cubans accepted it. How could he accept it if neither he nor the Cubans had ever been "under obligations to obey, but rather had rights to *demand?*" The only thing which he would always accept was the manifest will of his country, even if it went contrary to his own.

Because he restrained impatience, would not conform to demagogical methods and asked that the war be adapted to the country's needs and not be forced upon it before the country gave a clear indication of wanting it; because he believed that many contrary elements might fall of their own accord or join the side of those who wanted to fight—for these reasons he was considered weak and opposed to action.

It was his patriotic mission to be on his guard. There were preliminary details that could be taken care of without bloodshed. And until the signals were clear and he saw evidence of the country's definite desire for war, he did not think the opportune moment for going to war had arrived. Meanwhile they should "study all the means of which they would avail themselves at the opportune moment and bring together, instead of separating, the forces necessary for the battle." It was his conviction, based on his study of circumstances in Cuba and Spain, that Spain could not give Cuba what she needed, for the Cuban was more advanced politically than the Spaniard, and what Spain could offer him would not suffice.

Around the beginning of November, Brigadier General Juan Fernández Ruz arrived in New York after being deported via Key West. He planned to organize an expedition to renew the war. In Key West, which was always restless, he aroused enthusiasm. In New York he had an interview with Martí in order to learn his opinion concerning the most practical way of putting into action the hopes and desires to see Cuba free. Martí thought it best to hold a meeting in order that as many Cubans as possible might express their ideas on the subject. He took the initiative in arranging a meeting in the home of Enrique Trujillo. Some twenty persons attended the meeting. Without reaching any definite agreement a record of the proceedings was drawn up as an initial effort. Afterwards they agreed to inform General Gómez of their work. Martí prepared the document, but it was signed also by many compatriots who were outstanding for their revolutionary ideas. The letter stated that the coming war should be organized in accordance with the morale of the country. And their work should be inspired by "a vast, cordial, firm political creed, the only one that can bolster up the weakened confidence of the nation." The message of the letter was determined by Martí's civilian, democratic ideas concerning the organization of the war. And his program for united effort was based on five essential points: a revolutionary solution by means of democratic procedures; organization of the leaders outside and of the work to be done within the country; union of the emigrant groups with the same democratic spirit; equilibrium of revolutionary sympathies between the different social classes and between military and civilian groups; counteraction against annexionist propaganda which might defeat the revolutionary plan.

The previous year General Gómez had witnessed the failure of his project begun in 1885, and not without bitterness had he abandoned his efforts in a proclamation to the Cubans. His reply to the New York committee was that of a soldier always ready to occupy "my place in the line of combat for the sake of Cuban independence, with no other ambition than that of having the Cubans love my men and remember me tomorrow with affection."

Martí possessed the virtue of knowing how to wait, a virtue which bore magnificent fruits in politics as in everything else. If it seemed that the time to organize had come he was ready to work. In his heart he had no faith in those incomplete, rootless attempts which appeared sporadically and were born more from the desire for personal glory than from faith in their efficacy. He was interested in maintaining connections, arousing enthusiasm and keeping watch over the awakening of Cuban feeling in order to direct it along the only road that would be possible in the long run. Flor Crombet was in Key West in April, 1888, and he tried to arouse the emigrant colony, which he found "in a state of complete demoralization." Martí encouraged him in that work because Key West must be prepared when the time came for action. He did not falter in this propaganda. Diego Vicente Tejera embarked for Europe in May, and two friends accompanied him on board, Gabriel de Zéndegui and Martí. The boat sailed late at night, and the three friends walked about on deck awaiting the moment of departure. When he said good-by, Martí told Tejera:

"The Cubans in Paris are more asleep than those of New York. Speak to them a great deal of war, my friend, even if they think you're mad. We must instill the idea of war in the Cuban mind."

The recently founded Hispano-American Literary Society was preparing a program in honor of its president, Santiago Pérez Triana, a Colombian. It was suggested that Martí preside. Martí did not think it best to take part in the program because of his political reputation and the accusation that had already been leveled against the Society, that of being the instrument of the Cuban revolutionists. Insistence finally obliged him to yield, and on Saturday, June 16, before a huge audience representing different countries in America, the program was held with Martí as presiding officer. His presentation of Pérez Triana was an analysis of the famous Colombian's life. With exquisite strokes he painted the portrait of the educator of two generations, the man who descended from the presidential chair to become again a plain citizen, loved by his compatriots, the statesman who thought in terms of America, the founder of a literary school. Martí revealed his own extensive knowledge of Colombian letters. The fiesta concluded by the reading of *Los Heróes del Polo,* filled with generous thoughts.

In July patriotic efforts were renewed, and the club called *Los Independientes* was organized under the leadership of Juan Fraga with the purpose of establishing a war fund to be used when the opportune time came. Flor Crombet and Martí, both of whom attended the meeting, had some differences of opinion which did not become serious. In September, plans were begun for the celebration of October 10. A circular was sent out to the Cubans inviting them to a preliminary meeting in which they would decide on "the best way to celebrate their country's fiesta without partiality or neglect."

The only precedent of this program was an analogous fiesta in 1884. Estrada Palma again presided, as he had then, and a large audience filled the auditorium of the Masonic Hall. Martí was in charge of the program. As he was about to step onto the rostrum a small group which had purposely placed itself near the entrance began shouting so that Martí could not make himself heard, asking to have Señor Armas speak. One voice rose above the others: "Let Armas speak! He's a patriot!"

The resulting excitement apparently did not disturb Martí, who yielded the floor to Armas. When the latter had finished, Martí took the floor. It was evident that his firm ideas, manifested since his separation from the Gómez-Maceo plans, provoked this unjust accusation.

Martí's address that night was certainly not the one he had planned, but rather the one which circumstances required. His words and ideas were serene and condensed. He spoke of passions, of an incomplete partial policy that was "lenient toward enemies and despotic toward its own people," of "civilian or military tyrannies," but he also spoke of firm adherence to principles, of confidence in the ideal.

And in concluding the address, he spoke these final, decisive words:

"We are the check on future despotism and the only true, effective adversary of present despotism. . . . We unite what others divide. We do not die. We are the reserves of the fatherland!"

19. America for Humanity

At the end of the year 1888 Martí was honored by two distinctions from American nations. He was made a corresponding member of the Academy of Science and Fine Arts of San Salvador, and the Press Association of Buenos Aires named him as its representative in the United States and Canada, "with full power to make reciprocal agreements in the name of the Association with societies in those nations."

From Mexico the new staff of *El Partido Liberal,* which was no longer in the hands of Colonel Villada, expressed an interest in continuing to publish Martí's news-letters. He received an offer from *La Opinión Pública* of Uruguay. Martí sent his first contribution, concerning the Washington centenary celebration, on April 18, 1889.

Martí had occasion to offer a bold, striking defense of Cuba when the Philadelphia *Manufacturer* printed and the New York *Evening Post* reprinted with approving comments, an article that was depreciatory and insulting to the Cubans. Their pretext was that they wanted to make it publicly known that they did not desire the annexation of Cuba and that it would not be advisable for the United States. After alluding to the Cubans' effeminacy and aversion to work, the article stated:

"They do not know how to take care of themselves. They are lazy, morally deficent and incapable by nature and by experience of assuming the responsibilities of citizenship in a great, free republic."

The commentary of the *Evening Post* condensed its endorsement in one phrase: "These arguments are practically the same ones we should have employed had not the *Manufacturer* done so first."

Martí replied to the double offense with a letter to the editor of the *Evening Post*, not to discuss the annexation of Cuba, for no Cuban who valued his dignity could wish to see his country united with another whose leaders held such opinions of him, but to proclaim loudly that Cuba was not "a nation of wretched vagabonds or immoral pygmies" as it had been portrayed. Using arguments with which the North American people themselves were familiar, he answered the hard phrases, justifying the victims of attack.

Was it not providential, this attack on the dignity of the Cuban man at a time when the annexation campaign was growing stronger with the support of those who sincerely believed that that might be the solution of Cuban problems? According to the Philadelphia newspaper, a lack of virility and self-respect was demonstrated by the apathy with which the Cuban had submitted for so long to Spanish oppression. How vigorously Martí responded, and with what efficacy and moderation he in turn accused the accusers!

". . . And the sad truth is that in all probability we should have renewed our efforts successfully if it were not for those among us who favored annexation and held the unmanly hope of obtaining liberty without paying the necessary price for it; and if it were not for the others who feared, with reason, that our dead, our sacred memories, our blood-soaked ruins would serve no other end than to fertilize the soil for the growth of a foreign plant."

A few days later he sent out a pamphlet entitled *Cuba and the United States* containing the two insulting articles, which he had translated into Spanish, followed by his *Vindication of Cuba*. This letter, which he said was written not by him but by his country, revealed his intellectual energy.

Wherever there was a great idea to encourage, an error to correct, praise to give, there was Martí. Now it was considered obligatory to consult with him and call on him. He always presided over the patriotic meetings, and his judgment was considered sound because he looked ahead, because he foresaw the country's ills and knew how to eliminate them before they could take root.

America for Humanity

A group of Cuban Negroes attempted to organize a society. Rafael Serra, outstanding for his good judgment, admired Martí and expressed to him his objection to founding a society with purely recreational ends. Martí agreed with him and recalled a group in Madrid which attempted to organize an analogous society, met with opposition and was disbanded. *La Liga,* the League, as the new organization would be called, should be founded for the purpose of education and advancement, and in it lessons in equality and generosity should be taught. For fear that his enthusiasm might be taken for meddling or adulation or a desire for popularity, Martí had not expressed himself fully concerning social problems. But this was the propitious moment for him to say that such associations must be used as a point of departure toward the right goal:

"For our goal is not so much a mere political change as a sound, just, social constitution, without demagogical flattery or the pride of a potentate. And let us never forget that the greater the suffering the greater the right to justice, and that men's prejudices and social inequality cannot take precedence over the equality which nature has created."

Gonzalo de Quesada, a youth who had felt intense admiration for Martí ever since his first contacts with him, founded the semi-monthly periodical, *La Juventud* (Youth) in May. Trujillo's *Avisador Hispanoamericano,* in a note greeting its appearance, alludes to the new colleague's profession of faith, which seemed to him "written by a master hand," referring doubtless to Martí. A few days afterward, the *Avisador* inaugurated its own new presses, and there Martí had occasion to praise work, constancy, the desire for progress, the doing of good by the sons of Cuba.

The good man, as Trujillo's newspaper called Martí, was the friend of children. He had thought a great many things about them which he had never been able to say. But in his new magazine, *La Edad de Oro* (The Golden Age), which he was able to publish, thanks to the generous Dacosta Gómez, it was evident that he could speak the language of children in such a way as to move men.

The children of America were his friends; he addressed himself to them. But he gave them something that would not only amuse them, it would stir their potential manliness. "We are working for the children because the children are those who know how to love, because the children are the hope of the world." Perhaps he had never before written any pages as lovingly as these of *The Golden Age*.

As he saw the possibility and necessity of war approaching, he made it the subject of his speeches: "We must speak of war to the women, that they may resign themselves, and to the men, that they may think about it." For promises could no longer be believed in good faith. The time had come for "the master, prepared, and the servant, unprepared," to meet each other face to face. In his address he quoted those words of Martos, the Spanish politician, in the memorable interview ten years ago in Madrid: "There is no room for both of us there. It is either you or we."

The press had expressed the opinion that no harm could come to Spanish America from the Pan-American Congress planned for November, 1889. On the contrary there was talk of reciprocal benefits to be derived from the establishment of steamship lines, banking facilities, a monetary unit, arbitration agreements and a "powerful league which will command the respect of Europe, always conquering and enslaving."

Never had Martí known more troubled times. Beset with fear, he glimpsed dangers which kept him awake. Toward the end of August a commercial newspaper, *Export and Finance,* interested in the increase of commercial relations between the United States and the Spanish American countries, printed an article about him as consul of Uruguay. Martí spoke favorably of friendship and commercial dealings between the American nations, but he stated his opposition to the intervention of politics in the discussions of the Conference:

"I have been very displeased to note that some newspapers and a few individuals have attempted to alarm the Spanish American republics with the idea that the United States wishes to oblige them to do business with them because they (the United States) constitute the natural market to supply their needs. I am also displeased by the more or less vague allusions to secret designs of the United States against the economic independence of Spanish America."

The representatives of the Argentine Republic, Roque Sáenz Peña and Manuel Quintana, and the representative of Uruguay, Alberto Nin, were, from the very beginning, in contact with Martí, the correspondent of the most important Argentine newspaper and the consul of Uruguay. One of the first interviews took place on September 26. Dr. William H. T. Hughes, manager of a steamship agency, gave a banquet for the delegates of the two American nations. It was attended by persons connected with the Congress, and Martí was invited in his capacity of Uruguayan Consul. Martí formed a very good opinion of the delegates from the southern countries, whom he advised to be watchful in the coming conference in order to combat the ambition of Blaine, who was counting, with evil intentions, "on the complicity of the little avaricious states of our America." He was comforted by the attitude of reserve which they maintained, their energetic opposition to the nomination of Blaine for president of the Conference. They had not come to serve either outside interests or their own, to sell themselves or put on a display of submissiveness.

The Conference opened on October 2. On the following day an excursion was begun through the cities of the Union with incessant celebrations and speeches. The group was back in Washington on November 15. The Argentine delegates did not attend the "pompous six weeks' fiesta."

Martí noticed that the Conference had caused a rising tide of feeling concerning annexation. In *La Discusión* of Havana a letter was published concerning a visit paid to Blaine with the purpose of promoting annexation, which was already promised. The letter was signed with Martí's initials. In Cuba it was believed that he wrote the letter and that revolutionists in New York were making arrangements with the North American government. Martí even received offers from agencies as a result of this trick. The Inter-American Congress seemed to him dangerous for America or at least futile. And for Cuba he could see no other advantage than the possibility of obtaining from the United States the declaration that "Cuba should be independent." Further, as matters stood he believed it necessary, in fact inevitable, for the Cuban question to be presented before the Congress. The United States stood upon Cuba's threshhold like an enigma, and a people in that state of uncertainty "needed to solve the enigma." It was necessary to exact from the United States a promise to respect the rights which the Cubans would know how to conquer with their own energy before plunging into an inevitable war which "might be rendered futile by their neighbors' tacit determination to oppose it again in order to leave the Island in such a condition that they could later lay hands on it." He thought about writing a petition to the Conference, with signatures that would command attention, as a way of forcing the necessary declaration for future action, although he did not expect the United States to make a decision that could hurt their own interests. But that was what his political duty at that time advised him to do. When this idea occurred to him he received news of another measure being taken in Washington. It was directed principally by José Ignacio Rodríguez. Rodríguez sincerely believed the United States capable of taking Cuba out of Spain's hands and then giving her the freedom she did not know how to win for herself. "This faith of yours is generous," Martí exclaimed, "but as a rational being I cannot share it." And what kind of position would Cuba occupy in America "as an artificial nationality created for strategic reasons?" He wanted "a firmer foundation for his people."

As the bugbear of annexation disappeared he became more calm and began to recover his faith in the prudence and pride of the American nations. And he became so proud of the manner in which the men of his America commanded respect that he thought that the foundations of what he called the new America had already been laid.

As an American he had something to be proud of: the Argentinians who had inspired such respect for the nations of his America. Roque Sáenz Peña's phrase—America for humanity—was the Spanish-speaking republics' most beautiful expression of Americanism. And that phrase, which caused so much comment, was inspired by Martí.

America for Humanity

During that winter "when through ignorance or faith or fear or courtesy" the Spanish American nations met in Washington "beneath the fearful eagle," his anxiety would not let him live in peace until the prudence of the nations of his America quieted him. During those moments he turned again to writing poetry. In order to restore his spirit and his body he went to the country. "Streams flowed and clouds gathered." He wrote verses. He wrote his *Versos Sencillos* (Simple Lines).

The anxiety of waiting for his son in Venezuela gave birth to *Ismaelillo*. The concern which this dangerous congress caused him gave origin to the *Versos Sencillos*.

La Liga was to be what Serra and Martí wanted. The date of the inauguration was set for Wednesday, January 22, 1890, at 178 Bleeker Street. If his reputation as a defender of just causes, a friend of the humble, and a champion of progress and liberty had already won him a special place in the hearts of the Cubans, the members of the League also showed that night in an eloquent manner, that Martí was close to their hearts. What he desired was to be truly useful in the new undertakings which he considered the only way of facing the future. The League had its evening work distributed throughout the week: Tuesdays and Thursdays for primary education, Wednesdays for literary conversation, two Fridays a month for a lecture on a special topic by one of the members. Martí not only contributed his knowledge, he was the inspiration, the guide. He looked for teachers, increased membership, helped overcome difficulties. He put all his enthusiasm and vigilance into this project as one of his best. The teacher and the students sat in a semi-circle around a table. Gonzalo de Quesada, Barranco and Trujillo taught English, grammar and history. Thursday was Martí's day. He would find his pupils waiting impatiently for him when he entered the classroom with hurried steps and his hands full of books and newspapers. These were truly heart-warming moments for Martí. Affectionately he pressed their dark, calloused hands. He was not one of those who sought connections that would bring them pomp and recompense.

Martí's class was encyclopedic. On his table were the papers which his pupils had written without signing their

Martí

names. Each student indicated the topics he wanted discussed. Martí examined and arranged them, read them and then praised those that deserved it, in his precise, sober way. He pointed out the errors gently. He approached the different themes serenely, precisely. Martí had not written books of philosophy, but he was himself true philosophy. His respect for man, his belief in his essential goodness, his optimistic hope for the future were a constant inspiring lesson. He had "faith in human betterment, in a future life, in the utility of virtue." That was why he was there, facing those eyes avid for light.

If he spoke of the fatherland it was evident that he was moved by something more than shallow patriotism. He thought of freedom, but not as an end in itself. Beyond freedom was the nationality, the Cuban nationality which must be forged out of the desire of his compatriots. One could live in a free country and nevertheless have little awareness of one's nationality. Therefore, he repudiated the country obtained indirectly, for reasons of strategy or because of the condescension of a foreign power. He wanted a country that was fought for and won by the efforts of its sons, one that could respect itself and be respected by others. The Cuban nation could be built only with pride in being a Cuban and a constant desire to be a better one. That pride, that duty was what he wanted to infiltrate in other souls.

And the social aspect? That was a part of the political side in Cuba, as everywhere. He did not fear it, for "the justice and the weight of things are remedies that do not fail." But in this, as in everything, only justice has rights, "injustice falls by its own weight." He left everything to man, man who was the measure of everything.

There were needs of society that must be met "if one wishes to make a realistic study of the Cuban problem." The colored man must be treated "according to his qualities as a man; the worker "as a brother," with the "consideration and rights which assure peace and happiness in a nation."

A few months after the League was opened, Martí was appointed as a Spanish teacher at Central High School in New York, at 74 East Sixty-Fourth Street. He worked from 7 to 9 at night, but he did not let that interfere with his

Thursday lessons at the League. Serra entertained his pupils until Martí came.

He kept receiving honors from America. Argentina, upon Roque Sáenz Peña's recommendation, named him her consul in New York on July 24, 1890, and on the thirtieth of the same month Paraguay conferred an analogous position upon him.

Disquieting news came from Cuba. It was said that revolutionary unrest was growing. Preparations were being made. Maceo was given a triumphal reception in Havana and the province of Oriente. In New York the club *Los Independientes* organized a program in order to take up a new collection. Martí spoke at the program, held on June 16. But the revolutionary effervescence which had been noted on the Island soon passed, and everything went back to normal when Polavieja took command at the end of August. One of his first measures was to deport Maceo. The deportation of Crombet and Angel Guerra soon followed. In October the traditional invitation to celebrate the patriotic date was again sent around. The slow, silent work of attracting followers and building a foundation continued "reviving the self-respect of those who have lost it, reviving the faith of the impatient ones who faltered on the first day's march, stretching out a hand; . . ."

In December he received two real honors—that of President of the Hispano-American Literary Society and that of representative of Uruguay at the Monetary Conference at Washington. Martí's participation in the latter began in February of the following year, when the activities of the conference really began. During the interval he studied the background and familiarized himself with the designs of Blaine, the director of the maneuver, which was no less than an attempt to "standardize currency in America, a project whose basic purpose is to pour into the Latin American markets the millions and millions of dollars in silver minted in the United States of North America." From the beginning Martí played an important role in the conference. He was the leader of the opposition to the silver plans and later represented other groups. Everything that would give credit to Spanish America would benefit its future project because the United States would hinder the now imminent action of Cuba less if it respected the rest of Spanish America. Any union between the two continents would be harmful to the interests of the revolution. The delegates of the American nations witnessed reluctantly this struggle which they supposed would have no practical results. Only Martí and Blaine matched wits. Martí displayed such prudence and superior judgment that his propositions were always accepted by the Conference. When the North American delegation tried to disband as useless the Conference in which it had appeared so interested at first, it was Martí, supported by representatives of his America, who opposed them. When an attempt was made to hold discussions on many topics at one time or make rapid decisions, Martí dissuaded them. The delegates familiarized themselves with each article separately and studied the propositions beforehand. Caution was the weapon which Martí wielded. And not only did they agree to a preliminary study of the report presented by the North American delegation, but also the report of a commission made up of the representatives of Chile, Brazil, Argentina, and Uruguay. Martí, who represented the last country, was put in charge of drafting the proposed resolution.

The very attitude of the country which had invited them and considered the conference inopportune and premature but nevertheless wanted it to continue, seemed unacceptable, especially when the United States recognized the futility of any attempt at monetary union which did not have the approval of the European markets. Martí drew up a resolution that the work be brought to a close. First with little support and finally by unanimous vote his resolution was approved. It was a great lesson that the countries of his America were giving to the country that invited them and closed its doors on them when they arrived, for as Martí said, "Guests should declare loudly that they came out of courtesy, and not out of servitude or necessity in order that their host may not think that they come on bended knee or that they are puppets that go and come wherever the one who holds the strings desires."

He managed to overcome the great danger of leaving existent "an assembly which, because of the complex, delicate relationship between many Spanish American nations and the United States, might, in the hands of a ruthless candidate, yield to the United States more than befitted the respect and security of the Spanish American nations."

The Hispano-American Literary Society was going through a period of intense activity with Martí as president. His supporting officers were Benjamín Guerra and Gonzalo de Quesada. Their work was deeply American and a unifier of different Spanish American elements. The reputation of the society had grown a great deal, just as the prestige of the countries of the other America had risen after the two conferences.

Patriotic activities had been temporarily suspended, but the proximity of the tenth of October enlivened the atmosphere. In a meeting in Martí's house the program was planned and announcements were first made. The sheet which Martí circulated and *El Porvenir* published contained something more than an invitation. It contained the hope that the two years had not passed in vain.

Martí raised the Cuban exiles, who had grown strong in ten years of study, sacrifice and zeal, to the level of the Cubans on the Island who were suffering the despotism of an incorrigible master. His call was to reach all who felt the imminence of something invisible but real which was taking shape. The good Spaniard, the freedom-loving Spaniard who did not block the Cubans' road to triumph merited their esteem. Martí's speech was not, as it had been in previous years, simply an evocation. It had definite revolutionary force.

Martí was now the consul of Argentina. In a Spanish newspaper published in New York an attempt was made to show that his attitude as a Cuban fighting to obtain for his country the same thing that the fathers of the Argentine Republic obtained for theirs, was incompatible with his position as consul of that republic. There even was mention of the possibility that some conflict might arise as a result. He did not retain his post even for a moment. He resigned by telegram.

Martí

The club, *Los Independientes,* was hastening to begin its activities, moved by the enthusiasm which Martí's address aroused. Early in November elections were held, resulting in a new board made up of Benjamín Guerra and Gonzalo de Quesada under the presidency of the enthusiastic Juan Fraga.

At the same time Martí resigned from the presidency of the Hispano-American Literary Society, just as a session over which he had presided was drawing to a close. In this session he had presented, eloquently, prose and poetry by several Spanish American authors, among them Julián del Casal. His resignation was based on a delicate matter—his political reputation might cause trouble for the Society, and he wished to avoid that.

The Ignacio Agramonte Club of Tampa, like the other emigrant clubs, was going through a period of inactivity, but it felt that the time for action would soon come. The organization decided to hold a literary and artistic benefit meeting in order to raise funds. The president, the patriot Néstor L. Carbonell, was a fervent admirer of Martí. He was, however, a personal friend of Trujillo, and he wrote him on October 16 asking him to extend to Martí an invitation to come to Tampa and take part in the program. To him this invitation meant a great advance in his work of uniting with the same purpose all the Cuban exiles. At twelve o'clock on the night of the twenty-fifth he reached Tampa, and on the following day, in the *Liceo Cubano,* where all his compatriots from that city had gathered, eager to hear him, he gave a vigorous address. It was a call to the deepest feelings of the men who wanted and needed freedom, to join forces in an effort to win it. He spoke of the war, not as a momentary impulse which could fall into disorder, but as a war of necessity, the organized, strong war. Cuba longed for the war, she was consumed with impatience for the inevitable moment to arrive. And he concluded his speech by reducing to an absurdity the doctrine of decadence and little faith which was being preached in a recent book entitled *A Pie y Descalzo* (On Foot and Barefoot). Its purpose apparently was to spread discouragement, persuade the Cubans to abstain from serving their country out of fear of the tribulations of war. Dishonorable people paid by the Spanish government—that was what Martí called those who stirred up "fear of going barefoot, which is a very common thing now in Cuba, for between the thieves and their helpers, the only ones left who have shoes in Cuba are the accomplices and the thieves." That same evening, as a result of the fervor which Martí's inspiration had aroused and channeled, some "Resolutions Adopted by the Exiles of Tampa" were read and approved. They declared the urgent necessity of "uniting in a common, republican, free action, all honorable revolutionary elements." In that document the general ideas which should be the guiding principles of revolutionary action were stated. They were the same ideas for which Martí had been fighting since 1884.

On the following day, November 27, at a program organized by the Cuban Convention he gave his second speech. The "surge of a people on the march" seemed to fill the hall. It was not words of lamentation that they heard, but words of triumph after the storm: "Others lament necessary death; I believe in it as the pillow and the leaven and the triumph of life."

That same day the *Liga de Instrucción,* similar to the New York league, was formed and Martí was initiated into the *Liga Patriótica Cubana.* He left the next morning. An hour before his departure a farewell program was held for him in the *Liceo.* Here it was made very evident that he had aroused indescribable enthusiasm among the Cubans.

A Cuban worker of Key West, Angel Peláez, inspired by Martí's words, began to recruit friends to help him bring Martí to Key West. His enthusiasm was so great that he communicated it to several friends, who constituted a committee. They began collecting the necessary funds to organize programs. Although they met with little enthusiasm at the beginning, finally their insistence and faith triumphed, and the trip was made possible.

Martí was ill when he arrived at Tampa on December 24. From there he sent a telegram to Peláez. From Tampa to Key West he was accompanied by the boards of the Ignacio Agramonte Club and the Liga Patriótica. At four o'clock in the afternoon of the twenty-fifth they reached their destination. General José Francisco Lamadriz, one of the leaders of the Cuban war of 1868, advanced to greet Martí.

"I salute the past revolution," said Martí.

"I salute the new revolution," responded Lamadriz, touched by hopes of redeeming Cuba.

Amid flags and music and followed by a crowd, they went to Mme. Bolio's Hotel Duval, where Martí was to stay. In the evening a banquet was held in his honor, at which he spoke several times. The next day his increasing illness kept him in bed but did not prevent his receiving the commissions that visited him. With them he discussed the organization necessary in order to channel so many revolutionary impulses that were dispersed. In order to check his illness it was necessary to forbid him to speak. Dr. Palma, the physician attending him, forbade him to have visitors. Friday, January 1, the restriction was lifted, and the Cuban colony crowded into the hotel. January 3 at San Carlos the program was held. Martí and other patriots spoke. On the fourth, which dawned with the flags of Cuba and the United States hanging from many flagpoles, the Club Patria y Libertad held a celebration. The *Círculo Cubano,* presided over by Lamadriz, held a program the following night. Meanwhile there was no end to the meetings in his room at the Hotel Duval with the representatives of the political groups, eager to decide upon the program upon which their future country would be built. On the afternoon of the fifth there was a meeting in the Hotel Duval of the presidents of the different political groups of local Cuban separatists, as well as the official representatives of the political group known as the *Liga Patriótica Cubana* and the Ignacio Agramonte Club of Ibor City in Tampa. There were also men not affiliated with political clubs but considered elements favorable to the cause of the liberty and independence of Cuba. Martí presided and offered for the consideration and study of the junta the projected resolutions constituting the Bases of the Cuban Revolutionary Party which was to be formed outside of Cuba. The resolutions had been written and presented two days before by Martí and had met with the approval of Lamadriz, Poyo, and Figueredo. It had now been approved by all who composed the assembly on the night of January 4. After the examination and study of each of the different clauses and the formulation of observations as each saw fit, Martí moved that they confirm "their unanimous approval in all of its parts of the aforementioned political document." After this approval it was agreed that each of the presidents of the different groups represented there should submit the document to the respective clubs and also to the associations of independent political clubs of other localities. It was also agreed that the Statutes by which the party was to be governed should be drawn up by Martí.

On January 6 the people "were milling about in the shops, stores and homes." They were preparing to bid Martí farewell with a festival in the San Carlos theatre.

A disagreeable incident awaited him in New York: the letter which Enrique Collazo sent him and published, containing the allusions Martí had made in his speech on November 26 in Tampa—allusions to those who had sold themselves to interests, those who were discouraging the Cubans because they were being paid a salary by the Spaniards. Collazo's letter, which he suspected was instigated by Roa, the author of the book, *On Foot and Barefoot,* besides proposing that Martí's authority be taken away, attempted to prejudice the soldiers of the last war against the spirit of the new war. Martí's letter, which bared both the knavery and the knaves, served to make all their followers abandon them and join the revolutionary ranks. He received many demonstrations of loyalty as a result of the incident, and demonstrations of protest were made against Collazo's attitude.

Part V:

Decisive Years

20. The Revolutionary Party

The Cuban Revolutionary Party was the instrument of prestige and action which Martí needed in order to carry out his work. In New York he called a meeting of Cubans in Hardman Hall on the night of February 17, 1892, and delivered his speech entitled *Tampa and Key West*.

In the Bases of the Cuban Revolutionary Party he brought out the ideas which had been ripening for ten years of meditation upon the best way to realize his country's independence. In this document he described the character of the war, "which should be generous and brief, intended to assure through peace and work the happiness of the inhabitants of the Island," and the spirit of the Republic, which should be that of "a new people and a sincere democracy." Among the concrete proposals were those of "uniting in a continued, common effort the action of all Cubans living abroad," "fomenting sincere relations between the historical and political factors within and outside of the island," "spreading in Cuba knowledge of the spirit and the methods of the revolution," collecting funds and establishing discreet, beneficial relations with friendly nations.

The party was governed by his Statutes. According to these, it would "function through the independent associations, which are the bases of its authority, through a Council, constituted in each locality by the Presidents of all of the associations of that locality and through a Delegate and a Treasurer, elected annually by the Associations."

Martí often thought that his people were not ready. Apropos of Bolívar he said that sometimes nations are ready and the man to lead them does not appear, and again the man is ready and the people are not. This was the case with him. For a long time his life had been a preparation, a process of ridding himself of whatever was useless for his enterprise, of tenaciously seeking, on the other hand, everything that might be necessary to him. Since his second deportation to Spain he had said this in a letter to Viondi. This wait had lasted for over twelve years. Now the people were beginning to be ready.

All circumstances had been converging toward this point. At the opportune moment almost all the bonds were broken. He had neither consulates nor correspondence nor translations, nor anything to tie him to daily realities other than those realities that were to serve the cause of Cuban liberation.

For a long time he had tried to found a newspaper that would channel the work of the revolution. A newspaper was indispensable, especially when the cause of the Revolutionary Party was faced with an enemy. Enrique Trujillo, editor of the *Avisador Hispano-Americano,* dissatisfied with the centralizing organization which the Party stood for, declared his support of a "New York headquarters" and spread the idea that "Key West was trying to dictate to New York."

Patria appeared on March 14, 1892. Concerning the necessity of the war Martí explained his already well-known ideas with remarkable clarity and penetration:

"He is a criminal who promotes war in a country that does not need it, or fails to promote a necessary war."

He did not attack the Spaniards living in the country, but rather the representatives of "a nation incapable of governing a people who can only be happy without her." He interpreted the war as a political procedure, a saving of time and a re-establishment of the equilibrium necessary between an oppressor-nation and an oppressed nation. But the war which brought about a mere change of form would not be worth the sacrifice.

The Party did not consider itself established until the majority of the emigrant clubs had accepted it. In order to give it efficacy and enter into complete activity it was necessary to hold elections and announce the results. It was thought best to set the election date for April 8 and the proclamation of the elected officers for the tenth. Delays in settling details made him nervous. He began to fear that the war would not materialize. They had waited long enough. In *Patria* the campaign of haste grew more intense, and it became the gospel of the new policy. To a friend in Key West he wrote: "Publish, publish. Reach Cuba through all possible means. Wars travel on roads of paper."

The presidents of the Key West clubs, representing their associations, accepted the dates proposed for the elections of the Delegate and Treasurer and for "the solemn, unanimous proclamation of the fatherland."

April 8 Martí and Benjamín Guerra were elected Delegate and Treasurer. On the tenth the proclamation of the Cuban Revolutionary Party was made in all the clubs in Key West, Tampa, and New York. On the seventeenth, in New York, in Hardman Hall, the program of confirmation was held with Tomás Estrada Palma as president and Juan Fraga as president of the New York Council.

The propaganda of *Patria* was continuous. Everything that furthered the work found a place on its pages. Clubs multiplied, formed spontaneously in order to aid the Party by the methods which it had established, or the clubs already in existence revised their organization to conform to that of the party. Martí's correspondence multiplied in order to carry his message to all. No one must consider himself privileged above others, no one must feel unnecessary. That was the norm that he inculcated in his friends in Key West. And the message of *Patria* reached Cuba.

At the beginning of July when the newspaper was well established and everything was in order, Martí began his propaganda trips. He was received at Key West by a much greater crowd than the previous one, and feted by clubs, *liceos,* schools, receptions, and banquets. In Tampa the crowd at the overflowing Liceo poured out into the street to hear him. Then a procession of Spaniards passed by, hundreds of Spaniards declaring themselves in favor of Cuban independence.

Martí

Ocala reminded him of Cuba, and there Cubans lived happily. The Americans put on demonstrations for Martí, and he gave a speech in English. Then the excursion continued to Jacksonville. They were to visit the tomb of Padre Varela.* The founding of the Padre Varela Club marked his passage through the Cuban colony in Saint Augustine.

In New York Martí had had an opportunity to know Serafín Sánchez. At that time Sánchez had not yet established a house in the north and longed to do so in Key West. He asked Hidalgo Gato to help him earn a living. Serafín Sánchez later settled in Key West. Máximo Gómez carried on a constant correspondence with Serafín, in whom he had complete confidence. Martí's name was mentioned frequently in their letters, and it came up again in connection with the Collazo incident. At that time Gómez considered Martí haughty and incapable of marching in the same ranks with other men to whom he considered himself superior. But he recognized in him a great Cuban, and he considered him a patriot capable of fighting on the battlefields of Cuba for the redemption of his country. In regard to the turn that affairs were taking in Cuba, the General expressed himself emphatically:

"All of us, all men of arms . . . must be, or try to be, the most pacific in peace and simply wait for them to arm us and order us to the battlefield." Serafín informed Martí of Gómez' attitude, for he knew that Martí was counting on him as supreme commander. Martí was preparing for another trip. Those were very busy, hurried days. But before his trip he sent an agent to cover the province of Oriente and prepare the people of Camagüey and Havana. He had to keep many responsibilities in mind all at the same time: the necessity of keeping the clubs active and occupied so that they would not become lethargic, the collection of contributions, the great care with which they must proceed in order not to be considered imprudent, and ways of avoiding the intervention of the North American government in the armed organization of the Party, against which the Spanish government was protesting. He prepared manifestos addressed to the Island and to the north, and he pondered ways of

* Father Félix Varela, a distinguished Cuban educator and patriot. (Ed.)

avoiding the reefs of scanty resources without losing prestige. It would be necessary to knock at many doors when the time came, but first they must "find someone to whom the doors would be opened."

To Gerardo Castellanos, the first agent sent to the Island, he gave written instructions dated August 4, in which no detail of interest was lacking. He was to explain the greatness, extension, and energy of the Party, familiarize himself with all revolutionary elements, and restrain compromising impatience. He must explain the entire policy of the Party and the character of the war and above all check the danger of an impulsive and unprepared revolution under some regionalist caudillo. There were also precise details concerning persons and places.

August was drawing to a close. Martí had returned from a brief trip to Philadelphia, and was already planning a trip to Santo Domingo and an interview with Gómez. There were those who reminded him of past incidents, but there was not a particle of egoism or pride in him. He would go to see Gómez. Before departing he left his manifestos to Cuba and the United States and charged Fraga with the commemoration of October 10.

September 3 *Patria* published an article entitled *Recomendaciones,* containing the suggestions which Martí passed on to the clubs and council. In that same number of the newspaper a separate sheet was published entitled *The Delegate on His Journey.* Although his destination was not stated, it was known that he was going to meet Máximo Gómez.

September 11 he reached La Reforma, Santo Domingo, where the General lived. Gómez was, as always, awaiting the time when his services should again be needed by Cuba, and he would serve with the same disinterest and loyalty with which he served her in 1868. "The old general opened simultaneously his doors and his arms to me. And the old man embraced again, during a long silence, the traveler who had come a long way to see him and tell him of the need and affection his unhappy people felt for him." Their conversations, which reviewed the past and present, lasted for three days.

Martí

Many thought that Gómez harbored resentment against Martí because of the incident in 1884. But Gómez was like Martí, and he took his place beside him to accompany him in the great undertaking. They left together on the thirteenth for the city of Santiago de los Caballeros. There Martí wrote his letter to the General concerning the spirit of the Party, in the name of which he requested his cooperation, with no promise of any reward but "the pleasure of sacrifice and the probable ingratitude of men." Gómez' reply was decisive, in keeping with Martí's offer. Both documents had a single purpose: to make known on the Island and among the emigrants that General Gómez was at the service of the new liberating plan, and considered it a "high honor" to occupy the position which he had been offered at Martí's side.

On the fifteenth they parted. Martí went on to the capital of the republic and General Gómez returned to La Reforma. In his notes the General wrote: "The triumph of the Cuban revolution is a matter of concord and unification and, in my opinion, the work Martí has done up to now is quite consistent, for he is gradually obtaining the desired unification of the discordant elements." Martí talked with prominent people in the capital and received demonstrations of love and respect for Cuba, which was what he sought. On the nineteenth he left for Barahona; he wrote to the General before his departure. On the twenty-fourth he arrived at Haiti, where he remained until October 4, when he left for Jamaica. Everywhere he carried out his work of unification and enthusiasm. October 13 he left Jamaica for New York, arriving the eighteenth. At the League all the clubs met together, eager to hear about his travels. He went to the League "like the student that he was of social problems rather than a man of purely political background." He described the Spanish American homes, pointed out the political faults and merits of the peoples he had just visited, and put his finger on the critical problems of society. He gave a description of the shops, fields, and homes of enterprising Cubans. He spoke of the unrest in the cities of Haiti, and of the home of Máximo Gómez.

He left for Tampa and Key West on November 7. The result of his travels through the Antilles, his interviews with

The Revolutionary Party

Gómez and Maceo, the work under way and more firmly established than ever before added to the value of this trip to the places from which the vigorous impulse sprang. In conversations and speeches he left people's faith strengthened with the certainty that the plan was taking root. But something even more important obliged him to stay for several weeks in Florida. Through the people he received news of Cuba. Martí needed detailed information concerning conditions in the Island and needed to send emissaries. The proximity of Key West favored this contact. He communicated frequently with Juan Gualberto Gómez, the representative of the Party in Havana. After his interview with Gómez he had to send new agents to the Island, to give account of the disposition of the leaders.

In Tampa a serious incident put his life in danger. An attempt was made to poison him, but he realized it in time and spat out the poison. Nevertheless he had to take to his bed and prolong his stay. At the end of December he was in New York again but in very poor health.

At the end of January, 1893, Gerardo Castellanos returned from his second trip to the Island. Martí was so well satisfied with his first commission that when his month's service was up Castellanos left again to visit Camagüey and Oriente besides having interviews in Havana with prominent figures within the movement, especially with the indefatigable Juan Gualberto Gómez. His second visit was also very fruitful.

The autonomist campaign was stirring again in Cuba, and it was necessary to intensify the work of the Party. On January 31 in Hardman Hall a meeting was held with the purpose of proclaiming the absolute independence of the Cuban Revolutionary Party from the autonomist policy. In his speech Martí affirmed and demonstrated "the fundamental, proven negativeness of the system of autonomy," "the patent inadequacy of the autonomous system dependent on a tyrannical, distrustful nation in order to put Cuba and Puerto Rico in a position for feasible competition and free commerce with the sovereign active nations of the continent to which they belong." Autonomism was the expression of a period of discouragement and truce in a people emerging from a war in which they had prepared themselves for liberty. It could have only one mission: that of preparing for the triumph of revolutionary ideas. It had failed in this preparatory mission, appropriating what the revolution had conquered, to convert it into a mere attempt at a useless system.

Martí toured Florida again. His presence aroused the energy and enthusiasm that started everything moving. Clubs were created where he passed by, or they began a new life. On February 14 he appeared in Fernandina, on the twenty-second in Tampa, and on March 9 he was in Central Valley, with Tomás Estrada Palma. On the twenty-third he was back in New York. Wherever he went he wrote to Quesada, who was taking his place on *Patria*, and he gave him precise instructions. He was always vigilant, that an imprudent word might not reveal the true state of the revolutionary movement or the unrest of the times. His steps were followed. Just as in 1880, an attempt was made to introduce espionage into the very nucleus of directors. Martí knew that this had caused the failure of the other attempt. As Delegate he revealed only what it was best to have known. This procedure sometimes served to deceive the enemy or to make him believe that they were stronger than they really were. From Fernandina he wrote to Quesada: "I have received and answered the telegram concerning the maritime attempt. Fernandina faces the sea, and that is all the maritime attempt there was. Deny it vigorously; you have probably done so already. It is an excellent announcement. When we leave they will not know it." He had to fight too for the contributions from the clubs in order to build up the war treasury which would soon be necessary.

The Party had proclaimed through its Delegates its opposition to all premature attempts, and it considered it a treasonable undertaking to send to Cuba a weak movement which would simply help the Spanish government which desired and fomented it. Nevertheless there were rumors that the rebellion was to break out in Cuba on March 20. *Patria* denied the news, declaring that "there had not been recently between the Cubans on the Island and the Revolutionary Party any agreement to foment or permit an armed movement which would compromise by its inadequacy the success of the war which is being organized . . ." What was the cause of this rumor? Was it that the tenth of October, the date of elections, was approaching? The Spanish newspapers commented on Martí's revolutionary attempts and plans for an expedition to Cuba under his leadership. He was portrayed as megalomaniac, a man ambitious for notoriety, a rabble-rouser, a "petty hero who has found around him a herd of Cubans and wishes, in the manner of a providential liberator, to fall as an intruder upon his country, which does not recognize him, and disturb the calm of the honorable authorities of the Island."

The purpose was evident: to arouse suspicion, create the idea that the Party permitted Martí to make immoderate, personal use of its facilities. In his article entitled *Persona y Patria* (The Individual and the Country), he dispelled all such thoughts. If there was something great in the Revolutionary Party it was the fact that "in order to found a republic it has operated as a republic."

In the elections on April 10 the Delegate and Treasurer were re-elected by unanimous vote. It was necessary to go on traveling, with this new confidence and pride in the unity and concerted action that he had just seen. In Philadelphia, where the Cuban group was "very loyal, and growing," there were interviews and a meeting. In the railroad stations he wrote on his lap the articles for *Patria*. By telegram he kept track of the number of columns needed to complete the newspaper. Martí wrote of these matters from Atlanta to Gonzalo de Quesada and went on to New Orleans, where he would not have a moment to himself. It would do no harm, it was decided, "to let the rumor pass around subtly that he had gone to see Maceo."

An unexpected event changed his plan and forced him to give up the trip: the news that was circulated on May 1 about a revolutionary movement headed by the Sartorius brothers and initiated on April 24 in Oriente. When Martí was en route to Key West to "face difficulties" he telegraphed to Quesada and Guerra to disclaim all connection of the Party with the uprising, which was "spontaneous or precipitated deliberately by Spain in order to catch the Island off guard." Although enthusiasm in the emigrant colonies rose to fever pitch and club funds were rapidly increased, the movement was put down in a few days. Martí remained at Key West in order to have information close at hand concerning the importance of the movement and the possibility of extending it to the entire Island if circumstances favored such action. It did not happen that way, but he converted the defeat of the Sartorius brothers, who were "hasty or deceived," into money and unification without discrediting the Party.

On May 20 he was back in New York. On the twenty-fourth in Hardman Hall he gave an address intended to point out the isolated character of the uprising of the rebel group, who had not acted according to orders or advice from the Revolutionary Party but simply acted on their own initiative. In spite of that, although the Party was strongly opposed to all partial, inadequate revolutions, the uprising, had it continued, would have received aid from the Party "like any other movement by which the country showed its desire to be free." And he reaffirmed his opinion, and that of the Party as well, that the revolution should not be attempted until they had made the necessary arrangements and acquired the resources necessary for their triumph. Martí's idea was not to discourage the impetuous ones, but to make sure the revolution was not discredited, and to assure the Island that thorough preparations had been made.

That night Martí met Rubén Darío, who had just arrived in New York. Gonzalo de Quesada went to Darío's hotel to meet him and took him to Hardman Hall. There he led him along a dark, narrow hall to a brightly lighted room where Darío suddenly found himself in the arms of a man of "small stature, an enlightened face, and a voice both sweet and compelling." Rubén Darío was escorted to the stage and greeted with applause from the audience. That night Martí and Darío went out for a walk together. They had gone only a few steps when someone called to Martí. "I have a little remembrance for you," said the Negro workman who approached him with humble affection. He gave him a silver pen. Darío and Martí continued their walk toward a Cuban home where Darío, as he listened to Martí, thought: "I have never found, even in Castelar, such an admirable conversationalist."

Martí had notified Máximo Gómez from Key West that he would visit him as soon as he finished urgent business in New York. He had written the same to Maceo from New Orleans when the Oriente events detained him. Two days after his speech, March 26, he embarked. On June 3 he set foot for the second time on the soil of Santo Domingo in order to inform General Gómez of the true progress of events. His report pleased the General a great deal, for he could see that every minute the time for action was drawing near. Two days later Martí continued on his journey.

On July 30 Martí reached Costa Rica. Pío Víquez, editor of *El Heraldo de Costa Rica,* welcomed him with a moving editorial tribute to the "illustrious Cuban" in which he told of the surprise he received from the "presence of that energetic American fighter for the triumph of the democratic rights and the culture of the peoples of America." On Sunday, July 2, he was given a banquet, and on the third, accompanied by Antonio Maceo he attended a lecture by Antonio Zambrana. Friday, July 7, he gave a lecture at the School of Law at the invitation of the Association of Students. He developed his theme around the originality of American life, the future of the continent, the mission of its youth. He referred to the artistic and political decadence of Spain and finished with a reference to Cuba, preparing to break her chains forever. At seven o'clock on the morning of July 8 he left Costa Rica.

He was bound for New York, but first spent a few days in Panama. In connection with his stay in Panama, the government in Madrid on September 20 issued a circular Royal Order which was transmitted to the Minister in Colombia. The vice-consul of Panama had already informed him of Martí's visit to the Isthmus and "the meetings which he organized among the Cubans of that locality, who favor the revolution. Their activities were reduced to unimportant outward show, after which Martí turned to the Republics of the Pacific." The Minister, in obedience to the order he received, recommended that the Vice-consul exercise "the greatest zeal in watching every move or activity of these groups." He recommended these precautions "especially since the serious turn that events in Morocco seem to be taking might give them the illusion that they have a good opportunity to promote an uprising."

As Martí left Costa Rica he was happy over Maceo's acceptance of the part which Gómez had planned for him to take in the revolution. Maceo received the instructions and was determined to fill his post as soon as the time came. When Martí arrived in the north, worried for fear the emigrant groups there had lost enthusiasm or unfavorable reports might have come from the Island, he was greeted on the contrary by the most favorable news. He gave a minute account of everything to Gómez in a letter dated August 29.

No sooner had he written Gómez that optimistic letter than he left for Key West. The prosperity which had provided a smiling appearance a year ago had changed to a state of increasing penury. The economic crisis which the U.S. was suffering was evident everywhere, and many factories in Key West were shut down. The exodus began. Contributions to the Party decreased considerably.

In Havana, at the Palace of the Captain General, some of the leaders of the 1868 revolution met and declared their decision to await the results of the Maura reforms. In order to strengthen morale the Tampa emigrants met on September 18 under the direction of the Council of the Revolutionary Party. They adopted resolutions declaring their firm decision to fight for the independence of Cuba by means of the separatist revolution no matter what obstacles they might meet. This resolution was inspired by Martí. His trip, purposely kept secret, produced the necessary results. When he returned toward the end of September he began preparations for the fiesta on October 10, another opportunity to strengthen morale.

From Havana Martí received news of the propaganda of the Cubans who had gone over to the side of the Spanish government and accused him of speculation with Party funds and said that he disdained the leaders of the past war. More than once he received letters from his own family revealing the attacks that were being made upon him. He could not answer. His friends, who knew the truth about his life, and the very men of the past war who knew of his devotion to his work must answer for him. Gómez had written in a letter: "I shall tell them that he is like us."

A new uprising took place at the beginning of November, 1893, in the region of Cienfuegos. The leader was Federico Zayas, feared on account of his popularity and his impulsiveness. Martí had restrained him twice, in September and in October, and he had made him promise to wait. Now, as previously, Martí did not begrudge credit to the uprising but he did not recognize it as a product of the orders of the Party. His tactics were the same as always: to give aid if the rebellion should maintain itself and have Gómez and Maceo ready to descend upon Cuba. This was not the war which he had prepared or desired. "I should like a wholesome, strong war, planned with all prudence, but when the war overleaps our preparations I think we should be prepared to aid it and to foresee the disastrous results of delay or, worse still, the criminal abandonment of those on the battlefield awaiting only enough opportune aid to give the world a new, free people." A few days later Martí learned that Zayas had obeyed instructions intended to precipitate war and cause its failure.

Martí visited Philadelphia, Tampa, Key West, and Jacksonville again in December. His presence brought renewed activity. He wrote Quesada, who was carefully looking after details concerning *Patria*:

"There should not be a single ungrammatical sentence. Commas help in this respect. Cultivate commas."

Cultivate commas and at the same time hold in his hands all the threads of great events that were preparing a definitive change for a people!

He had no sooner left Key West than an unexpected conflict arose which might have dangerous consequences: the strike of the Cuban workers in the factory *La Rosa Española*, aggravated by the introduction of Spanish foremen brought from Havana. In order to solve one problem and keep the factory from transferring its activities to Tampa, local authorities went to Havana and obtained workers to take the place of the strikers. The conflict grew worse, and Martí intervened, putting the defense of the Cuban case in the hands of the North American lawyer, Horatio Rubens. The introduction of new men to end the strike constituted a violation of the country's laws. But Martí saw in the incident more than a mere conflict over unemployment, he saw the division among the workers, favored by the North Americans, who controlled the majority of the factories and by Spain, who was financing this industry. Thus began a year which Martí considered decisive. The earlier uprisings and then this new conflict increased his anxiety.

For months he had been tormented by the fear that Máximo Gómez might not appreciate the real situation of the country and the real necessity for direct, rapid action on his part. The plan made with him and Maceo was to "attack Cuba from three directions at once." Finally, Gómez seemed to be receiving confirmatory notices and fixed the date for action vaguely for the end of February, 1894. In accordance with this plan Martí was to put "into the hands of each leader the necessary means to send to each one his private order, thus providing the uniformity which is indispensable."

Even from the hard blow at Key West he wished to derive some immediate benefit. When the incident ended with the transfer of the factory that had caused the trouble to Tampa, more than 400 laborers were left without work, and danger threatened. Martí foresaw the slow disintegration and disappearance of the revolutionary capability of Key West. But that very danger and that hard blow meant a fiercer, more determined resolution to win a country for themselves. He published in Spanish and in English his vigorous article *A Cuba!* which appeared in *Patria* on January 27, 1894.

Those were sad days for the once prosperous Key West, and Martí had felt the people's suffering as deeply as they did, but his prudence was equal to his indignation and sorrow. On January 18 he left Tampa, where he had stayed during the conflict in order to be near but not near enough to make matters worse.

Toward the end of March he wrote Maceo concerning final details. The understanding was that he was to send to a place they would agree upon with Gómez the necessary amount for Maceo's departure to Cuba. In his letter he expressed his opinion of the situation at that time: "The entire mass is boiling, and I do not think it can be kept boiling very long, or that this thing can be done by isolated thrusts. We must do it before it is expected and all at once." But Gómez did not share Martí's excitement over the situation. Gómez proceeded cautiously and suggested making a trip to New York. Martí hinted at the danger of being too much in evidence or revealing immediate military arrangements.

It was almost April 10, the date for Party elections. Two days earlier, the eighth, the steamer *State of Texas* arrived in New York bringing Máximo Gómez, accompanied by his son, Francisco. Gómez had decided to make the trip in order to see for himself the progress of the revolutionary plans in the north and know the true position of the emigrant colonies. On April 10 the New York Council met with Gómez present. Martí and Benjamín Guerra were re-elected. As presiding officer Martí gave a moving speech welcoming Gómez, whom he considered the prototype of unlimited abnegation for the redemption of Cuba.

Gómez left for Santo Domingo on April 21. His son, Francisco, stayed with Martí. Together they set out for Florida on May 12. There was a meeting at San Carlos the nineteenth. In his speech Martí pointed out that everywhere spirits were vibrant with eagerness, and it was at last necessary that their plans be executed.

They arrived in New Orleans on the thirtieth. The boat was to sail at dawn the thirty-first. Martí spent the early hours of the morning writing, with young Francisco at his side trying to help him. He counted the letters and notes written that night: 48, and there were still more to write.

The steamer, *Alberto Dumois*, left on the thirty-first. On June 5 they entered Puerto Limón, Costa Rica, and on the seventh arrived at San José where Martí invited the

Cubans to a meeting on the tenth and founded the Antonio Maceo Club. On the eleventh they went on to Puntarenas, where he met with Antonio Maceo and his brother, José, and with Crombet and Cebreco. He stayed in Puntarenas until the eighteenth—seven days of activity and exceptional attentions, of which he carried away "all sorts of pleasant memories." He also prevented a duel that had already been arranged between José Maceo and Flor Crombet, winning them over through his appeal to their enthusiasm for the work they had in common.

On the twenty-first they reached Panama. The next day they left for Jamaica hoping to have news in Kingston. Everywhere there were codes to be used in urgent telegrams, committees that visited Martí, emigrant colonies giving him a good reception. And everywhere, as in Kingston, where they arrived the twenty-fifth, contributions were gladly made. Each place paid the amount which Martí had estimated beforehand to be necessary for their needs, now imminent. On the twenty-sixth they sailed for New York, where they landed on July 7. They had not received all the contributions they had expected. Key West had not given a cent, although it had subscribed to three thousand pesos. It was necessary to make a new effort "to put something more into the treasury." Martí decided to go to Mexico. On July 15 he was in New Orleans waiting for a boat.

El Universal of Mexico, on July 22, published a notice concerning his visit.

He spent very few days there. He paid a touching visit to the Mercado home, filled with affectionate memories. With the aid of the few Cubans in Mexico City he tried to make up the deficit in the funds. But his old friends also came to his aid. He obtained the amount he desired and could have had even more. He visited an "important person," General Porfirio Díaz, President of the Republic, and explained to him "with a prudent combination of pleas and self-respect" the significance of the enterprise, without revealing its penurious state in order that they might not be looked down upon. He left Díaz "disposed to help them in case they were desperate" with "the way open to future possibilities." He met with his old friends at a gathering of writers presided over by Justo Sierra in the Bouret book store.

Martí personally obtained aid from Veracruz during the few hours he spent there on July 26. A Spaniard—José M. Pérez Pascual—was one of the most generous contributors. Everything was ready, "as if at any minute the final order should come and the reins be released," when he reached New York early in August. From Paris Betances wrote to him insisting that it would be worthwhile for him to make a trip there. The gravity of the situation prevented him from leaving. He was preparing ships and weapons and making incessant tours of the emigrant colonies in Florida. In Cuba everything would be ready within two months. The arrangement of details to attain unanimity kept him anxious and nervous. He allayed his impatience by anticipating contingencies through letters and telegrams of warning. He continued to be vigilant without relaxing his eagerness or his action for a moment, consumed by fatigue or radiant with enthusiasm when he fingered a good report and it seemed to him that the road opened before him straight and clear. "Today my life is like the vortex of all of our torment," he told Maceo. And the greatest of all his worries was the possibility of error: "With our poverty and difficulties we must not err." On October 27 he still lacked five thousand pesos, which he requested of Hidalgo Gato, guaranteeing their repayment "if you will advance them to Cuba."

The delay continued, against his will. Gómez was still in contact with the Island, and Martí's order was slow in arriving. The proximity of the revolution gave rise to new obstacles and intrigues. There was talk again of reforms in Cuba. And the greatest risk was that "such a strong, beautiful movement might fall into the hands of its enemies." Martí's plan was to go from Santo Domingo to Cuba with General Gómez. Gómez tried to dissuade him, believing that he could be more useful in the north. Martí insisted. He knew that he could be useful enkindling enthusiasm, uniting, destroying obstacles. And above all, what authority could he have if at the hour of danger he did not keep his promises and join those who were facing danger?

Martí

He wanted to say good-by to his mother before his departure. He sent Martín Herrera to bring her to him at Key West. But Doña Leonor could not go. Almost blind, she was about to be operated on at that very time. On November 18, when Martí was about to return to New York, he wrote from Key West to her doctor, an old schoolmate:

"Take good care of her for me, for now, you see, she has no son. The son that nature gave her is using the last years of his life in an effort to save his greater mother."

During those final moments difficulties arose at every step, events accumulated, things were done and a moment later seemed to be undone. Financial difficulties increased. Everything cost twice the estimated sum, and they had only enough resources for the expenses predicted. In order to satisfy demands, allay suspicions and face unjust attacks he could not have a moment of calm. Instructions were put into final form. A plan was formulated and communicated to the Island through Juan Gualberto Gómez, a plan which did not reveal the three expeditions in preparation but was "related with it in regard to timing and places." It was accepted according to a declaration signed by Collazo, in the name of the province of Oriente, Mayía Rodríguez representing Gómez, and Martí.

The *Amadis* would sail to meet Maceo, carrying machinery and workmen for an imaginary Dr. Mantell of Santiago de Cuba. John Mantell, his son, who was none other than Manuel Mantilla, would be on board, as would Patricio Corona, as harbor pilot, with sufficient money to meet emergencies. As soon as the boat appeared it would take on five or six friends of Mr. Mantell and continue its journey. That was how Martí planned Maceo's expedition. In order to convey Máximo Gómez, another boat was prepared on which Martí would go, accompanied by Mayía Rodríguez. After they left a third ship would go to Las Villas, with exactly the same preparations and resources. Serafín Sánchez would be in charge of this expedition.

Martí had not revealed the details of these preparations to anyone. His dealings with Mr. Borden, who owned a dock in Fernandina, Florida, and could freight the ships

The Revolutionary Party

without arousing suspicion, were kept in absolute secrecy. The time came for the ships to be handed over to the leaders designated by the respective groups. By a separate route the arms and munitions arrived in cars freighted up to Mr. Borden's own dock. No one could suspect a failure. Those were extraordinarily tense moments for Martí.

Patricio Corona was now informed about the expedition. Serafín Sánchez had designated a colonel of the last war, Fernando López de Queralta, to take charge of his ship. Manuel Mantilla and Patricio Corona were ready to leave, for the Lagonda was to sail first because of having farther to go, to Costa Rica. López de Queralta received his instructions without making any objections. All documents were in legal form. The ship was to pick up workers in the Antilles and take them to a port which would be indicated. On board, in a suitable place, a thousand pesos would be handed over to the captain in order that he take them to the coasts of Cuba. Only in the event of his refusal would they resort to force. At the last minute López de Queralta raised objections and refused to undertake the voyage under the conditions agreed upon. In conversation with the captain of a ship he revealed the true object of the expedition. Martí discovered the betrayal but tried to render it ineffective. He visited the ship brokers' office, conducted there by López de Queralta. He realized then, because the conversation was so public, that the plan was discovered. At the same time that this was taking place López de Queralta had sent his materiel to the indicated warehouse and dock declaring the shipment as military articles.

When the object of freighting the ships was revealed, the ship brokers complained to the government in Washington, and the plan was soon divulged. The Lagonda, already loaded at Fernandina, received an order for embargo and search. An order for confiscation was issued to the Amadís and the Baracoa, declared suspicious.

It was indeed a surprise for the representative of the Spanish government. It was also a surprise for the Cubans on the Island and the emigrants. The Washington representative of the Spanish Government could hardly recover from his astonishment. He could never have conceived that an undertaking of such magnitude could be carried out by the Cubans with such efficiency and secrecy.

Martí hid in the home of Dr. Ramón Miranda, Quesada's brother-in-law, for several days in January, eluding the reporters who were looking for him everywhere in pursuit of sensational information.

21. "Now My Time Has Come"

The very secrecy with which Martí had proceeded made his position more difficult in the eyes of those who, out of prudence or discipline, had placed themselves under his orders without knowing the plans. When Mayía Rodríguez and Enrique Collazo, in hiding in a hotel in Jacksonville while they waited for the *Lagonda,* on which they were to sail, received news of the failure, they regretted bitterly their ignorance of the real state of the conspiracy, for they had limited themselves to hearing only what Martí told them, which was very little. Martí was staying at the Travellers' Hotel, in the same city, with another group of Cubans. With the intention of asking him for an explanation, Mayía and Collazo left their hotel, accompanied by Charles Hernández, the bearer of the news.

They found Martí seized with an extraordinary nervous excitement. Ceaselessly he repeated the same words: "It is not my fault! It is not my fault!" When Collazo and Mayía entered, the latter with a changed, hard expression, they realized that something extraordinary had happened. Those who were going to demand an explanation soon gave him back their loyalty and faith.

When Martí felt calmer, he spoke of the impossibility of abandoning the enterprise which had aroused such hopes. Only the means had changed.

The failure of the Fernandina plan had an unexpected effect on the Island. It revealed a vast movement which awoke the sleepers, restored faith to the incredulous and made everyone reflect that the Cuban war was not only imminent, it was a powerful attack. The Junta in Havana, meeting with Juan Gualberto Gómez, received at that moment the news divulged by the American press and the cable. General Julio Sanguily, who belonged to the Junta but did not have sufficient confidence in the work Martí was doing, had a real surprise. He rose from his seat and uttered words that revealed to his fellow conspirators how much he had doubted Martí until that moment, and how firmly he believed in his work from then on. All the Cubans who had thought about the independence of their country reacted the same way to a greater or lesser extent.

On January 17 when his work crumbled before his eyes, Martí was already thinking of renewing his efforts in a different direction. The work undone was such that it would serve to further unity and to increase public respect. Perhaps, outside of the material losses, the worst thing was the disappearance of the coordination of efforts which he had obtained, between the movement on the Island and external aid. It was no longer possible to subordinate the movements in Cuba to those from outside, and the revolution was free to arise by itself in Cuba without being shackled by the wait which it had had thus far. He hastened to promote coordination again without the loss of any aid, with the speed and precision which the frustrated movement had demonstrated and with the help of the emigrants, who gave him evidence of their confidence and loyalty.

On January 29, having saved as much as it was possible to save, he drew up in New York the call to arms which the impatient Island demanded. Mayía Rodríguez and Enrique Collazo signed the document with Martí. The authorization demanded that the actions of the regions involved be simultaneous, or as nearly so as possible. Any uprising in Occidente that did not take place at the same time as those in Oriente was considered dangerous, and it should be planned as closely in accord as possible with Camagüey and Las Villas. The declaration also assured immediate, continual outside aid. With this order Quesada left for Key West. He was to see that it reached Juan Gualberto Gómez. He had another

"Now My Time Has Come"

charge: that of taking up a new, indispensable collection in order to cover the expense (two thousand pesos) of the trip which Martí and Gómez had now decided to make from Santo Domingo to Cuba. Quesada bore letters from Martí to Figueredo, Poyo, Serafín Sánchez, Gato, and Paulina and Ruperto Pedroso, Martí's Negro friends. Now the time for sacrifice was near, and Martí asked them to make it, to give their house to the cause if it was necessary.

He sailed for Santo Domingo on the thirty-first. A few minutes before his departure he wrote to Maceo. All he could offer him, at that difficult time, was the same amount that he had for the trip with Gómez: two thousand pesos.

Gómez was very anxious, for he had received no news. But Martí arrived on February 7 accompanied by Mayía Rodríguez and Collazo. It was necessary to face the new facts, and this adjustment was the subject of their conversations during the first few days. They made long trips on horseback in search of men who might help them. They went from Montecristi to La Vega, Santiago de los Caballeros and Puerto Plata, returning at the end of February. On the twenty-sixth in Montecristi they received news of the uprising in Cuba. In March Martí again visited towns and settlements in Haiti: Cap Haitien, Fort Liberté, Guanaminthe, Petit Trou. They were beginning to solve the greatest problem, that of money, and in March they were offered a schooner with some men. Enrique Collazo and Manuel Mantilla left for New York. They had orders from Gómez to invade the Island in the province of Occidente as soon as the news of his arrival in Cuba was received.

The inactivity of waiting gave him the opportunity of approaching the life of the humble in all its rough, natural details. Never had he portrayed with fewer strokes and greater depth the man of the country in his poor retreat, the countryside around him, his keen, thoughtful judgments, his inner fineness. The pages Martí wrote seemed like lessons in human understanding. He wrote them, not for any newspaper, but for "his little girls"—Carmen and María.

In his letters to *Patria* he stressed two points of the constant, necessary campaign. They must preach the true character of the war, which was not directed against the

Martí

Spaniard, but against a distant, usurping, inefficient regime. They must also convince the autonomists that the revolutionary forces did not look down upon them or have different goals. The generous war was the kind he was preaching and the kind he intended to wage, the war without hatred, the war to restore dignity to man.

Those were times when he surpassed even the faith he had always had, as he felt the happiness of putting the crowning touch on something great after overcoming the accumulated obstacles.

While they were detained by the material impossibility of finding a way to leave, Martí did not cease writing, during that month of March, to clubs, to *Patria,* to Maceo, impatient and dissatisfied with the amount allotted to him, and to Flor Crombet, willing to lead an expedition with what he had. Martí's manifesto from Montecristi explained to the world the legitimate, natural causes of the revolution for independence. His thoughts were ordered and precise. He made a thorough analysis of the facts on which a people based its search for liberty and renewed the efforts of its heroes.

In his letter to Henríquez y Carvajal his ideas seethed like an essence, and his sacrifice as a man and prophet of America were like a prayer. His was the work of a great mystic of action, the action that redeems men:

"To me the fatherland will never mean triumph, but . . . duty."

"From me you may expect absolute, continual devotion. . . . But my only desire is to stay there, standing firmly by the last tree-trunk, the last fighter, and to die silently. Now my time has come."

On April 1 Martí and Gómez, with four companions—Francisco Borrero, Ángel Guerra, César Salas, and Marcos del Rosario—left Montecristi at midnight. At ten the following morning they were in Inagua, where they found the schooner they had contracted waiting for them. But the Captain betrayed them. On April 5 a German freighter carrying fruit arrived in a destitute condition. With the aid of the Consul of Haiti they obtained passage on this boat with the intention of putting to sea in a small boat as they passed near the coasts of Cuba. On the sixth the ship neared Cap Haitien and they disembarked, spreading out in the town in order not to be recognized. Martí locked himself up to write. On the ninth, the day of departure, he sent a long letter to his daughter, María, and also *L'Histoire Générale* in order that she might translate it into concise, clear Spanish as it was written in the original French. He gave her a great deal of advice concerning a good translation and an individual style, which reminded him of the one he used in writing *La Edad de Oro*.

"And when you have *L'Histoire Générale* well translated with clear handwriting and even lines and fine, clean pages with a good margin, will there not surely be someone who will print and sell for you, for your home, this clear, complete text on the history of man, better and more attractive and pleasant than all the history books in Spanish? A page a day, my little daughter. Learn from me. I have life on one hand and death on the other, and a nation on my shoulder, and see how many pages I write you."

He thought of the school he wanted her and her elder sister to establish in order to help with their support. He made an outline of what they should teach, and how:

"And it would be well for you to make an effort and teach French, as I taught it to you, by translating from books that are pleasing and realistic."

He was very concerned about leaving María provided for the necessities of life. But he thought that his letter would be effective, for he asked her in such a way that she could not fail to do as he asked. And he added a sorrowful sentence:

"Wait for me as long as you know that I am living."

On April 9 they embarked again and at eleven they were back in Inagua. At two in the afternoon that day the boat sailed, and in the evening they made out the peaks of the mountains of Cuba. At eight in the evening the *Nordstrand* stopped and lowered in a small boat into the water for them. Even the captain hesitated a moment about delivering them to a rough sea on that dark night. General Gómez gave the order. The expeditionaries, with their equipment, leaped

245

into the small boat. Because of the strong waves they were in danger of capsizing, but they were guided by good fortune. At ten in the evening they were climbing up the rocks on the coast. The place where they set foot on Cuban soil is Playitas.

Like Columbus, General Gómez kissed the earth. It was ten o'clock at night. Soon they began to walk under the brilliant light of the moon, which had just come out. They stopped two hours later. General Gómez took out his compass, and they continued their march straight north. They walked all night with their heavy bags on their backs. At dawn they heard a cock crowing, and General Gómez perceived a "smell of burnt fields." He glanced at Martí and noticed, in the dim light, "how radiant his face was with pride in taking part in these things." Shortly afterward they approached a settlement: Cajobal. They knocked at one of the first houses they came to. They were received with misgivings at first, then with overflowing joy when the people learned from Gómez' questions that they were Cubans who knew the region and its people. Shortly afterward, with a guide who was provided for them, they went in search of a place where they could stay until they contacted the revolutionists. In a cave in the mountains of Baracoa they spent the night. The next day, the thirteenth, a guide reached them. He was to conduct them to Felix Ruenes' group. They spent a second night in the cave, which now made them feel confident. From hammock to hammock Martí and the General carried on their nocturnal dialogue. "Everything, General," said Martí, "is compensated for by the happiness of this night." Two days later, in camp, Martí sat down to dispatch communications everywhere, even to New York. In a note in the diary he was writing for "his little girls," he expressed his happiness of feeling himself at last in his element. He gave an account of his activities from that night when they put to sea, "under a sky darkened by a rainstorm," until that moment. He spoke of his troubles as lightly as if they were games, and danger did not count at this time. "It is a great joy to live among men in the hour of their greatness," he wrote to Estrada Palma in reference to Gómez. People called Martí "General" and he was embarrassed by the undeserved title. That same day, April 16, Gómez called the others together, and Martí was unhappy, thinking it was a question of some danger from which they were excluding him. Soon Ángel Guerra appeared and told him that Gómez as Chief of Staff, supported unanimously by the others, not only recognized him in the war as a Delegate of the Cuban Revolutionary Party but named him Major General of the Liberating Army. "With an embrace they raised my poor life to the level of his [Gomez'] ten years' experience!"

For thirteen days they marched through the mountains of Baracoa without a single difficulty, curing those wounded in the first combat of José Maceo's column. Just as the two revolutionary groups met the first combat took place, and Martí heard bullets whistling over his head. During intervals between fighting he wrote notes and letters and the first proclamations. Now he was going out to face the "first Spanish campaign, the political campaign to suppress the war." From without they needed a "fervent resolution to help" while from within they fought with all their strength and skill. They must be prepared on the outside as well. "Force against force."

He served as a nurse when the camp was asleep. He stretched out his hammock at the foot of a large tree. From his knapsack he extracted medicine for the wounded. "How lovingly the stars look down at three in the morning," he wrote. "At five I am wide awake and mounted on my horse."

The circulars gave meaning and order to the war. One was entitled *War Policy,* and its words were the same that he had said previously:

"The war must be sincerely generous, free of all acts of unnecessary violence against persons and property and all demonstrations or indications of hatred toward the Spaniard."

On May 2 he wrote for the *Herald,* at the request of its editors, an article defining the war in Cuba. He declared:

"Cuba wishes to be free in order that here man may fully realize his destiny, that everyone may work here, and that her hidden riches may be sold in the natural markets of America. . . . The Cubans ask no more of the world than the recognition of and respect for their sacrifices."

By May 9 he had held a conference with Maceo, and they went out in search of Masó. Martí's description of the trip is vivid:

"How erectly the brave Rabí rode his horse! How triumphant and hopeful was Antonio Maceo. Until today we have been riding about the region unharmed. Today we left the camp of Quintín Bandera with a very small escort. And from Masó on to Camagüey. Soon, everywhere, simultaneously, we shall begin against our stunned, frightened enemy the most active operations that the order, enthusiasm and continual growth of our forces permit."

Such was his impetuosity and enthusiasm at that time, and so firm his old idea, already expressed, of a rapid decisive war, a speedy war, that he found even Maceo not sufficiently eager, and he spoke to him of "the paucity of operations, the continual supply of cattle for the cities, and the idleness of many good people who want more fighting than there is." His fear that the war might come to a standstill must have assaulted him when he wrote those lines to Maceo. Doubtless that was another of the causes of the prolongation and inglorious end of the War of 1868. Only by redoubling their efforts day by day with the firm determination to bring the war to a swift, victorious end could another period of stagnation be avoided. That was why he shouted to Maceo: "Get into your stirrups and set men on fire with your voice." This was Martí's cry from La Jatía on May 12 when he was looking for Masó. On the fifteenth they reached the place known as Dos Ríos. From there he wrote a new letter to Masó:

"We have been looking for you now for six days with great anxiety and dire need of seeing you."

They camped at Dos Ríos while they awaited Masó's arrival. Martí had placed great hopes in Masó for "the attack in which, for historical and strategic reasons, such a brilliant initial part will be played by the forces united by your prestige and aided by such distinguished officers. When we are at your side our work can be enlarged, and we can say more to our country without ceasing to move onward all the time."

Thus, an as incessant movement and a compelling drive that did not leave a moment for repose until the predicted end was attained, thus he conceived and desired the war. And he was an example for the leaders.

While waiting at the camp, he began to write on the eighteenth to Manuel Mercado, his friend in Mexico. He wanted Mercado's family to know that he was in danger every day of giving his life for his country and for his duty, just as he had wished to do twenty years earlier, in those unforgettable conversations among his family gatherings.

The camp received news that a large convoy manned by enemy forces was going in the direction of Ventas de Casanova. Gómez decided to attack it and went out with forty well-armed men, leaving Martí in the camp awaiting Masó. At dusk, just as Gómez was entering Remanganaguas the convoy was sighted, and he waited in hiding. At dawn on the eighteenth he prepared his ambush. But the leader of the Spanish column, Ximénez de Sandoval, was notified and, thinking Gómez' forces were superior, he let the day pass without continuing his march. Gómez withdrew with his men to rest. The next morning he found that Sandoval had tricked him and left early.

Returning to the camp at approximately one p.m., April 19, he was greeted with enthusiasm by Martí and Masó. They organized their forces and gave speeches of patriotic feeling and warlike ardor. Gómez had just finished speaking and was about to rest when the advance guard stationed along the road by which he entered warned them of the presence of the enemy. Sandoval's forces, after taking the convoy to its destination, were retracing their steps in pursuit of the rebels.

"To horse!" shouted General Gómez. And to Masó:

"Follow me with all your forces."

They advanced rapidly and soon found themselves face to face with the already formed squadrons of the enemy in the small plain of Boca de Dos Ríos. General Gómez had hoped to station his men there in order to maneuver his cavalry. Now it was impossible. His position was disadvantageous, the onslaught terrible.

Martí also came out. General Gómez ordered him to retreat, for that was not the place for him. Could Martí obey an order to withdraw at such a time? He had never asked anyone to face a danger he was not willing to face himself. That was what he had said and proclaimed. He had longed for this moment in order to be like them, like those who fought and knew danger, in order to put an end to the doubt that had made him suffer so. What right had he to expect to be respected, he who a few hours before asked Maceo to rise in his stirrups because he found the war inadequate, if now that the time had come he stood aloof like a distant spectator? No one stopped him. But no one could have stopped him.

What was he thinking at that instant when he perceived that Gómez' efforts were futile, that he was doomed to hurl himself to destruction against a disciplined, astute resistance? At strategic points from which they defended their troops the Spaniards had laid their ambushes. At a frenzied gallop Martí approached the Spanish ranks, resigned to his fate but willing to be the first. A friend, de la Guardia, rode beside him. A shot sent Martí tumbling to the ground at the same time that his companion's horse fell. In vain he tried to lift Martí. "Martí has fallen wounded over there," Guerra told the General. But it was not known just how he died, and his body could not be recovered from the enemy.

In the camp that night the deepest silence reigned, and perhaps their consciences tormented them. There had been first a lack of premeditation and then neglect. Martí's excitability, well known by his friends, and his inexperience required special care for his person.

On the pine board that served him as a table there was an unfinished letter—his letter to Mercado. The last sentence was hardly begun: "There are some affections which involve such delicate points of honor . . ."

The soul of the revolution was no longer there. In his place there was an immense void.

"Now My Time Has Come"

Every man who had known and loved him must have felt a great loss. And through the battlefields filled with confused yearnings and humble heroism the tremor of a great sorrow must have passed, as every heart repeated, "Martí is no more!"

But his spirit lives on in the blue of our sky, in the depths of our souls. It will always live, like the breeze that hovers over our green fields.

A Summary

A Summary of Martí's Life

1853. January 28. Born in Havana.

1857. January. Taken to Spain with his parents.

1859. June. Returned to Cuba.

1865. March 19. Inauguration of Municipal School for Boys under direction of Rafael María de Mendive. Martí enrolled.

1866. September 29. Examined for entrance into Institute of Havana.

1869. January 22. So-called "incident of the Villanueva Theatre" resulted in Mendive's arrest.

January 23. Publication of first issue of *La Patria Libre*, edited by Martí and others. Contained his drama, *Abdala*.

March 23. Mendive's school closed.

October 21. Accused of disloyalty, sent to Havana jail.

1870. March 4. Sentenced by Court Martial to six months in the penitentiary.

April 4. Entered penitentiary.

October 13. Transferred to Isle of Pines.

1871. January 15. Deported to Spain.

January. Published *El Presidio Politico en Cuba*, in Madrid.

May 31. Matriculated at Central University of Madrid.

1873. February. Published pamphlet, *The Spanish Republic and the Cuban Revolution*.

May 17. Petitioned Rector of University of Madrid for transfer of registration to University of Zaragoza.

August 30. Petitioned for and passed examinations in Institute of Zaragoza.

1874. January. Fall of the Spanish Republic. Defense of Zaragoza by the republicans against the attack of General Pavía. Martí spoke at public benefit program for widows and orphans of fallen republicans.

255

June 27. Completed work for degree of *bachiller.*

June 30. Received degree of *Licienciado en Derecho Civil y Canónico.*

August 31. Registered in Faculty of Philosophy and Letters.

October 24. Examined for degree of *Licenciado en Filosofía y Letras.*

1874. December. Left Spain for Paris.

1875. January. Embarked for Mexico in Southampton.

February 8. Reached Veracruz.

March 7. Revista Universal of Mexico published Martí's first contribution.

May 5. Assigned "bulletin" section of *Revista Universal.*

December 19. Opening performance of Martí's *Amor con Amor se Paga* at Teatro Principal de Mexico.

1876. January. Represented Chihuahua workers at labor congress.

November 16. Battle of Tecoac Heights (Oaxaca). Defeat of troops of Lerdo's government.

November 19. Last number of *Revista Universal.*

November 20. President Lerdo abandoned capital.

November 23. Triumphal entry of Porfirio Díaz.

December. Martí collaborated on *El Federalista.*

December 29. Left for Veracruz bound for Havana.

1877. January 6. Reached Havana, using second Christian name and surname: Julián Pérez.

February 24. Embarked for Veracruz.

Went from Mexico to Guatemala.

May 29. Appointed Professor, Central School, Guatemala.

May. Met María García Granados, "girl from Guatemala."

July. Orator at literary gathering in Normal School.

Made Vice President of literary society *El Porvenir.*

September 15. Wrote a drama commemorating Independence Day. (This work appears to have been lost.)

December. Obtained permission to go to Mexico.

December 20. Marriage in Mexico.

1877. January. Returned to Guatemala.

April 6. Resigned position at Normal School.

April 15. Announced that on this date he would publish first number of *Guatemalan Review.* (No numbers have been found.)

July 6. Left Guatemala for Honduras.

September 3. Reached Havana, accompanied by his wife.

September 16. Applied for permission to practice law on condition he would obtain title later. Petition rejected.

November 12. Birth of his son.

A Summary of Martí's Life

1879. January 12. Elected Secretary of Literature Section of *Liceo of Guanabacoa.*

January 29. Applied for permission to teach, offering to present title of *Licenciado en Filosofía y Letras* later.

April 21. Declared opposition to autonomy.

April 27. Program in honor of violinist Díaz Albertini at Liceo of Guanabacoa. Captain General commented on Martí's speech: "I am going to conclude that Martí is a madman. . . . But a dangerous madman!"

July 26. Authorization to teach in secondary school annulled. Worked in Viondi's office.

August 26. Uprising in Oriente, led by leaders of past war.

September 17. Martí imprisoned for conspiring.

September 25. Deported to Spain.

December. Left Spain, passing through Paris.

1880. January 3. Reached New York.

January 24. Read address, later published as pamphlet entitled *Cuban Affairs* in New York, 1880.

February 21. Martí's first art criticism appeared in *The Hour,* newly founded New York weekly.

May 13. Proclamation of Revolutionary Committee of New York. Written by Martí.

Contributions to *New York Sun.*

1881. February. Left for Venezuela.

July 1. First number of *Revista Venezolana.*

July. Incident with dictator Guzmán Blanco obliged him to leave country suddenly.

July 28. Sailed for New York.

August 20. Began sending news-letters from New York to *La Opinión Nacional,* Caracas.

1882. April. Finished printing *Ismaelillo,* book of verse. Wrote most of *Versos Libres,* left them unpublished.

Translated various books for Appleton Co.

July 15. Sent first news-letter to *La Nación of* Buenos Aires.

1883. February 28. Finished translating Stanley Jevon's *Logic.*

March. Began collaboration on *La América* of New York.

October. Editor of *La América.*

1884. October 20. Wrote Máximo Gómez announcing his withdrawal from revolutionary plans being formulated by Gómez and Maceo.

1885. Published *Amistad Funesta* in *El Latino-americano,* N. Y.

December. Finished translation of *Called Back.*

1886. Wrote for La Republica of Honduras.

August. Gómez-Maceo revolutionary plans failed.

Martí

1887. Collaborated on *El Economista Americano,* New York.

April 16. Named Consul of Uruguay.

December. Translated Helen Hunt Jackson's *Ramona.*

1888. October 12. Named Representative in United States and Canada of Press Association of Buenos Aires.

1889. March 21. Published in the *Evening Post* a *Vindication of Cuba.*

April 18. Sent his first article to *La Opinión Pública,* Uruguay.

July. Published first number of *La Edad de Oro,* children's monthly.

December 19. Spoke at meeting held in honor of Delegates to Inter-American Conference.

1890. January 22. Inauguration of *La Liga,* educational society in New York.

Appointed Spanish teacher, New York Central High School.

June 16. Named Consul of Argentina in New York.

July 24. Named Consul of Paraguay in New York.

December 23. Designated Uruguayan representative at Inter-American Monetary Conference in Washington.

December. Elected President of Hispano-American Literary Society of New York.

1891. March 30. Read report at Monetary Conference in Washington.

Published *Versos Sencillos.*

October 11. Resigned as Consul of Argentina and Uruguay.

October 30. Resigned from presidency of Hispano-American Literary Society.

November 25. Arrived in Tampa in response to invitation of Ignacio Agramonte Club.

November 27. Founded *Liga de Instrucción.*

November 28. "Resolutions Adopted by the Cuban Emigrants of Tampa," as preamble of Bases of the Cuban Revolutionary Party.

1892. January 5. Meeting of Club presidents, under Martí's leadership, resulted in organization of Cuban Revolutionary Party.

January 8. Submitted to Liga Patriótica of Tampa the plan of the Cuban Revolutionary Party, which was approved.

March 14. Published first issue of *Patria,* organ of new revolutionary activities.

April 8. Elected Delegate of Cuban Revolutionary Party.

August 4. Instructions issued to Commander Gerardo Castellanos, first agent of Revolutionary Party sent to Cuba.

September. Sailed for Santo Domingo.

A Summary of Martí's Life

September 11. Arrived at La Reforma, Santo Domingo, met Máximo Gómez.

September 24. Arrived in Haiti.

October 4. Left for Jamaica.

October 13. Sailed from Jamaica to New York.

October 18. Arrived in New York.

November. Life endangered by plot to poison him.

1893. January. Gerardo Castellanos returned with satisfactory reports from second propaganda trip to Cuba as Martí's agent.

January 31. Meeting in Hardman Hall, proclamation of total independence of Cuban Revolutionary Party from policy of autonomist.

May 24. Spoke at Hardman Hall and met Rubén Darío, introduced him at the program.

May 24. Manifesto of Cuban Revolutionary Party.

May 26. Sailed for Santo Domingo.

June 3. Arrived in Santo Domingo for second time. Conferred with Máximo Gómez.

June 30. Arrived in Costa Rica.

July 8. Left Costa Rica, bound for Isthmus. Spent several days in Panama, went on to New York.

November. New uprising in Cuba.

December. Trip through Philadelphia, Tampa, Key West.

1894. April 8. General Máximo Gómez arrived in New York to confer with Martí.

May 4. Martí toured Philadelphia, Key West, Tampa, Jacksonville, other places in Florida accompanied by General Gómez' son.

May 30. Arrived at New Orleans.

June 7. Arrived in Costa Rica.

June 21. Arrived in Panama.

June 25. Arrived in Kingston, Jamaica.

July 7. Arrived in New York.

July 16. Sailed for Mexico.

August. Returned to New York.

December 25. Finished plans to invade Island with three well equipped boats.

1895. January 10. Betrayal and failure of Martí's plan, known as Fernandina Plan.

January 29. Order authorizing revolution in Cuba signed in New York.

January 31. Sailed for Santo Domingo.

February 26. Heard news in Montecristi of uprising in Cuba.

March. Month spent in preparations for sailing.

259

Martí

March 25. Wrote from Montecristi to Federico Henríquez y Carvajal the letter considered his political testament.

March 25. Drew up manifesto of Montecristi, signed by Martí and General Máximo Gómez.

April 1. Wrote to Gonzalo de Quesada the letter considered his literary testament. Embarked with five companions on a schooner at Montecristi, bound for Cuban coast.

April 2. Arrived at Inagua.

April 5. Obtained passage on German freighter Nordstrand.

April 11. At 8 p.m., three miles from Cuban coast, Martí and his five companions were lowered in a boat into the sea. Around 11 p.m. they disembarked at Playitas.

April 13. Met Felix Ruenes' column, which escorted them.

April 16. Proclaimed Major General of Liberating Army.

April. Marched through mountains of Baracoa in search of Maceo.

April 26. Sent out circulars concerning meaning of the war.

May 2. Wrote to Editor of *New York Herald* concerning purposes and methods of the war of independence in Cuba.

May 5. Interview with Maceo and Gómez at La Mejorana.

May 18. Began his last letter, never finished, addressed to Manuel Mercado.

May 19. Killed in action at Dos Ríos.